INDIAN INSURANCE SECTOR IN 21st CENTURY : AN OUTLOOK

INDIAN INSURANCE SECTOR IN 21st CENTURY

An Outlook

A. VIJAYAKUMAR

KALPA

Indian Insurance Sector in 21st Century : An Outlook

Rs. 890

ISBN: 978-81-7835-782-9

Published in 2009 in India by
Kalpaz Publications
C-30, Satyawati Nagar,
Delhi-110052
E-mail: kalpaz@hotmail.com
Phone : 9212729499

Laser Type Setting by: Rudra Computer Graphics, Delhi
Printed at : Singhal Print Media, Delhi

Contents

Preface

The reforms in the insurance sector leading finally to the opening of the insurance sector for private participation have brought in its wake major changes not only in the design of the products available in the market but also the manner in which they are marketed. We have today a host of products coupled with a large number of intermediaries who market them. The post-liberalized insurance industry panorama in India is witnessing dramatic changes in terms of a slew of latest products and services, new channels of distribution, greater use of I.T. as a service facilitator etc. There is also the phenomenon of noticeable shifts in consumer preferences impacting the product mix being offered by insurers. The market structure dominated by a few stabilized public sector players and the 'new' players in the market (some of whom claim their lineage from established international insurance behemoths) is in a state of flux- in terms of figure out market shares but is full of potential.

Added to these are the rising trends of convergence of financial services, especially in the areas like wealth management and evolution of newer risk management tools, particularly in the context of reinsurance management. Greater attention is also being bestowed on the areas like Agricultural Insurance and risk coverage of export-import trade. Then there is impact of visible socio-economic changes like greater urbanization, greater job mobility, growth of the services industry, weakening of traditional family structure, impact of globalization etc. All in all, interesting things are happening in the Indian insurance scene. Insurance undergone rapid and massive changes in all aspects of their business: product and services, sectoral structure, market segmentation, competitive environment. This has encouraged many overseas insurance companies, having a required amount in their reserve, to open their branch in our country.

This book is based on thought provoking empirical research articles, relevant to the field, that help the reader to understand the subject better and to strengthen the fundamentals of the subject. I am confident of the view point that the series of students pursuing research in the field would acquire balanced knowledge about the subject and it is surely going to stand in a good stead for those aiming for developing command over the latest developments in the field and would help them to explore the research areas beyond the given contents of the book. This book has been designed to meet the requirements of academicians, students and research scholars in their pursuit in the area of Indian Insurance Sector and the like.

I ventured to bring this publication containing 28 research papers focusing on varied aspects of Indian Insurance Sector penned with an in-depth analysis, by academics and research scholars and duly edited by me, as a useful compendium on the Indian Insurance sector for the benefit of all. In this book an attempt has been made to highlight the challenges and responses that have been taken place in the Indian Insurance sector during post – liberalization. The research papers prepared by the ardent research scholars and academics drawn from different parts of the country have been classified in such a manner to facilitate a proper and fuller understanding of the fast changing role of Indian Insurance Sector in developing the national economy.

This is truly a product of collaborative efforts. I wish to express my sincere gratitude to all the contributors who responded generously to my request, without their response this volume would not have taken in its present shape. The co-operation and support of all the contributors has been a great source of encouragement to this academic venture. It is hoped that volume would be welcomed by the academic community and found useful by researchers, policy makers and institution builders concerned with working and performance of Insurance Industry.

I also extend my profound thanks to Kalpaz Publications, Delhi, for giving shape to my idea by publishing this book in a record time. I am solely responsible for any omission and inconsistencies in the book and look forward for constructive suggestions from readers.

This is only a humble beginning of a great event contemplated for a wider understanding of the emerging trends and the changing role of Indian Insurance sector, thus, benefiting the community to a greater extent.

A. VIJAYAKUMAR

List of Contributors

1. **J. Jayashree and N. Sumathi,** Lecturers in Commerce, Dr.SNS Rajalakshmi College of Arts and Science, Coimbatore.
2. **K.K. Saradha,** Lecturer in Economics, Vellalar College for Women, Erode.
3. **S. Brindha,** Lecturer-HR, GRD Institute of Management, Coimbatore.
4. **J. Udhaya Kumar, M. Thyagarajan and A. Sivakumar**, Lecturers in Commerce, Dr. SNS Rajalakshmi College of Arts and Science, Coimbatore.
5. **Dr. A.Vinayagamoorthi,** Reader in Commerce, Periyar University, Salem.
6. **Dr. V. Renugadevi,** Lecturer in Commerce, Vellalar College for Women, Erode.

   M. Vidhya, Lecturer in Commerce, KSR College of Arts and Science, Tiruchengode.
7. **G. Tamizh Chelvan**, Lecturer in Commerce, Dr.GRD College of Science, Coimbatore.
8. **M. Thyagarajan and J. Udhayakumar**, Lecturers in Commerce, Dr. SNS Rajalakshmi College of Arts and Science, Coimbatore.
9. **Dr. R. Easwaran and M. Vidhya,** Lecturers in Commerce, KSR College of Arts and Science, Tiruchengode.
10. **Dr. S. Kalaiselvi,** Lecturer in Commerce (MFC), Vellalar College for Women, Erode.

11. **S. Lakshmi,** Lecturer in Commerce, Paavendhar College of Arts and Science, Manivizundhan South, Attur.
12. **Dr. T. Nagananthi**, Lecturer in Commerce, R.V.S. College of Arts and Science, Sulur, Coimbatore.
13. **Dr. B. Baskaran**, Reader in Commerce, D.A.Arts College, Dharmapuram, Mayiladuthurai.
14. **Dr. B. Sekar,** HOD of Commerce, Swami Dayananda College of Arts and Science, Manjakkudi.
15. **N. Deepa,** Lecturer in Commerce, Sri Vasavi College, Erode.

    S. Thenmozhi, Lecturer in Commerce (CA) Vellalar College For Women, Thindal.
16. **Dr. A. Selvaraj**, Reader in Commerce, Gobi Arts and Science College, Gobichettipalayam.

    Shinie Poulose, Lecturer in Commerce, PKR Arts College for Women, Gobichettipalayam.
17. **N. Sumathi and J. Jayashree,** Lecturers in Commerce, Dr. SNS Rajalakshmi College of Arts and Science, Coimbatore.
18. **M. Karthigai Priya,** B.Com Student, Rose Mary College of Arts and Science, Thirunelveli.
19. **K. Muthulakshmi,** Bishop Heber College, Trichirapalli.
20. **J. Jayashree and N. Sumathi,** Lecturers in Commerce, Dr.SNS Rajalakshmi College of Arts and Science, Coimbatore.
21. **K. Abirami**, III B.B.M, Vellalar College for Women, Erode.
22. **Dr. A. Kumudha,** Reader in Management, PSGR Krishnammal College for Women, Coimbatore.

    V. Shripria, GRD School of Management Studies, Coimbatore.

    Dr. V. Srividya, Assistant Professor, PSG Institute of Management, Coimbatore.
23. **G. Jothi,** Lecturer in Commerce, Parks College, Tirupur.
24. **Dr. K. Subramanian,** Reader in Commerce, Sadakathullah Appa College, Thirunelveli.

25. **Dr. G. Shanthi,** HOD of Commerce(CA), Vellalar College for Women, Erode.
26. **Dr. I. Narsis,** Department of Commerce, Bishop Heber College, Trichy.
27. **Dr. R. Easwaran and Dr. M. Balasubramaniam,** Arulmigu Kalasalingam College of Arts and Science, Krishnankoil.
28. **Dr. C. Arjunan,** SNR Sons College, Coimbatore.
    Dr. L. Manivannan, Reader in Corporate Secretaryship, Erode Arts College, Erode.

1

Globalisation of Insurance

J. Jayashree, N. Sumathi

Concepts of insurance evolved thousands of years ago. The Chinese, for example, divided their cargoes among many boats to reduce the severity of loss from the perils of the seas, while the biblical story of Joseph and the famine in Egypt illustrates the storing of grain during the seven good years to relieve shortages during the seven years of famine. Marine insurance emerged in London when ships sailed for the New World. Fire insurance arose from the great fire of London in 1666, in which 14,000 buildings were destroyed. In 1752 Benjamin Franklin founded the first mutual fire insurance company in the United States, the Philadelphia Contributor ship for the Insurance of Houses from Loss by Fire. In 1759, he helped establish the first life insurance company, now known as the Presbyterian Ministers Fund. In 1887 the first auto-liability policy was written. Advancing technologies and a dynamic marketplace constantly change society's insurance needs. The insurance industry's goal is to respond to those needs with available and affordable insurance.

Indian Insurance Industry

Research and Markets (has announced the addition of the "Booming Insurance Market in India (2008-2011)" report to their offering. With a huge population base and large untapped market, insurance industry is a big opportunity area in India for national as well as foreign investors. India is the fifth largest Lifeinsurance market in the emerging insurance economies globally and is growing at 32-34% annually. This impressive growth in the market has been driven by liberalization, with new player's significantly enhancing product awareness and promoting consumer education and information. The strong growth potential of the country has also made international players to look at the Indian insurance market. Moreover, saturation of insurance markets in many developed economies has made the Indian market more attractive for international insurance players, according to "Booming Insurance Market in India (2008-2011)."

This research report will help the client to analyze the leading-edge opportunities critical to the success of insurance industry in India. Based on this analysis, the report gives a future forecast of the market that is intended as a rough guide to the direction in which the market is likely to move.

- Total life insurance premium in India is projected to grow Rs. 1,230,000 Crore by 2010-11.
- Total non-life insurance premium is expected to increase at a CAGR of 25% for the period spanning from 2008-09 to 2010-11.
- With the entry of several low-cost airlines, along with fleet expansion by existing ones and increasing corporate aircraft ownership, the Indian aviation insurance market is all set to boom in a big way in coming years.
- Home insurance segment is set to achieve a 100% growth as financial institutions have made home insurance obligatory for housing loan approvals.

- Health insurance is poised to become the second largest business for non-life insurers after motor insurance in next three years.

The other proposed amendments to the insurance laws

- To lower the capital requirement of standalone health insurance companies to Rs 50 crore from Rs 100 crore
- To increase LIC's paid-up capital to Rs 100 crore from Rs 5 crore
- To allow insurance companies to appoint insurance agents, surveyors and loss assessors
- To demarcate the distinction between a beneficiary nominee and a collector nominee
- To allow the collector nominee to distribute the claim among legal heirs
- Not to question any policy on any ground after 5 years

Emerging Insurance Markets

Promoters of Indian insurance companies can also hope to get some relief on the clause prescribing mandatory listing after 10 years. Sources said with the life insurance companies pushing for easing – if not doing away with – of this clause, the government is set to propose an amendment when it moves the Bill. Many cash-rich Indian promoters are keen on staying as majority shareholders in life insurance ventures. In addition, the comprehensive amendments to insurance laws will also seek to allow public sector general insurance companies to raise capital from the market to finance their expansion. With the Left withdrawing support to the Man Mohan Singh government, the finance ministry is hopeful of pushing through key reform proposals, including amendment to the Insurance Act, 1938, and other laws governing the public sector general insurers and Life Insurance Corporation (LIC).

While it was ready with the amendments as far as 36 months ago, the government was unable to introduce a Bill in the Parliament as the Left parties were opposed to the move.

At that point of time, the UPA did not want to be seen as seeking the opposition's support to push through key economic legislations. Insurance companies have been pushing for a relaxation of the foreign investment limit as they are governed by stringent solvency margin norms and continuously need capital infusion to support business growth. Many Indian promoters are constrained to chip in with their 74 per cent share every few months due to pressure for capital from other businesses. The increase in FDI is urgently required for creating additional capacity, flow of technical know-how from overseas and better customer service, the CEO of a life insurance company said. While mooting 49 per cent FDI in insurance, the finance ministry has also proposed to remove restrictions on Indian promoters, who were required to bring down their holding to 26 per cent after the tenth year of commencing business.

In addition, the Insurance Act, 1938, does not permit foreign re-insurers to function independently in the country and they can hold a maximum of 26 per cent stake in a local joint venture with a minimum paid-up capital of Rs 200 crore. Even though the insurance sector was opened up since 2000, public sector General Insurance Corporation (GIC) continues to be the only re-insurers in the country as foreign reinsures have stayed away from having a presence that is bigger than a branch office. The absence of an amendment to the law prompted the Lloyd's syndicate to withdraw its key India representative recently. With industrial risks rising, it is proposed to allow foreign re-insurers, like Lloyd's of London, to open branches in India. This will result in lower cost of re-insurance and such branches will create a hub for the Asian reinsurance business in India.

U.S. Insurance Industry

The U.S. insurance industry is comprised of approximately 1600 life (life/health) and 3000 non-life (property/casualty) insurance and reinsurance companies; it is the world's largest insurance market, accounting for $736 billion or 34 percent of 1998's worldwide premiums of $2.2 trillion. Insurance is sold either directly by insurers (direct insurers)or through the independent agency system, exclusive agencies, and brokers. Based on the 1997 U.S. Bureau of Labor Statistics, the life and health insurance industry employed 909,000 persons and the property/casualty insurance industry, 635,000; 706,000 persons were engaged in agency or brokerage activities and in insurance service organizations.

Globalization

While reinsures have always had an international presence and brokers have moved in that direction, primary insurers, with one notable exception, have been reluctant to expand internationally. The rapid growth of computer technology, however, has transformed the world into one global economy, in which U.S. and foreign insurers must, along with all other businesses, compete. Global insurance premiums grew by 9.7 percent in 2004 to reach $3.3 trillion. This follows 11.7 percent growth in the previous year. Life insurance premiums grew by 9.8 percent during the year, thanks to rising demand for annuity and pension products. Non-life insurance premiums grew by 9.4 percent, as premium rates increased. Over the past decade, global insurance premiums rose by more than a half as annual growth fluctuated between 2 percent and 10 percent. Advanced economies account for the bulk of global insurance. With premium income of $1,217 billion in 2004, North America was the most important region, followed by the EU (at $1,198 billion) and Japan (at $492 billion). The top four countries accounted for nearly two-thirds of premiums in 2004. The United States and Japan alone accounted for a half of world insurance premiums, much higher than their 7 percent share of the global population. Emerging markets accounted for over 85 percent of the world's population but generated only 10 percent of premiums. The volume of UK insurance business totaled $295 billion in 2004 or 9.1 percent of global premiums.

Distribution Channels

The insurance industry continues to explore new distribution systems, including the Internet and formation of alliances with banks and other financial services organizations in an effort to become more efficient and focused on the customer, who today places as much importance on service and convenience, as on price.

Life/Health Insurance

Life/health insurance in the United States in 1998 represented 27.6 percent of the worldwide market, second to Japan's 28.6 percent and well ahead of the United Kingdom's 9.8 percent, which ranked third. A variety of life insurance (which provides income for a beneficiary at the insured's death), annuities (provides income for life for the annuitant), and health care products are offered. In 1997 Americans purchased $1.97 trillion of new life insurance; the average new policy totaled $97,358. Term policies and ordinary/whole life policies account for virtually all of the total life insurance in-force of $13.2 trillion. At the end of 1997, 373 million policies were inforce with an average size of $165,800 per insured household. Term policies provide "pure insurance" (no cash value) and maximally cost-effective protection to growing families.

Ordinary/whole life policies provide protection as well as building up cash values (investment component), which the policyholder can either borrow on or obtain by surrendering the policy. Life/health policies are sold on an individual or group basis—(the employer or association receives the master policy and the insured members receive certificates of insurance). Annuities-fixed (predetermined amount) and variable (varies with investment returns) can be purchased by making a single payment or a series of payments. The annuity income can start immediately or at some future date. Different types of annuity contracts meet different needs. Today there is a strong demand for individual annuity products, driven by the movement of the baby boomers through the preretirement phase, increased life expectancy and the fear of outliving savings, and concerns about the long-term viability of Social Security. Health (medical, disability, long-term care) insurance plans are offered by insurance companies, managed health care organizations, and medical prepayment organizations. Long term care products provide for reimbursement for covered nursing home and home health care expenses incurred due to physical or mental disability.

Table 1
Top Ten U.S. Life Insurers Ranked by Life Insurance (In Millions)

Insurance Companies	*Amounts*
Metropolitan Life Insurance	1,545,453
Prudential Insurance Company of America	1,013,109
Connecticut General Life Insurance	543,369
Northwestern Mutual Life Insurance	536,379
Transamerica Occidental Life	498,247
New York Life Insurance	440,527
Aetna Life Insurance	385,525
RGA Reinsurance	381,634
Lincoln National Life Insurance	367,155
State Farm Life Insurance	347,430

Property/Casualty (P&C) Insurance: The United States dominates the world in P&C insurance (also known as general insurance). In 1998 the U.S. generated 43.4 percent of worldwide P&C premiums, Japan was next with 10.3 percent and Germany third with 8.8 percent. P&C insurance is broken down into personal lines (auto/private passenger and homeowners) and commercial lines (farm, commercial auto, aviation, marine/ocean/inland, crime, surety, boiler and machinery, glass, commercial credit, workers' compensation, public liability (including environmental pollution), professional liability (directors and officers, errors and omissions), product liability, commercial multiple-line, nuclear, title, and surplus and excess lines insurance).

Table 2
Top Ten U.S. Property/Casualty Insurers Ranked by Net Premiums Written (NPW)

Property / Casualty Insurers	*NPW* (in millions)*	*Combined Ratio***
State Farm Group	34,755.3	108.2
Allstate Insurance Group	19,072.1	95.5
American International Group	10,727.9	99.5
Farmers Insurance Group	10,316.4	101.7
CNA Insurance Group	10,044.0	115.2
Nationwide Group	8,494.9	108.9
Travelers Property Casualty Group	209.8	102.3
Berkshire Hathaway Insurance Group	7,731.8	95.7
Liberty Mutual Insurance Group	7,197.2	117.0
The Hartford Insurance Group	6,028.4	105.9

* Net premiums written includes only premiums written by domestic companies.

**A combined ratio of less than 100.0 indicates an underwriting profit.

Conclusion

All the governments play important roles in managing large social insurance programs, such as social security, medicare, unemployment compensation, federal deposit insurance, and pension benefit guaranty. In these areas the government acts either as a partner or competitor to the insurance industry, or as an exclusive provider. Federal and state governments also manage property and casualty programs, such as "all-risk" crop, crime, flood, and workers' compensation.

Reference

Text Books:

1. Tripathy & Pal "Insurance theory and Practice", Prentice-Hall of Indian Private Limited, 2005.
2. Dr.P.K.Gupta "Insurance and Risk Management", Himalaya Publishing House, 2005.
3. Life Insurance Fact Book, (Washington, D.C., American Council of Life Insurance), 1998.
4. "Securitization Frontierland," Best's Review Property/Casualty, (Oldwick, N.J., A. M. Best Company), July 1999.

Web Sites:

1. www.licindia.com
2. www.irdaindia.org.

2

Insurance Industry - Opportunities, Challenges and Strategies

K.K. Saradha

Insurance has come up as a very important financial service in most of the part of the world. The insurance is considered as one of the important segment in an economy for its growth and development. This industry provides long term funds that are essential for the development of basic infrastructure. The Indian Insurance Industry is more than 150 years old. This industry has witnessed many phases of the working from the days when there were many private sector companies initially and they moved to nationalization and again to the private sector.

Growth

If we go back to ancient times, we realize that the first insurers of life were the marine insurance underwriters. They used to issue life insurance policies on the lives of their master and the crew of the ship and the merchants. These policies were issued only for short periods. The first life insurance policy was issued on 18th June 1583 on the life of William Gibbons, for a period of 1 year. People always felt the need to have security of their lives and the property they owned. Somewhere in 18th century, societies like the Amicable Society, Equitable Life Assurance Society, Hand in Hand Society etc. were formed for issuing life insurance policies. During the early 19th century, a large number of life insurance companies were formed in India as well, which eventually became part of today's Life Insurance Corporation of India.

As far as the evolution of non-life insurance is concerned, it all began with the boycott of British goods and the British administration. These nationalists' movements made Indians come together for the common cause of protection of life and goods. This was the time when the swadeshi movement began. Thus over the years it forced the Government to have it's own autonomous bodies like LIC and GIC taking care of the life and the general insurance in India. Insurance today is not restricted just to life alone. But it has become the trend or the need of the hour to insure each and everything one has. So the different areas wherein insurance business can be done are - Life insurance, Health insurance, Automobile insurance, Property insurance, Casualty insurance, Liability insurance, Title insurance, Credit insurance, Terrorism insurance, Political risk insurance.

The Indian economy has undergone major reforms in the past decade with the liberalization of trade and investment, as well as regulatory reforms in the key sectors of the economy. Boasting of the largest number of operational life insurance policies in the world, the Indian insurance industry has emerged as a serious destination in the global insurance market. Until 1999, the business of insurance in India was the exclusive privilege of two State-owned corporations – the Life Insurance Corporation of India (LIC) and the General Insurance Corporation of India (GIC).

The Government of India took a major step towards liberalization of this industry in March 2000 and brought into effect the Insurance Regulatory Development Authority Act (IRDA Act). The IRDA Act opened the market by doing away with all entry-level restrictions on private insurers. Therefore, it has been four years of consistent growth. With the current potential premium income of the country estimated at about $80 billion, India is seen as the sixth largest market in the world. Insurance in India has now become a phenomenon that is worth reckoning. In the short post- liberalization span, the market has evolved manifold. India's enormous population and ever-growing middle class continue to offer huge potential to the insurers.

Present Scenario

From the Indian Life Insurance Company Act in 1912 to the IRDA Act in 1999, regulation of insurance business in the country has come a long way. Insurance is a subject of Central law and the two major legislations dealing with insurance are the Insurance Act, 1938 and the IRDA Act, 1999.The IRDA was set up in 1999. Companies aspiring to carry on insurance and reinsurance business in India are required to register with IRDA, which is the sole authority for granting licenses to agents. In tune with the Indian government's system of checks and balances imposed through sector-specific Foreign Direct Investment (FDI) limits, the IRDA prohibits 100 percent foreign ownership of an Indian insurance company. An Indian promoter is required to invest either wholly or team up with a foreign insurer, which can own no more than 26 percent of the shares in any new venture.

Entry of private players and foreign collaborations: It was on the recommendation of the Malhotra Committee that private players were allowed to enter into the insurance market. Today there are almost 22 players who have entered the Indian insurance market besides the giant Life Insurance Corporation of India (LIC). Another major development that has taken in the field of general insurance is the de-linking of the 4 subsidiaries of the General Insurance Corporation of India (viz. Oriental Insurance Company Ltd., New India Assurance Company Ltd., National Insurance Company Ltd. and United India Insurance Company Ltd) from the parent company.

Marketing strategies and approaches: The entry of private players and their foreign partners has given domestic players a tough time, because the opening up of the sector has not brought in only foreign players, but also professional techniques and technologies. The present scene in India is such that everyone is trying to put in the best efforts. One can see strategies being more for survival than growth. But the most important gift of privatization is the introduction of customer-oriented services. Utmost care is being taken to maximize customer satisfaction. The opening up of insurance sector for competition offers ample opportunities to both existing as well as new players to penetrate into untapped areas, sectors and sub-sectors and unexploited segments of population as presently both insurance density and penetration are at low level. Both indices being at very low level in the country even compared to the countries with the same level of economic development and per capita income are indicative of the vast potential of the growth of this sector in future.

Opportunities

As compared to the Western countries, where they have already reached a stage of saturation, India can exploit some golden opportunities in the following fields.

- **Mass Marketing**

India is a highly populated country and would continue to be so in the near future. New players may tend to favour the "creamy" layer of the urban population. But, in doing so, they may well miss a large chunk of the insurable population. A strong case in point is the current business composition of the dominant market leader - the Life Insurance Corporation of India. The lion's share of its new business comes from the rural and semi-rural markets. In a country of 1 billion people, mass marketing is always a profitable and cost-effective option for gaining market share. The rural sector is a perfect case for mass marketing. Competition in rural areas tends to be "kinder and gentler" than that in urban areas, which can easily be termed cutthroat. Identifying the right agents to harness the full potential of the vibrant and dynamic rural markets will be imperative. Rural insurance should be looked upon as an opportunity and not an obligation. A smaller bundle of innovative products in sync with rural needs and perceptions, and an efficient delivery system are the two aspects that have to be developed in order to penetrate the rural markets.

- **Job Opportunities**

Job opportunities are likely to increase manifold. The liberalization of the insurance sector promises several new job opportunities for those who are equipped with degrees in finance. Finance professionals who had witnessed a slump in the job market would be much relieved. There will be demand for marketing specialists, finance experts and human resource professionals. Apart from this, there will be high demand for professionals in streams like underwriting and claims management, and actuarial sciences.

- **Inflow of Funds**

There could be a huge inflow of funds into the country. Given the industry's huge requirement of start-up capital, the initial years after opening up are bound to see a strong inflow of foreign capital. A rise in the equity share of foreign partners to 49 percent will act as a boost to them.

- **Reinsurance**

Huge capacity is likely to be created in the area of reinsurance. Apart from pure reinsurance activities, which involve providing insurance protection, there will be a revolution in service-related fields like training, seminars, workshops, know-how transfer regarding risk assessment and rating, risk inspections, risk management and devising new policy covers, etc.

- **Marketing Strategies**

With more players in the market, there will be significant increase in advertising, brand building, and this will benefit whole lot of ancillary industries. A substantial shift is likely to take place in the distribution of insurance in India. Many of these changes will echo international trends. Worldwide, insurance products move along a continuum from pure service products to pure commodity products.

- **Banc assurance**

In other markets, notably Europe, this has resulted in bank assurance: banks entering the insurance business. The Netherlands led with financial services firms providing an entire range of products including bank accounts, motor, home and life insurance, and pensions. Other European markets have followed suit. In France, over half of all life insurance sales are made through banks. In the UK, almost 95% of banks and building societies are distributing insurance products today. In India too, banks hope to maximize expensive existing networks by selling a range of products. Many bankers have shown an inclination to enter the insurance market by leveraging their strengths in the areas of brand image, distribution network, face to face contact with the clients and telemarketing coupled with advanced information technology systems. Insurers in India should also explore distribution through non-financial organizations. For example, insurance for consumer items such as refrigerators can be offered at the point of sale.

Banks with their wide area network with branches in all the parts of the country will have very good opportunity to enter the insurance business. They will success in this sector because they have data base of customers, trained staff, a good network of branches besides synergy benefits.

- **Information Technology**

Worldwide interest in E-commerce and India's predominant position in Information Technology and software development are also likely to be major factors in the marketing of insurance products in the immediate future. The number of Internet account is increasing and the trend has already been set by some of the leading insurers and insurance brokers worldwide.

- **Potential Market**

New comers will get the benefit of potential market. While nationalized general insurance companies and LIC of India have done a commendable job in extending their services throughout the country but the choices available to the insuring public are inadequate in terms of services, products and prices the untapped potential is quite large. The Malhotra Committee, which went into various aspects of India's insurance industry, estimated that in life insurance, 22% of the insurable population has been tapped so far. In India, premium per capita is only 2 and premium as percentage of GDP is 0.55%, which is very less in comparison of USA where premium per capita is 1381 and premium as percentage of GDP is 4.80. This huge gap from the global bench mark is itself lucrative.

- **Force Insurance**

In disaster prone areas, Government of India is going to make insurance force. The interim report of the high powered committee set up by the centre on disaster management, has proposed mandatory insurance of life and property by people residing in disaster prone area such as coastal belts, flood prone areas, near nuclear, chemical and hazardous industries and thickly populated areas.

- **Products Development**

A state monopoly has little incentive to offer a wide range of products. It can be seen by a lack of certain products from LIC's portfolio and lack of extensive categorization in several GIC products such as health insurance. More competition in this business will spur firms to offer several new products and more complex and extensive risk categorization.

- **Customers Services**

It would result in better customers services and help improve the variety and price of insurance products. Competition will compel the players to bring new and innovative product, wider choice of prices and quality service to consumers.

Growth of Economy

Insurance business in India is growing at the rate of 15.20 percent annually and IRDA has estimated that it is currently of the order of Rs. 812. 50 crore. When combined with banking services, it adds up to about 7 percent of the country's GDP. Insurance penetration (i.e. premium per capita) has increased from 2.32 percent in 2000 to 2.88 percent in 2003. Likewise, insurance density (i.e. premium per capita) has increased from Rs. 435.897 in 2000 to Rs. 722.092 in 2003. Such changes have caused a climb in the country's ranking from 23rd in the world, in terms of total premium volumes, in 2000, to 19th in 2003. India's share in the world market has increased from 0.41 percent to 0.59 percent during the same period.

Challenges

If one has opportunities, one has to face challenges; it is like two sides of the same coin. No doubt India has a lot of opportunities coming her way, but there are a few challenges and threats as well. The four main challenges facing the industry are product innovation, distribution, customer service, and investments. Unit-linked personal insurance products might find greater acceptability with rising customer awareness about customized, personalized and flexible products. Flexible products and new technology will play a crucial role in reducing the cost and, therefore, the price of insurance products. Finding niche markets, having the right product mix through add-on benefits and riders, effective branding of products and services and product differentiation will be some of the challenges faced by new companies.

- **Technology**

In today's highly competitive financial services environment, effective organizations will employ technology in a strategic way so to achieve a competitive edge. Technology will play an increasing role in aiding design and administering of products, as well in efforts to build life-long customer relationships. At the same time, investment in technology will only help as long as firms find the right people: people with the right attitude, values, and ethics, commitment to excellence, and focus on customer service. The critical success factor is a top-down emphasis on exceeding customer expectations with quality people, excellent products, and legendary service. As has been seen in other financial services, the entry of private players ensures that the customer will be the beneficiary in the long run. It will also result in enlarging the market and extending the reach of insurance across the country.

- **Competition**

Thus, apart from the normal issues facing any new company, many new Indian private insurance players will need to cope with the challenges of working with a joint venture partner. They will be competing with large and well-entrenched government-owned players. They have to overcome regulatory hurdles, change the attitude of new recruits and satisfy some very high customer expectations. Also, the players will have to consider the Indian market as a long-term investment, and maintain clear-cut objectives and constant monitoring at all levels.

- **New Client**

New insurance will have to invest a minimum capital of Rs. 100 crore. The normal gestation period is of five years. Hence, the new insurers will have to lock up their capital for at least five years before earning any profits. Besides they will face problems of shortage of trained manpower for the insurance industry. The setting up of various offices and distribution network is a time consuming process. Further, the new insurers will have to compete with the established insurance companies like LIC and GIC which have a corporate image and market presence for several years.

- **New Products**

Today, LIC has more than 60 products and GIC has more than 180 products to offer in market. But most of them are outdated, as they are not suitable to the needs of the consumers. Hence, all the insurers will have to offer innovative products to the consumers. The consumers are particularly expecting good pension plans, health insurance, term insurance, and investment products like unit linked insurance from the life insurers. Similarly, the consumer expect innovative products from the general insurance for managing health care, property insurance, accident insurance and other products at an attractive terms and premium. The consumers also expect reduction 15 in the premium of the insurance products as the mortality rate in India has come down by three times in the last five years.

- **Premium on**

The days of giving fixed insurance products are over. Now customers need insurance solutions that match their wants. The large scale of operation, public sector bureaucracies and cumbersome procedures hampers nationalized insurers. Therefore, potential private entrants expect to score in the areas of customer service, speed and flexibility. It may mean better products and choice for the consumer. For giving better services insurance companies will have to build call centres to provide call free telephone-based sales and service. The call centres will provide product-related information, customer account information, query and complaint handling. These call centres can also be used for outbound sales and marketing campaigns.

- **Distribution Channel**

In the liberalized insurance market, there will be multiple distribution channels, which will include agents, brokers, corporate intermediaries, bank branches, affinity groups and direct marketing through telesales and internet. There will be competition among the channels. Intense competition will grow among the old and new insurers in the market to win consumers. This will pose a great challenge to the insurers in the liberalized insurance market.

- **Consumer Education**

The existing level of awareness of the consumers for insurance products is very low, it is so because 62% of the population is literate and less than 10% well educated. Even the educated consumers are ignorant about the various products of insurance. Hence, it is necessary that all the insurers should undertake the extensive plan for education of consumers.

- **Grievance Handling**

The insurers will have to face an acute problem of the redressal of consumers' grievances for deficiency in products and services. The IRDA has already appointed ombudsman for looking into the grievances of the policyholders, its judgement will be binding on insurers. In the competitive market, awareness level of consumers will increase and it will help consumers to fight for their legal right for deficiency in services.

- **New Product Innovations**

One researcher shows that two products of LIC dominate with majority share of 52 products. With more competition good products will become an important differentiator among the various competiting insurance products. A lot will depend on the kind of products that these outfits launch. Initially after launching simple products multinationals will shift to specialized products.

- **Positioning of Insurance**

Products on the ground, the biggest challenge for the insurance companies will be to change the mindset of people, especially in life insurance. In India, life insurance is seen more as a tax saving mechanism rather than safety net in case of death. ICICI Prudential Life Insurance chief marketing officer Sangata Gupta also says that "working on consumer attitude will be the greatest challenge." New types of products should be futuristic in outlook. To start with, low premium high cover policies should be introduced and better savings products at a latter stage.

- **Rural Market**

It is said that the life insurance business suffers from high premium and low returns. A normally competitive industry should be able to increase coverage, mobilize large savings, and provide high returns. India is ranked at 2T" in the world in terms of mobilizing savings in the form of insurance. In countries like U.K. and South Africa, life insurance premiums account for over 50 per cent of gross domestic savings (GDS). Insurance in India has been a priority of the urban few. Now with numerous companies set to enter, the rural areas are expected to be tapped as well. IRDA has made it mandatory for life insurers to sell 5 per cent of their aggregate policies in the rural areas during the first year of operation that will be progressively increased to 15 per cent by the fifth year. But with gestation period long and investments large new entrants will feel very difficult to do it.

Strategies

After the entry of the new players the insurance sector has witnessed some remarkable changes in market shares. From its monopoly status the LIC of India's market share came down to 94.34 percent in 2002-2003 and to 87.05 percent in 2003-2004. The new players are trying hard to capture the market by diversifying their activities and trying out innovative techniques. To achieve sustained competitive advantage, the existing as well as new players are adopting various differentiation strategies.

Differentiation Strategies of Insurance Companies

The objective of differentiation is to create inimitable sustainable competitive advantage over competitors for a period of time. Insurance companies can differentiate themselves in the areas of product, customer service, distribution channels, promotion, brand building and so on.

- **Product Differentiation**

In case of product differentiation, new products, customized products, tailored products, bundled products can be introduced and new target segments can be identified. For example, life, health and personal accident insurance can be bundled together. Similarly Home Loan and insurance covering fire and burglary can be put together. The LIC of India provides only packaged policies whereas new players have been providing several Riders. Rider in insurance parlance is an option that gives the policyholder additional coverage without disturbing the fundamental risk coverage. This enables the customer to diversify his risk coverage. For example, in case of HDFC Standard Life Endowment Policy, the premium is Rs.4,835 and the rider accidental death benefit has a premium of Rs.144. Similarly money-back and term benefit, whole life and health can be the additional riders given.

- **Customer Service**

In case of customer service more than e-sales, e-servicing needs to be developed by the insurance companies. Ease in the payment of premiums through credit cards or Internet, will save the time of the customers. Similarly the claim settlement procedures need to be simplified. Training of agents and customer relationship management will take the insurance companies a long way in this regard. Online personal information will greatly improve the customer service. In case of life insurance, owing to the long-term nature of contracts, the consumer looks forward to efficient servicing of his policy with regard to any possible change of address, change in nominations and assignments, receiving premium and other notices, if any, and any other service that is required by him from time to time.

- **Distribution Channels**

In the field of distribution channels, many innovative techniques can be adopted. For example, Banc assurance and selling through postal network will make a great deal of difference. In Europe 25 percent of insurance policies are sold through banks. Banc assurance, as a package of financial services that can fulfill both banking and insurance needs, if implemented correctly can bring vast benefits to stakeholders such as banks, insurance companies, shareholders and consumers. Banc assurance will facilitate mass selling of insurance products through banks. Banks can act as large financial supermarkets.

- **Promotion**

Creating awareness among the people is the biggest challenge before the insurance companies for expanding the markets. People should realize and feel the need for insurance and know about some specific products designed for special needs. Mass media advertising is widely being resorted to by a number of new players in this regard. They are exploring all the existing and new channels for the purpose of promotion.

- **Brand Building**

Till today, at least in the field of life insurance, LIC is the strong brand but in the field of general insurance there was no such strong brand. For effective brand building, securing and retaining the customer is very necessary. The promise of the company is authentic – this has to be made known to the customers. In order to successfully hold a brand image a company must ensure to preserve the key values of legitimacy, distinctiveness, relevancy and consistency.

- **Environment Analysis**

The companies should concentrate on environmental change, its direction, magnitude and its short-term and long-term impact, formulating strategies to meet the challenges of high competition, preparing contingency plans and then designing action plans for effective implementations of formulated strategies.

- **Restructuring Organisations**

The traditional hierarchy system is very slow in making decisions due to several levels of management, due to its procedural inflexibility and slow communication. A manager in the privatized scenario is required to be an organizational specialist, country specialist and a global specialist.

- **Speed, Cost Effectiveness and Innovations**

The insurance companies will have to make substantial investments in customer relationship management technologies. They will be required to have wide area networks (WAN) connecting branches spread across wide geographical locations and workout modalities facilitating premium payment through the internet.

- **Human Resource**

Development Human capital is important for any organization especially for organizations whose activities revolve around special human interactions. Along with products and services the new insurers need people with the right set of knowledge, skills and aptitude for insurance. The persons who are involved in selling the product and those who are doing the back office work need to equip themselves with newer skills and insights into every aspect of company's functioning. They have a daunting task of exploiting potential in the industry and at the same time bring good risks to the company for providing insurance coverage. They have to retain the existing customers for which they need to have better understanding of products and services by creating healthy internal environment with group harmony. Existing companies will have to frame their human resource policies to retain the competent and motivated staff since new entrants will be eying them by offering lucrative salaries.

- **Efficiency in Distribution**

  It is very important factor and my prove bottleneck to the new players. Insurance companies are making the products available through the ready distribution channels of banks, non-banking finance companies and housing companies. One has to be careful doing this, since creating distribution and distances does not automatically mean controlling them.

- **Risk Management**

  Like all intermediaries in financial markets, insurances companies will have to bring sophistication in market research techniques future portfolio expansion.

The Way Ahead

With the entry of competition, the rules of the game are set to change. The market is already beginning to witness a wide array of products from players whose number is set to grow. In such a scenario, the differentiators among the different players are products, pricing, and service. Consumers are increasingly more aware and are actively managing their financial affairs. Today, while boundaries between various financial products are blurring, people are increasingly looking not just at products, but at integrated financial solutions that can offer stability of returns along with total profits. To satisfy these myriad needs of customers, insurance products will need to be customized. Insurance today has emerged as an attractive and stable investment alternative that offers total protection - Life, Health and Wealth Protection. Consumers today also seek products that offering flexible options, preferring products with benefits unbundled and customizable to suit their diverse needs.

The trend in developed economies where people live longer and retire earlier is now emerging in India too. With the breakdown of traditional forms of social security like the joint family system, consumers are now concerned with the need to provide for a comfortable retirement. This trend has been further driven by the long-term decline in interest rates, which makes it all the more necessary to start saving early to ensure long term wealth creation. Today's consumers are increasingly interested in products to help build wealth and provide for retirement income.

This all adds up to a major change in the demand for insurance products. While sales of traditional life insurance products like individual, whole life and term will remain popular, sales of new products like single premium, investment linked, retirement products, variable life and annuity products are also set to rise. Firms will need to constantly innovate in terms of product development to meet ever-changing consumer needs. However, product innovations are quickly and easily cloned. Pricing will also not vary significantly, with most product premiums hovering around a narrow band.

In this competitive scenario, a key difference will be the customer experience that each life insurance player can offer in terms of quality of advice on product choice, along with policy servicing, and settlement of claims. Service should focus on enhancing the customer experience and maximizing customer convenience. Long-term growth in the business will depend greatly on the distribution network, where the emphasis must evolve from merely selling insurance to acting as financial advisors, helping customers plan their finances depending on life stage and personal requirements. This calls for a strong focus on training of the distribution force to act as financial consultants and build a lasting relationship with the customer. This would help create a sustainable competitive advantage that cannot be easily matched.

The insurance sector has had one of the smoothest entries into the liberalized era with multiple providers from the public and private sectors. It is time to look ahead and see what needs to be done for the further development of this sector.

Conclusion

Over the past three years, around 40 companies have expressed interest in entering the sector and many foreign and Indian companies have arranged anticipatory alliances. The threat of new players taking over the market has been overplayed. As is witnessed in other countries where liberalization took place in recent years, we can safely conclude that nationalized players will continue to hold strong market share positions, but there will be enough business for entry to be profitable. Competition will surely cause the market to grow beyond current rates, create a bigger "*pie*", and offer additional consumer choices through the introduction of new products, services, and price options. Yet, at the same time, public and private sector companies will be working together to ensure healthy growth and development of the sector. Challenges such as developing a common industry code of conduct, contributing to a common catastrophe reserve fund, and chalking out agreements between insurers to settle claims to the benefit of the consumer will require concerted effort from both sectors.

However, everyone is quite excited about the opportunities, growth and development of the insurance industry in India. This market has the potential to grow into one of the largest markets in the world in the foreseeable future. However, if appropriate steps are not taken now to get the structural aspects right, this industry will face many challenges that might adversely affect its growth.

References

1. *Insurance in India Changing Policies and Emerging Opportunities*, Palande, P.S, Shah, R.S, Lunawat, M.L Sage Publications India Pvt. Ltd., New Delhi.
2. *Elements of Insurance*, Murthy, A. Margham Publications, Chennai.
3. *Insurance HRD Practice*, Mamta Jain, Ritu Publications, Jaipur.

Website

www.google.com
www.yahoo.com
www.rediff.com

3

Market Potential for Insurance in Rural Areas

S. Brindha

The growth of Insurance Industry in the India was found to be minimal in 1960s and 1970s, due to factors like low savings, low investment, inadequate infrastructure, and illiteracy. However, changes in the economy in 1980s, such as growth in the rate of industrialization, infrastructure, the capital markets, savings rate and capital formation resulted in a tremendous growth in the life insurance industry, which helped to track the potential of the Indian life insurance industry to uncover key challenges to its growth. It was also estimated that by 2012, Indian household would be paying premium of up to Rs 4,100 from the current Rs 1,300. India's ratio of life insurance premium to its GDP is around 4% against 6-9% in the developed world. But, the report claims it could rise to 6.2% by 2012 and almost 40% of the urban population is likely to have some form of life insurance cover, while in rural areas too it could touch 35%. Currently they are 30% and 25%, respectively. It must be emphasized that the opening of the insurance market is far from a bad thing for nationalized insurers. With a strong presence, a wide network and considerable brand equity, they are in a good position to tap the very same segments profitably, while improving their product and service offerings.

Besides other areas can be focused to grow and survive in the Indian Market

1. Understanding Customer needs
2. High-level Training and Development
3. Alliance and Tie up
4. Agent Relationship
5. Market Segmentation
6. Revamped Marketing Strategy

Enormous contributions have to be made to spread the awareness about insurance, and expanded the market. It was recognized that their reach was still limited, the range of products offered restricted and the service to the consumer inadequate both in urban and rural set up. It was also predicted that India has a vast potential that is waiting to be tapped and this could be achieved when sufficient competition is generated and it is exposed to the developments in the rest of the world. The insurance sector was, therefore, opened up for private sector participation with provision for limited foreign equity exposure.

The limited coverage in the rural areas and the vulnerable sections of the society continues to be a source of concern for the regulatory body. Since we are witnessing a demographic change in the country and the younger generation, which is exposed to, the outside world demands products and services, which are at par with what is available in the advanced countries. There is no doubt that the Indian insurance companies would face this challenge and provide services on par with services provided in the advanced countries. Hence the major objective of identifying the market potential would be to be to spread life insurance to every nook and corner of the country especially rural areas, to socially and economically backward classes.

The statement could really True that "Rural life insurance to grow 4-fold by 2015".

The country's under-utilized rural market holds tremendous growth opportunities for insurance companies with their revenues expected to grow as much as four times to reach Rs 7,800 crores ($2.9 billion) by 2015, a latest report says. High competition and relatively high market saturation in the urban areas have led insurance players to start focusing on rural and semi-urban India. According to international consultancy firm Clement, Over 70 crore people reside in the rural areas of the country with insurance penetration rate as low as three per cent, providing huge opportunity for, mainly, private life insurance firms. However, life insurance companies can tap the tremendous growth opportunities in the under-penetrated market only if they can develop a viable and cost-effective distribution channel and create client awareness and confidence in the product, the report said.

Interestingly, most insurance companies have found that addressing the rural opportunity in India would require innovative products and innovative methods.

Penetration of insurance products

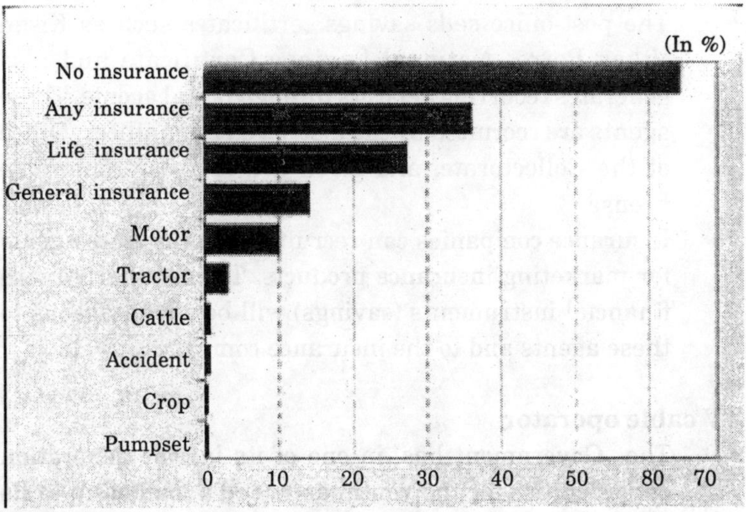

The rural market is vibrant and holds tremendous potential for growth of insurance business, particularly because of the strong saving habit.

The prospects in the rural sector are promising; the real challenge lies in distributing and delivering systems cost-effectively and efficiently. It is common knowledge that the cost of building exclusive delivery systems for selling insurance would be prohibitive. However, valuable data are available on the existence of extensive network built by the rural development agencies, banks, cooperative institutions, NGOs, micro-financing institutions, women's SHGs, youth clubs, panchayats and some industrial houses in the rural sector. Insurance companies can, therefore, be well advised to harness this infrastructure and work out collaborative arrangements with these institutions to their mutual advantage.

Possible rural agents to market insurance policies

The following categories of persons could be identified as potential agents, their competency to sell insurance products has to be ascertained by companies.

Postal agents

- The post-office sells savings certificates such as Kisan Vikas Patra, National Savings Certificate and also generates recurring deposits through postal agents. These agents are recruited by the district savings officer, Office of the Collectorate, and given a three-year renewable license.
- Insurance companies can recruit and train these agents for marketing insurance products. The familiarity with financial instruments (savings) will be advantageous to these agents and to the insurance company as well.

TV cable operator

- The Government has, in one of its income generation opportunities for the youth, extended a loan of up to Rs

40,000 to set up satellite cable TV connections and to select number of educated unemployed youth.

- Cable TV operators are educated and have access to all homes in the village that have a cable connection, that is, about 400 households in villages with a population of more than 5000. He visits the homes at least once a month to collect the subscription for the cable TV.
- His accessibility to rural homes makes him a potential insurance agent.

Youth Club Members

- The youth clubs in the villages should be active in activities such as starting a library, digging village ponds, processing official documents for villagers and organising rural sports events and cultural shows to ensure better quality of life in the village. They are also part of government programmes where they get involved in spreading information and awareness on health and sanitation, government schemes and assist in government health camps.
- These youth are educated and seek avenues for generating income for themselves.
- Leaders of youth clubs can be selected and recruited for marketing insurance products by companies.

Doctors and School Teachers

Registered medical practitioners and teachers are the more educated persons in a village and command considerable respect and influence. Many of them are working as agents for LIC, post-office and other financial institutions. As these persons are well-educated, they can be easily trained under the IRDA curriculum and appointed as insurance agent by the private agencies. The general notion is that it is expensive to do business in the rural areas due to its inaccessibility and other factors, like inferior infrastructure, poor educational background, and deprived living standards. The challenge of developing a cost-effective delivery system is not insurmountable and there is enough scope for innovative collaborations. The process of penetration in the rural areas could be pushed further through an appropriate use of IT.

Agents Training

The expanding market demands a large agency force. Presently there are more than 20 lakh individual agents and nearly 5000 Corporate Agents. In order to introduce an element of professionalism in the insurance intermediaries elaborate training and testing arrangements were introduced. Being the person on the spot as a representative of the insurer, it is essential that the agent recognizes and understands the need of the prospect. Having identified the need, it is his duty to ensure a need-based selling. In the absence of a need-based selling, the contracts are not likely to last long and the policyholder looks for the earliest opportunity to quit.

Corporate Agents

The opening of the sector is accompanied by entry of new set of intermediaries in the insurance market. The Corporate Agent model is expected to bring down costs of procurement of business substantially to the insurance company while benefiting the corporate with fee based income which improves its revenue stream. The insured himself, should feel comfortable with this model as he would be dealing with an Institution that is familiar to him.

Brokers

The introduction of brokers in the Indian insurance industry in the liberalized scenario is another significant development. Brokers act as representatives of the policyholders although the insurers pay them. As a result, they are expected to bring better service to the clients in several areas like:

- Monitoring the insurance market, the credibility of the players and the quality of services they render
- Analyzing the various products available in the market and assist the clients in choosing the products that suit their requirement
- Helping the client in the completion of the proposals, conclusion of the contract and render subsequent service, if any
- Assisting the client in the settlement of claims.

Although the agent is also expected to render most of these services, for several reasons this has not been achieved in the Indian context. Being better equipped with higher level of training and with no obligations to the insurers, the brokers are expected to deliver these services to the client in a more objective fashion. In spite of the constraints inherent in a tariff regime, a significant growth in the number of applicants for grant of broker's license has been witnessed. The brokers were obviously testing the market in preparation for the detariffing that should normally take place when the market is freed from monopoly.

Insurance Education and Research

One of the spin-offs of liberalization of the insurance sector has been rise in demand for insurance education, training and research. The Insurance Institute of India's role appears to have been confined to professional examinations conducted by it. The course is a recognized qualification for professional competence in the area of insurance. What was perhaps ignored is the need to innovate by way of introduction of new subjects in tune with the demand and expectations of an evolving market after a thorough review of the existing course curriculum.

Research in insurance remains a neglected area and there is need for a concerted effort to develop and define areas of focus for research in tune with the requirements of the industry. Without a research focus no institute can expect to make tangible gains in the near future in terms of value addition and meeting the expectations of its members and the industry at large.

Rural and Social Focus

Insurance sector irrespective of it being private or public sector owned chase the niche markets in the relatively well off regions and their activities would, therefore, be mostly urban centric and they would ignore the rural markets and the weaker sections of the society. It was indicated that when the state has monopoly of the sector the public sector companies were being used as instruments of state for implementing welfare schemes benefiting the rural masses and the vulnerable sections. The Insurance Act was, therefore, amended authorizing the Regulator to lay down certain obligations on the insurers towards rural areas and weaker sections.

The insurers recognized the potential of the rural markets; particularly in the context of these markets having exhibited the ability to procure goods and services with the growing income levels. There is also awareness about the need for insurance particularly life and health. The new players are making an effort to tap these markets in a commercial way. This fact is duly reflected in the premium underwritten in the rural sectors/ lives covered in the social sectors by some of the insurers which is in excess of the stipulated obligations. The welfare of the weaker sections and providing reasonable cover to them at affordable rates will be a challenge. The low income people live in risky environments and are lot more exposed to risks.

Conclusion:

The country has benefited enormously from the reforms process. The average annual growth rate of GDP has been steadily rising and the 8% plus growth rate that is the present norm speaks volumes of how India has been progressing. Inspite of the Inflation threat, the foreign exchange reserves present a very health picture and foreign debt is being paid ahead of schedule. India has become a production base and an export hub for diverse goods from agricultural products to automobile components to high end services. Indian firms are now a part of global product chains. Large international corporations have established R&D centres in India. With such a constant support and development, it is quite feasible to tap the existing market potential of the insurance sector in the rural and the weaker sections of the society.

References

1. Insurance – Bodla BS, Garg MC, Singh K
2. Insurance and risk management by Gupta P K
3. Insurance – Weipess; Bill
4. Rural Development – Verma SB, Pawan YT
5. Kurulshetra – A journal on Rural Development, April 2008, Vol. 56 No 6.
6. www.irda.com
7. www.licindia.com
8. www. www.indiainfoline.com

4

Information Technology in Insurance -An Outlook

J.Udhayakumar, M.Thyagarajan and A.Sivakumar

The rapid innovations in the field of information and communication technology have posed serious challenges for the insurance industry in India. The use and application of information technology in wide variety of insurer's operations has now become strategic in the sense that it has direct impact on the productivity of resources and a sweeping impact on reducing the cost of various activities. With the arrival of private insurance players, the competition has become more intense and an important role is being played by the insurance sector. Even though the use of information technology is not a new to the insurance sector, yet we may find tight compartmentalization regarding the use of information technology in various departments of the insurance companies including the major player since last 50 years. The most visible of these departments are accounting, policy issue and servicing, claim processing, sales management etc.

The imperative for all the insurers, especially LIC and GIC is to build up an efficient interface between the various departments and segments. This would reduce the paper work, improve efficiency of service delivery and provide competitive advantage to the insurance companies

Technologies for Insurance

The effective use of information technology has been more crucial to the success of the insurance industry. The insurance markets are being revolutionized by technology at a high speed pace. IT and software solutions, allowing cross-border trade to become electronic and paperless, are increasingly on offer to importers, exporters, shipping companies and financial institutions. Following technologies advancements can really enhance the performance of insurance companies

- **Database Management Systems**

The principles of tracking and measuring responses can pay off for the conventional insurance industry. To find more clients, insurer needs to consider many factors, including lapsation, cash value, premium and competition. But the need to record and study the characteristics of persistency the length of time we retain policies, customers and agents is most important for insurance companies.

- **Data Warehouse**

Data warehousing technology is based on integrating a number of information systems into a one stop shopping database to achieve vision of making company national in scope, but regional in focus. Data warehousing allows managing by profit level with an integrated approach rather than by limiting losses. Data mining can be used as a means to control costs and increase revenue resulting in enormous earning for effective users.

- **Group Linking Software**

Group linking software enables sharing of information and particularly suits document heavy insurance business. Tracking of policy application shows how information that is input and accessed from a number of locations can increase efficiency.

Mapping

Insures to meet different needs, such as identifying loss prone areas or geographic claim analysis can use mapping technology. It helps the insurers to analyse the extent of its network i.e., the insurer can determine whether it has too many or too few agency force in a particular area.

- **Call Center Technology**

Good customer service is a crucial element in gaining, maintaining and retaining profitable customer. Call centre concept based on interactive voice response services (IVRS) is gaining importance in this aspect. Employees based the primitive concept of call centre on an enquiry system providing information services to customers through telephone line answers. The totally automated computerized exchange but lacks in flexibility i.e. only predefined queries are serviced.

- **Video Linking**

A video linking facility between two remote units of an insurance company in between an insurer and a broker allows underwriters at one place and brokers at other unit to discuss risk inherent in a proposal face to face.

- **Cat Models**

Catastrophic models use data from the recent spate of natural disasters that helps develop more predictions of insurers' proper!y exposures in future disasters. Using this data curious "what if" scenarios of probable maximum loss (PML) using the best estimate available at an insurer's exposures are tested. Finally an underwriting policy that limits the company's exposure to catastrophic losses is implemented.

Information technology applications in functional area

Even though the information technology has wide application in all the spheres of the insurance business yet following are the most important ones in respective functional areas.

Marketing

The scope for use of information technology in marketing function is tremendous. It may start from the consumers' acquaintance to an insurance product to claims settlement or further selling of new products or developing consumers for the products.

- **Consumer Awareness**

The use of information technology may be path breaking for the insurance companies since conventionally the awareness of the insurance products in India is low. With the use of internet the information about the products and pricing policies can be made available to the public in few seconds and much transparency in operations can be establishes. There are numerous websites availed which can help the prospective customers to compare the insurance products of various issuers and decide the product suited to his needs.

Finance

Information technology can be effectively used for internal management viz. accounting treasury management, financial performance reporting etc. and as well as in resource mobilization, portfolio management, investment planning etc.

Human Resource Management

Application of IT in human resource management is obvious. It can be effectively utilized in recruitment and selection training, performance appraisal, promotions transfer and dismissals valuation etc.

E- Insurance in India

Insurance companies will probably have to wait for internet penetration to increase and the still ambiguous e-commerce rules to take concrete form. However, what is not debatable is that new private entrants will change the rules of the game for the Indian insurance business, both in the life and the non-life segment, unfolding opportunities for software engineer and professional agents. Life insurers were among the first to go online with informative content and features like actuarial calculators. In the non-life sector, automobile policies are popular over the internet, premium income, points out the paper, is expected to raise $18billion from about $1 billion currently. The growth of global online insurance business augurs well for the Indian IT sector. The exponential growth in the online insurance business will unfold significant business opportunities for software companies/consultants.

The opportunities that rise out of this will be both global and local, because new entrants will have to either fine tune or prepare customized packages for the Indian market. Online insurance will also help companies reduce costs and keep premium low, a perquisite in a price sensitive market in India. The government however will have to address problems relating to bandwidth on an urgent basis to make online insurance a reality in India. Other major challenges to face Indian insurers will be to design and develop strategies for delivering services to well segmented customers. The third challenge lies in developing the right combination of customer segments and applicable distribution strategies.

Most web sites offer contact numbers of their branch officers where we can get further details of the products on offer. The agent locator feature, available on maxneyorklife.com, iciciprulife.com and on bimaonline.com help one locate an insurance agent most accessible to you based on a search facility. On would expect downloadable proposal and claim forms for few of the schemes.

Benefits of Electronic Insurance

E – Insurance provides multiple benefits to the insurer and the existing and prospective insured.

- Information collected is better and cheaper
- Speed of response – issuance of policy and settlement of claims is faster
- Provides new ways of doing business in competitive market.
- Flexible pricing and customized services
- Global accessibility i.e. lapse of physical boundaries
- Increased sales without additional sales force
- Immediate premium collection
- Reduced cost per transaction
- 24*7 availability i.e. round the clock availability of information
- real time knowledge base building

Life Insurance on The Web

Insurers	*Website*
LIC of India	www.licindia.com
Om Kotak Mahindra	www.omkotakmahindra.com
Max New York Life	www.maxnewyoirklife.com
Birla Sun Life	www.birlasunlife.com
ING Vysya Life	www.ingvysyalife. com
HDFC Standard Life	www.hdfcinsurance.com
ICICI Prudential1 Life	www.iciciprulife.com
Portals On Life Insurance	www. bimaonline.com
	www.bimaguru.com

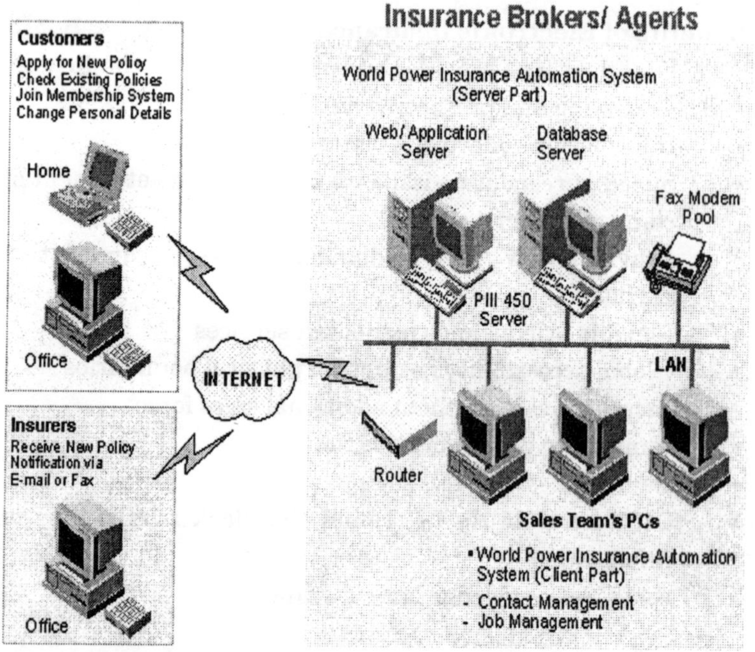

Major Factors Affecting E-insurance

Growth of net

It is estimated that India would have about 150 million net users by 2010.these figures represent a huge buying potential

Competition Pressures

Insurance companies because of competitive pressures would be driven into internet rather than a clear ROI justification

Customer

The availability of net based services will be a huge factor for customer retention

Costs

In the beginning e-insurance will be a cost factor rather than a profit driver, but in the long run it will be a cost reducing factor

Conclusion

The use and application of information technology in wide variety of insurer's operations has now become strategic in the sense that it has direct impact on the productivity of resources, and a sweepening impact on reducing cost of various activities. The greatest impact in online technology has been achieved by e-commerce. E-commerce is attractive both to buyers and sellers as it reduces search costs for buyers and inventory costs for seller. The recent growth of Internet infrastructure and introduction of economic reforms in the insurance sector have opened up the monopolistic Indian insurance market to competition from foreign alliances.

References

Books

- Dr.P.K.Gupta, Insurance and Risk Management published by Himalaya Publishing House 2005
- R.K.Agarwal, Role of Information Technology in the Insurance Industry, the Chartered Secretary, 2001

Websites

Www. Insurance technologies.com

5

Indian Insurance: Modern Marketing Approach

Dr. A. Vinayagamoorthy

The Insurance sector plays a vital role in the economic development of our nation. It acts as a mobiliser of savings, financial intermediary, promoter of investment activities, stabiliser of financial markets and a risk manager. India is still an under-insured country in the world. It is at the 18th position among Life Insurance markets and 28th in Non-Life Insurance markets in the world. This indicates that there is a huge potential, yet to be explored. The insurance sector in India has come a full circle from being an open competitive market to nationalization and back to a liberalized market again. In our daily life whenever there is uncertainty there is an involvement of risk. The instinct of security against such risk is one of the basic motivating forces for determining human-attitudes. Life Insurance is universally acknowledged to be an institution, which eliminates 'risk', substituting certainty for uncertainty and comes to the timely aid of the family in the unfortunate events of the death of the bread winner.

Superiority of Life Insurance:

Through insurance, one can enjoy the benefits of protection, aid to thrift, liquidity, Tax relief etc. Importance of insurance has increased both vertically and horizontally. From individual point of view, insurance provides security and safety, affords peace of mind, enhances the habit of savings, eliminates dependency, protect the mortgaged property, promotes investments and above all it fulfills the needs of a person like family needs, old age needs, readjustment needs, special needs and clear up needs.

From business point of view, it reduces uncertainty of business losses, increases business efficiency, indemnifies keymen, help continue business and increase labour welfare. From society's point of view, it protects social wealth like cattle, crop, machine, vehicle etc., promotes economic growth and controls inflation. It also proves social benefits like employment opportunities, develops human facilities like housing, electricity, water, and sanitation and improves the standard of living of the people. From national point of view, it increases the national savings, national investment and contributes to the implementation of national economic planning. It also promotes exports and earns foreign exchange.

History of Insurance in India

The business of life insurance in India in its existing form started in India in the year 1818 with the establishment of the Oriental Life Insurance Company in Kolkata.

Some of the important milestones in the Life Insurance Business in India are:

1912 : The Indian Assurance Companies Act enacted as the first statue to regulate the Life Insurance business.

1928 : The Indian Companies Act enacted to enable the government to collect statistical information about Life Insurance.

1938 : Earlier legislation consolidated and amended to by the Insurance Act with the object of protecting the interest of the insuring public.

1956 : 245 Indian and Foreign Insurers and provident societies taken over by the Central government and nationalised. LIC formed by an Act of Parliament viz. LIC Act, 1956 with a capital contribution of Rs.5 crore from the Government of India.

The General Insurance Business in India, on the other hand, can trace its roots to the Triton Insurance Company Ltd., the first General Insurance Company established in the year 1850 in Kolkata by the British.

Some of the important milestones in the General Insurance Business in India are:

1907 : The Indian Mercantile Insurance Ltd., set up, the first company to transact all classes of general insurance business.

1957 : General Insurance Council, a wing of the Insurance Association of India, frames a code of conduct for ensuring fair conduct and sound business practices.

1968 : The Insurance Act amended to regulate investments and set minimum solvency margins and the Tariff Advisory Committee set up.

1972 : The General Insurance Business (Nationlisation) Act, 1972 nationlaised the general insurance business in India with effect from 1st January 1973. 107 insurers amalgamated and grouped into four companies viz. the Nation Insurance Company Ltd., the New India Assurance Company Ltd., the Oriental Insurance Company Ltd., and the United India Insurance Company Ltd. GIC incorporated as a company.

The funds generated by LIC and Public Sector General insurers are invested in the avenues that benefit the society.

They solely acted as public undertaking insurers and catered the life cover and general risk cover of the public till the enactment of Insurance Regulatory and Development Authority (IRDA) Act, 2007.

Current Scenario

Global integration of financial markets resulted from de-regulating measures, technological information explosion and financial innovations. Liberalisation and Globalisation have allowed the entry of foreign players in the Insurance sector. With the entry of private and foreign players in the Insurance business, people have got a lot of options to choose from. Radical changes are taking place in customer profile due to the changing life style and social perception, resulting in erosion of brand loyalty. To survive, the focus of the modern insurers shifted to a customer-centric relationship.

1. Liberalization and Privatization

India's economic development made it a most lucrative Insurance market in the world. Before the year 2007, there was monopoly state run LIC transacting life business and the General Insurance Corporation of India with its four Subsidiaries transacting the rest. In the wake of reform process and passing Insurance Regulatory and Development Authority (IRDA) Act through Indian parliament in 2007, Indian Insurance was opened for private companies. Liberalisation on the Insurance sectors has allowed the foreign players to enter the market with their Indian partners. Most of the foreign Insurers have joined within the local market. India offers immense possibilities to foreign Insurers since it is the world's most populous country having over a billion people.

Insurance industry had ten and six entrants in life and non-life sector respectively in the year 2000-2001. The industry again saw two and three entrants in the life and non-life business respectively in the year 2001-2002. One additional entrant was made both in the life and in non-life business in 2004 and 2005 respectively. At present there are fourteen companies each in Life and General Insurance. The Funds earlier generated by the state owned insurers have been diversified with other new insurers. We should wait and see how the new players are going to boost up our economy.

2. Competition

Private and Foreign entrants in the Insurance Industry made others difficult to retain their market. Higher customer aspirations lead to new expectations and compel him to move

MARKET SHARE (%) - December, 2007

	Life Insurers			*Non – Life Insurers*	
1.	LIC	76.07	1.	New India	21.41
2.	ICICI Prudential	6.91	2.	National	17.11
3.	Bajaj Allianz	4.75	3.	United India	17.11
4.	HDFC Standard	2.98	4.	Oriental	17.02
5.	Brila Sunlife	1.72	5.	ICICI- Lombard	8.04
6.	Tata AIG	1.66	6.	Bajaj Allianz	6.15
7.	SBI Life	1.46	7.	IFFCO-Tokio	4.00
8.	Max New York	1.28	8.	Tata-AIG	2.89
9.	Aviva	1.08	9.	ECGC	2.50
10.	Kotak Mahindra Old Mutual	0.71	10.	Royal Sundaram	2.17
11.	ING Vysya	0.54	11.	Cholamandalam	1.22

(Contd.)

(Contd. Table)

Market Share (%) - December, 2007					
Life Insurers			*Non – Life Insurers*		
12.	AMP Sanmar	0.46	12.	HDFC-Chubb	0.89
13.	Met Life	0.37	13.	Reliance General	0.75
14.	Sahara Life	0.03	14.	Agriculture Insurance Co.	--
Private Total		**23.93**	**Private Total**		**27.35**
Public Total		**76.07**	**Public Total**		**72.65**
Grand Total		**100.00**	**Grand Total**		**100.00**

Source : www.irdaindia.org

towards the insurer who provides him the best service in time. It becomes less viable for them even to maintain the functional networks or competitive standards and services. To survive in the Industry they analyse, the emerging requirements of the policyholders / insureds and they are in the forefront in providing essential services and introducing novel products. Thereby they become niche specialists, who provide the right service to the right person in right time.

In December 2007, the private players in the life insurance business have increased their market share to 23.93 per cent. Among them ICICI prudential is ranked first in capturing the market followed by Bajaj Allianz and HDFC Standard. In the General Insurance sector the private players have captured 27.35 per cent. Among them ICICI-Lombard is ranked first, followed by Bajaj Allianz and IFFCO-Tokyo.

The healthy competition in the sector enabled the State owned insurers of our mother country to reduce its market share to 76.07 per cent and 72.65 percent in life and non-life business respectively. Moreover, private insurers have planned to increase their market share in the next five years. The public insurers have to enrich its approach to with held its share.

3. Information Technology

Insurers are the earlier adopters of technology. Because of the Information revolution, customers are free to choose from a wide range of new and innovative products. The Insurance companies are utilizing the Information technology applications for better customer service, cost reduction, new product design and development and many more.

New technology gives the policyholders / insureds better, wider and faster access to products and services. The impact of Information Technology in Insurance business is being felt at an accelerating pace. In the initial years IT was used more to execute back office functions like maintenance of accounts, reconciling broker accounts, client processing etc. With the advent of "database concepts", these functions are better integrated in an administrative efficiency.

The real evolution is however emerged out of Internet boom. The Internet has provided brand new distribution channels to the Insurers. The technology has enabled the Insurer to innovate new products, provide better customer service and deeper and wider insurance coverage to them. At present, Insurance companies are giving customers a distinct claim id to track claims on-line, entertaining on-line enrollment, eligibility review, financial reporting, billing and electronic fund transfer to its benefit clan customers.

4. Product Innovations

Insurers are continuously innovating new products based on forward looking models. They have developed new products addressing the new challenges in society and products to address the hazards from new environmental issues. Companies will need to constantly innovate in terms of product development to meet ever-changing consumer needs. Understanding the customer better will enable Insurance companies to design appropriate products, determine price correctly and to increase profitability. Since a single policy cannot meet all the Insurance objectives, one should have a portfolio of policies covering all the needs.

Product development is made possible by integrating actuarial, rating, claims and illustration systems. At present, the Life Insurers are concentrating on the pension schemes and the Non-Life Insurers on many innovative schemes of various realms and thereby enriching their market share. Moreover, with increased commoditization of insurance products, brand building is going to play a vital role.

5. Distribution Network

While companies have been successful in product innovation, most of them are still grapping with right mix of Distribution Channels for capturing maximum market share to build brand equity, building strong and effective customer relationships and cost effective customer service.

While the traditional channel of tied up advisors or agents would be the chief distribution channel, insurer should innovate and find new methods of delivering the products to customers. Corporate agency, Brokerage, Bancassurance, E-insurance, Cooperative societies and Panchayats are some of the channels, which can be tapped by the insurers to reach the appropriate market segments. Now-a-days, the urban masses are tapped with the new techniques provided by Information Technology through Internet. Rural masses are attracted by the consultative approach adopted by the Insurers. Moreover, they attract the customers through telephone and mobile also.

6. Customer Education and Services

Insurance is a unique service industry. The key industry drivers are related to life style issues in terms of perceiving insurance as a savings instrument rather than for risk cover, need based selling, quality of service and customers awareness.

In the present competitive scenario, a key differentiator is the professional customer service in terms of quality of advice on product choice along with policy servicing. Servicing is focusing on enhancing the customer's experience and maximizing his convenience. This calls the effective CRM system, which eventually creates sustainable competitive advantage and enables to build long lasting relationship.

Modern Marketing Approach

Marketing strategies for insurance in the emerging scenario could be understood in terms of the following steps:

[R] → [STP] → [MM] → [I] → [C]

Here,			
	R	=	Market Research
	STP	=	Segmentation, targeting, positioning
	MM	=	Marketing Mix
	I	=	Implementation
	C	=	Control

Having done market research and finalising on segmentation, targeting and positioning the strategy would focus on the marketing mix namely, Product, Price, Place and Promotion. While determining the implementation methodology, the four characteristics viz. Intangibility, Inseparability, Perishability and Variability gives rise to certain unique requirements that deserve careful attention while formulating the marketing strategy for insurance. After implementation, the insurers should concentrate on the effective control that would enhance their business.

In India Insurance is sold and not bought. The agents / Advisors by using various strategies sell the product by convencing the customers. Moreover, they push Policies with the highest premium to pocket a higher commission. The consultative approach to selling is the modern approach, which helps customers and prospects to buy. A consultant makes calls and sells just like any other sales person. The difference is in their attitude, their approach and their commitment. Here, the customer is seen as a person to be served and not a person to be sold. It helps the purchaser to make an intelligent decision. The four-step process includes:

- Need discovery
- Selection of the product
- Need satisfaction presentation, and
- Serving the sale

This approach to selling their products requires understanding of concepts and principles borrowed from the fields of psychology, communications, and sociology and needs a lot of personal commitments and self – discipline from the seller.

The commitments referred are:

- Finding and understanding the needs of the customers.
- Partnering with the customers.
- Helping the customers to achieve his business and other objectives by the purchase of the product or service.
- Believing that your products / services are a great fit with your customer's needs, and
- Believing in yourself and your ability to help the customers in solving their problems.

A consultant is willing to forego short-term gains to achieve greater long – term benefit to him and to the customers he serves. He builds relationships on a foundation of trust, respect and performance. Moreover, consultants don't sell – they're specialists who make recommendations to help the prospect to buy. They act as a professional and offer real–world solutions that make sense to the customer. Today, the insurers adopt this technique and thereby go on increasing their market share.

Suggestions:

Awareness Building

LIC has nearly 80 products and GIC has more than 150 products to sell. But investor knows only about handful. This can be ratified by proper awareness building measures. Agents can be instructed not to sell only the high commission yielding policies.

Risk Education

People seek and find shelter in insurance sector whether it is life or non-life policies, not just for investment alone but to meet the contingencies in the life. Hence, it is the duty of the insurance sector to educate the people from mere savings to risk hedging.

Innovation

The insurance sector should introduce innovative products offering a right mix of flexibility, risk and return to give suitable appetite of the customers need. Their target should also be focused on specific niches, which are poorly served or are not saved at all.

Branding

To face competition, insurance needs to be sold more vigorously. More competition in this business will spur firms to offer several new products and more complex and extensive risk categorization. Internet can be used as a tool to improve the productivity of existing distribution and increase the level of customer satisfaction rather than as a direct source of sales.

Agents' Welfare

The system of selling insurance through commission agents needs a better incentive structure. A Eminent persons like marketing specialists, finance expects, human resource professionals, engineers, statisticians, medical professional etc.

can also be get involved in this sector. Remuneration will be linked with performance and opportunities will be given to the existing personnel's to upgrade their skill technology and knowledge for restructurings themselves towards the betterment of the industry.

Market Extension

Privatization of the insurance sector has opened the doors to innovations in the way business can be transacted. Among the techniques that seem to catching up fast, the participations of NGOs and self help Group (SHGs) can also be encouraged in selling insurance products to the rural areas.

Conclusion

In the global era, Insurance companies are increasingly willing to spend more on the customer satisfaction and brand building exercises. Though it is one of the highly regulated industries, it still provides lot of scope for creativity and innovations. As our industry is predominantly dominated by personal selling and personalized services many a time the service standards vary based on the intermediary involved in the process. In order to achieve the competitive edge over others standardize the process and bring about quality improvement and get feed back from the customers regarding the quality of services rendered. This will result in customer satisfaction, customer retention, customer acquisition, employee retention and cost reduction. Dins dale observes "No one is the modern world can afford to be without insurance". So, to increase marketability, customer services should be increased. Creating a core efficient and competitive financial system suitable for the requirements of both national economy and individual economy will give a suitable solution. Insurance industry is like a Banyan tree giving shelter to both savers and employment seekers. If its activities are properly cultivate and maintained, their fruits can be reaped successfully all through the years.

Hence it is needless to say that insurance industry is a source of investment and employment. This paper is focusing on the marketing approach adopted by the modern insurers to withheld their existing customers and attract new ones.

References and Notes Books

1. Insurance Principles and Practice - M. N. Mishra, S. Chand and Company Ltd., New Delhi. (2005)
2. Introduction to Insurance - Marks S. Dorfman, Prentice hall, Inc, Engle Wood Cliffs, N.J. 07632 (2004)
3. Indian Insurance Industry - D.C. Srivastava and Shashank Srivastava, New Century Publications, Delhi. (2005)

Journals

1. Southern Economist, March 1, 2006.
2. Insurance Watch, August, 2007.
3. Insurance Watch, September, 2004.
4. Insurance Chronicle, February, 2007.
5. Insurance Watch, March, 2006.
6. Insurance Watch, July, 2005.
7. Indian Journal of Marketing, July, 2007.
8. Life Insurance Today, September, 2007.
9. Life Insurance Today, December, 2007.

Websites

1. **www.irdaindia.org**
2. **www.bimaonline.com**
3. **www.licindia.com**
4. **www. asiantradehub.com**

6

Impact of Liberalisation and Globalisation on Insurance Sector

Dr.(Mrs). V. Renugadevi
Mrs. M. vidhya

Introduction

The Insurance sector plays a vital role in the economic development of our nation. It acts as a mobilize of savings, financial intermediary, promoter of investment activities, stabilizer of financial markets and a risk manager. India is still an under-insured country in the world. It is at the 18th position among Life Insurance markets and 28th in Non-Life Insurance markets in the world. This indicates that there is a huge potential, yet to be explored.

Insurance Business in Pre-nationalization Era

In India, the history of insurance, in its present form, can be traced with the establishment of a British Firm, Oriental Life Insurance Company in Calcutta in 1818. This was followed by the formation of Bombay Life Insurance Company in 1823, the Madras Equitable Life Insurance Company in 1820 and the Oriental Government Security Life Insurance Company in 1874. The first general insurance limited company was established in 1850. The Indian Mercantile Insurance Company Limited, which was set up in Bombay in 1907, was the first Indian Company to transact all classes of general insurance business. Even though the first life insurance company was established as early as 1818, there was no exclusive legislation to govern the activities of insurance companies during the nineteenth century. The Indian Companies Act passed in 1866 regulated all companies, including insurance companies.

To control the operations of life insurance business in India, the Indian Life Insurance Companies Act was enacted in 1912. This act was based on Assurance Companies Act, 1909 of U.K. In 1938, the Indian Insurance Companies Act was passed. This act amended the 1912 Act and provided for collection of statistics concerning insurance business other than life business. It also covered the foreign companies operating in India. The Act made provisions for required equity capital to carry out insurance business, ceilings on share holding patter, strict controls on investments, ceilings on management expenses and agency commission, etc. Subsequently, a separate wing was established in the Ministry of Finance to administer the provisions under the Act.

After the Indian Insurance Companies Act, 1938 was passed; there was mushroom growth of insurance companies in India. In spite of mushrooming of many insurance companies per capita insurance in India was merely Rs. 8 in 1944 as against Rs. 2000 and Rs. 600 in US and UK respectively. Even this limited growth is marked by many malpractices, deficiencies, and frequent liquidations of insurance companies shaking public confidence and depriving policyholders of their savings and security. It is reported that in those days insurance and banking was in the control of big industry houses resulting in interlocking of funds between banks and insurance companies.

These dark deeds of dishonest insurance men helped to intensify the public chauvinism and invited public demand for nationalization. As a consequence Government of India nationalized life insurance by amalgamating all the private companies under one corporation.

Insurance Business in Post-nationalization Era

Life Insurance Corporation of India set-up by Government of India in the year 1956 dominated life insurance sector, General insurance Sector still was in private hands. It was mainly confined to small entrepreneurs and ancillary units attached to big industrial plants. With the growth in the process of industrialization in India, number of companies in the general insurance sector increased steadily and by 1972 their number had gone to 107. But many of these companies did not have a strong financial base as they were mainly dependent upon premiums received from industrial units to run their operations. Business of three wars in a decade (1962, 1965 and 1971) focus of Central Government shifted form industrial sector to defense sector. This shift caused economic slowdown, which resulted in fund shortage faced by industrial units. All these developments had a bad effect on the general insurance sector. Of the 107 companies in existence at the end of 1972, more that 50% were in financially bad shape.

Taking into account the bad health of private operations and vast fund mobilization potential in this sector, Government of India nationalized the general insurance sector with effect from 1 January 1973. It formed four subsidiaries (The New India Assurance Company Ltd., the United India Insurance Company Ltd. and the National Insurance Company Ltd.) with a holding company (General Insurance Corporation of India). Presently, all these subsidiaries are working independently. GIC will now be the Indian reinsurer. Since 1973, the insurance sector has been totally under the control of Government of India through LIC and GIC and its subsidiaries. As a result, revenue of both of them increased significantly in the last years.

Recent Development in Insurance Industry in India

The Government of India in 1993 has set-up a high powered committee by R.N. Malhotra, former Governor, Reserve Bank of India, to examine the structure of the insurance industry and recommend changes to make it more efficient and competitive keeping in view structural changes in other parts of the financial system of the economy.

Major Recommendations of Malhotra Committee

The committee submitted its report in January 1994 recommending that private insurers by allowed to coexist along with government companies like LIC and GIC companies. This recommendation had been prompted by several factors such as need for greater and deeper insurance coverage in the economy and a much greater scale of insurance sector is at least partly driven by fiscal necessity of tapping the big reserve of savings in the economy. Committee's recommendations were as follows:

- Raising the capital base of LIC and GIC up to Rs. 200 crores, half retained by the government and rest sold to the public at large with suitable reservations for employees.
- Private sector is granted permission to enter insurance industry with a minimum paid up capital of Rs.100 crores.
- Foreign insurance companies are allowed to enter by floating an Indian company preferably joint venture with Indian partners.
- Steps to be initiated to set-up a strong and effective insurance regulatory in the form of statutory autonomous board on the lines of SEBI.
- Limited number of private companies to be allowed in the sector. But no firm is allowed to operate in both lines of insurance (life or non-life).
- Tariff Advisory Committee (TAC) is delinked from GIC to function as a separate statutory body under necessary supervision by the insurance regulatory authority.

- All insurance companies be treated on equal footing and governed by the provisions of the insurance act No special dispensation is given to government companies.
- Setting up of strong and effective regulatory body with independent source for financing before allowing private companies into sector.

Introduction of Insurance Regulatory and Development Authority (Irda) Act, 1999

On the basis of the recommendations of Malhotra Committee the government constituted through an interim Insurance Regulatory Authority on 23 'January, 1996. IRDA bill was introduced in Parliament in 1996. The bill was retitled as Insurance Regulatory and Development Authority and introduced again in 1999 along with three schedules containing amendments to the Insurance Act, 1938, LIC Act, 1956 and GIC Act, 1922 and was passed.

Main Provisions of Irda Act

Preamble of IRDA Act, 1999 reads "An Act to provide for the establishment of an authority to protect the interest of holders of insurance policies, to regulate, promote and insure orderly growth of the insurance industry and for matters connected therewith and incidental thereto. "Section 14 of IRDA Act, lays the duties, powers and functions of the authority. The power and function of the authority shall include the followings:

- Issue to the applicant a certificate of registration to review, modify, withdraw, suspend or cancel such registration.
- To protect the interest of policyholders in all matters concerning nomination of policy, surrender value of policy, insurable interest, settlement of insurance claims, other terms and conditions of contract of insurance.
- Specifying requisite qualifications and practical training of insurance intermediary and agents.
- Specifying code of conduct for surveyors and loss assessors.

- Promoting efficiently in the conduct and insurance business.
- Promoting and regulating professional regulations connected with the insurance and reinsurance business.
- Specifying the form and manner in which books of accounts will be maintained and statement of accounts rendered by insurer and insurance intermediaries.
- Adjudications of disputes between insurers and intermediaries.
- Specifying the percentage of life insurance and general business to be undertaken by the insurer in rural or social sectors, etc.
- Section 25 provides that Insurance Advisory Committee will be constituted and shall consist of not more than 25 members.
- Section 26 provides that authority may in consistent with insurance advisory committee make regulation consistent with this Act and the rules made there under to carry out the purpose of this Act.
- Section 29 Seeks amendment in certain provisions of Insurance Act, 1938 in the manner as set out in First Schedule. The amendments to the Insurance Act are consequential in order to empower IRDA to effectively regulate promote, and insure orderly growth of the insurance industry.
- Section 30 and 31 seek to amend LIC Act, 1956 and GIC Act 1972.

Impact of Liberalization on Insurance Industry

The opening up of insurance sector for competition offers ample opportunities to both existing as well as new players to penetrate into untapped areas, sectors and sub-sectors and unexploited segments of population as presently both insurance density and penetration are at low level. Both indices being at very low level in the country even compared to the countries with the same level of economic development and per capita income are indicative of the vast potential of the growth of this sector in future.

Opportunities

- **Potential Market**

New comers will get the benefit of potential market. While nationalized general insurance companies and LIC of India have done a commendable job in extending their services throughout the country but the choices available to the insuring public are inadequate in terms of services, products and prices The untapped potential is quite large. The Malhotra Committee, which went into various aspects of India's insurable population, has been tapped so far. In India, premium per capita is only 2 and premium as percentage of GDP is 0.55%, which is very less in comparison of USA where premium per capita is 1381 and premium as percentage of GDP is 4.80. This huge gap from the global bench mark is itself lucrative.

- **Force Insurance**

In disaster prone areas, Government of India is going to make insurance force. The interim report of the high powered committee set-up by the centre on disaster management, has proposed mandatory insurance of life and property by people residing in disaster prone area such as coastal belts, flood prone areas, near nuclear, chemical and hazardous industries and thickly populated areas.

- **Products Development**

A state monopoly has little incentive to offer a wide range of products. It can be seen by a lack of certain products from LIC's portfolio and lack of extensive categorization in several GIC products such as health insurance. More competition in this business will spur firms to offer several new products and more complex and extensive risk categorization.

- **Growth of Economy**

With allowing of holding of equity shares by foreign company either itself or through its subsidiary company or nominee not exceeding 26% of paid up capital of Indian Insurance Company, various joint ventures between foreign investors and Indian partners will be operated resulting into supplementing domestic savings and economic progress of the nations.

- **Bank assurance**

Banks with their wide area network with branches in all the parts of the country will have very good opportunity to enter the insurance business. They will success in this sector because they have database of customers, trained staff, and a good network of branches besides synergy benefits.

- **Customer Services**

It would result in better customer's services and help improve the variety and price of insurance products. Competition will compel the players to bring new and innovative product, wider choice of prices and quality service to consumers.

Challenges

- **New Client**

New insurers will have to invest a minimum capital of Rs.100 crore. The normal gestation period is of five years. Hence, the new insurers will have to lock up their capital for at least five years before earning any profits. Besides they will face problems of shortage of trained manpower for the insurance industry. The setting up of various offices and distribution network is consuming process. Further, the new insurers will have to compete with the established insurance companies like LIC and GIC which have a corporate image and market presence for several years.

- **New Products**

Today, LIC has more than 60 products and GIC has more than 80 products to offer in market. But most of them are outdated, as they are not suitable to the needs of the consumers. Hence, all the insurers will have to offer innovative products to the consumers. The consumers are particularly expecting good pension plans, health insurance from the life insurers. Similarly, the consumer expect innovative products fro the general insurers for managing health care, property insurance, accident insurance and other products at an attractive terms and premium. The consumers also expect reduction 15 in the premium of the insurance products as the mortality rate in India has come down by three times in the last five years.

- **Distribution Channel**

In the liberalized insurance market, there will be multiple distribution channels, which will include agents, brokers, corporate intermediaries, bank branches, affinity groups and direct marketing through telesales and internet. There will be competition among the channels. Intense competition will grow among the old and new insurers in the market to win consumers. This will pose a great challenge to the insurance in the liberalized insurance market.

- **Consumer Education**

The existing level of awareness of the consumers for insurance products is very low, it is so because 62% of the population is literate and less than 10% well educated. Even the educated consumers are ignorant about the various products of insurance. Hence, it is necessary that all the insurers should undertake the extensive plan for education of consumers.

- **Grievance Handling**

The insurers will have to face an acute problem of the redressal of consumers' grievances for deficiency in products and services. The IRDA has already appointed ombudsman for looking into the grievances of the policyholders, its judgement will be binding on insurers. In the competitive market, awareness level of consumers will increase and it will help consumers to fight for their legal right for deficiency in services.

- **New Product Innovation**

With more competition good products will become an important differentiator among the various competitive insurance products. A lot will depend on the kind of products that these outfits launch. During recent times, global life insurance, industry being driven by single premium and unit linked plans.

- **Positioning of Insurance**

Products on the ground, the biggest challenge for the insurance companies will be to change the mindset of people, especially in life insurance. In India, life insurance is seen more as a tax saving mechanism rather than safety net incase of death. New types of products should be futuristic in outlook. To start with, low premium high cover policies should be introduced and better savings products at a latter stage.

- **Rural Market**

It is said that the life insurance business suffers from high premium and low returns. A normally competitive industry should be able to increase coverage, mobilize large savings, and provide high savings in the form of insurance. In countries like U.K. and South Africa, life insurance premiums account for over 50 percent of gross domestic savings (GDS). Insurance in India has been a priority of the urban few. Now with numerous companies set to enter, the rural areas are expected to be tapped as well. IRDA has made it mandatory for life insurers to sell 5 percent of their aggregate policies in the rural areas during the first year of operation that will be progressively increased to 15 percent by the fifth year. But with gestation period long and investments large new entrants will feel very difficult to do it.

- **Information Technology**

Information technology (IT) has become an intrinsic part of the insurance industry world-wide from general accounting to customer service, reinsurance, underwriting, and risk management. Further, Indian insurance industry, IT is used as a reporting tool whereas overseas it is used more as a decision-making instrument. Once on the line customers with net connectivity would be able to check policy details from their balance to nominee schemes, the type of loans available and the amount in their investment accounts. Similarly, insurance advisors can check their customer's accounts as well as their own account.

Strategies

- **Environment Analysis**

The companies should concentrate on environmental change, its direction, magnitude and its short-term and long-term impact, formulating strategies to meet the challenges of high competition, preparing contingency plans and then designing action plans for effective implementations of formulated strategies.

- **Restructuring Organisations**

The traditional hierarchy system is very slow in making decisions due to several levels of management, due to its procedural inflexibility and slow communication. A manager in the privatized scenario is required to be an organizational specialist, country specialist and a global specialist.

- **Speed, Cost Effectiveness and Innovations**

The insurance companies will have to make substantial investments in customer relationship management technologies. They will be required to have wide area networks (WAN) connecting branches spread across wide geographical locations and workout modalities facilitating premium payment through the internet.

- **Human Resource**

Development Human capital is important for any organization especially for organizations whose activities revolve around special human interactions. Along with products and services the new insurers need people with the right set of knowledge, skills and aptitude for insurance. The persons who are involved in selling the product and those who are doing the back office work need to equip themselves with newer skills and insights into every aspect of company's functioning. They have a daunting task of exploiting potential in the industry and a t the same time brings good risks to the company for providing insurance coverage. They have to retain the existing customers for which they need to have better understanding of products and services by creating healthy internal environment with group harmony. Existing companies will have to frame their human resource policies to retain the competent and motivated staff since new entrants will be eyeing them by offering lucrative salaries.

- **Efficiency in Distribution**

It is very important factor and many prove bottleneck to the new players. Insurance companies are making the products available through the ready distribution channels of banks, non-banking finance companies and housing companies. One has to be careful doing this, since creating distribution and distances does not automatically mean controlling them.

- **Risk Management**

Like all intermediaries in financial markets, insurance companies will have to bring sophistication in market research technique future portfolio expansion.

- **Efficient Marketing Strategies**

Marketing strategies for insurance predicts in the emerging scenario could be understood in following steps:

R → STP → MM → I → C

Where, R = Market research,
STP = Segmentation, Targeting, Positioning,
MM = Marketing Mix,
I = Implementation, and
C = Control

The focus of emerging strategies would centre on the prepositions like reduce costs, increase profitability, reduce time to market, improve customer intimacy, retain customers for life, establish strong partnerships. Formulating a marketing strategy is more a process than an event.

Conclusion

In the global era, Insurance companies are increasingly willing to spend more on the customer satisfaction and brand building exercises. Though it is one of the highly regulated industries, it still provides lot of scope for creativity and innovations. As our industry is predominantly dominated by personal selling and personalized services many a time the service standards vary based on the intermediary involved in the process. In order to achieve the competitive edge over others standardize the process and bring about quality improvement and get feed back from the customers regarding the quality of services rendered. This will result in customer satisfaction, customer retention, customer acquisition, employee's retention and cost reduction. This paper focuses on the marketing approach adopted by the modern insurers to withhold their existing customers and attract new ones.

References

- Insurance Principles and Practice (2006) M. N. Mishra, S. Chand and Company Ltd., New Delhi.

- Introduction to Insurance (2006) Marks S. Dorman, Prentice hall, Inc, Engle Wood Cliffs, N.J. 07632.
- Indian Insurance Industry (2006)D.C. Srivastava and Shashank Srivastava, New Century Publications, Delhi.
- Internet sources.
- Insurance journals of various issues.

7

Export Credit Insurance in India

G. Thamizh Chelvan

The advent of globalisation and liberalisation has paved the way for international trade flourishment. To be successful, an exporter should offer good quality at a competitive price. Hectic competition that exists in the market compelled the exporters to go for liberal terms of credit to the buyer. This credit term involves huge risk to the traders. Payments for exports are open to risks even at the best of times. The risks have assumed large proportions today due to the far-reaching political and economic changes that are sweeping the world. An outbreak of war or civil war may block or delay payment for goods exported. A coup or an insurrection may also bring about the same result. Economic difficulties or balance of payment problems may lead a country to impose restrictions on either import of certain goods or on transfer of payments for goods imported. In addition, the exporters have to face commercial risks of insolvency or protracted default of buyers. The commercial risks of a foreign buyer going bankrupt or losing his capacity to pay are aggravated due to the political and economic uncertainties. Export credit insurance is designed to protect exporters from the consequences of the payment risks, both political and commercial, and to enable them to expand their overseas business without fear of loss

Genesis of ECGC

Export Credit Guarantee Corporation of India Limited was established in the year 1957 by the Government of India to strengthen the export promotion drive by covering the risk of exporting on credit. Being essentially an export promotion organization, it functions under the administrative control of the Ministry of Commerce and Industry, Department of Commerce, and Government of India. It is managed by a Board of Directors comprising representatives of the Government, Reserve Bank of India, banking, insurance and exporting community. ECGC is the fifth largest credit insurer of the world in terms of coverage of national exports. The present paid-up capital of the company is Rs.800 crores and authorised capital Rs.1000 crores.

Major Functions of ECGC

ECGC provides the following services to the exporters as well as to the export financing institutions.

- Provides a range of credit risk insurance covers to exporters against loss in export of goods and services
- Offers guarantees to banks and financial institutions to enable exporters to obtain better facilities from them
- Provides Overseas Investment Insurance to Indian companies investing in joint ventures abroad in the form of equity or loan
- Provides guidance in export-related activities
- Makes available information on different countries with its own credit ratings
- Makes it easy to obtain export finance from banks/financial institutions
- Assists exporters in recovering bad debts

- Provides information on credit-worthiness of overseas buyers

Performance of ECGC

The following table explains the achievements of ECGC

Value of business covered: Rs. Crores

Year	*1999*	*2000*	*2001*
Standard policies and transfer guarantees	3139.00	24633.00	23530.00
Policies-Project Exports	1815.00	574.00	360.00
Factoring	0.00	0.00	0.00
Guarantees – Short term Exports	148088.00	158962.00	157274.00
Guarantees & Term projects	493.00	323.00	744.00

(Contd. Table)

Year	*2002*	*2003*	*2004*
Standard policies and transfer guarantees	26411.00	28117.00	35696.00
Policies-Project Exports	737.00	1720.00	1436.00
Factoring	47.00	223.00	291.00
Guarantees – Short term Exports	237084.00	296870.00	311914.00
Guarantees & Term projects	699.00	1088.00	1408.00

Policies

With the objective of providing insurance services to the exporters ECGC has introduced various policies suitable to the exporters interest and requirements of policies have been launched. Following are the major policies of ECGC.

(1) Standard Policy

Shipments (Comprehensive Risks) Policy, commonly known as the Standard Policy, is the one ideally suited to cover risks in respect of goods exported on short-term credit, i.e. credit not exceeding 180 days. This policy covers both commercial and political risks from the date of shipment. It is issued to exporters whose anticipated export turnover for the next 12 months is more than Rs.50 lacs. Under the Standard Policy, ECGC covers, from the date of shipment, the following risks:

(a) **Commercial risks:** Which encompasses the

- Insolvency of the buyer
- Failure of the buyer to make the payment due within a specified period, normally four months from the due date.
- Buyer's failure to accept the goods, subject to certain conditions

(b) **Political risks:** Which encompasses the

- Imposition of restriction by the Government of the buyer's country or any Government action, which may block or delay the transfer of payment made by the buyer.
- War, civil war, revolution or civil disturbances in the buyer's country.
- New import restrictions or cancellation of a valid import licence in the buyer's country.
- Interruption or diversion of voyage outside India resulting in payment of additional freight or insurance charges which can not be recovered from the buyer.

- Any other cause of loss occurring outside India not normally insured by general insurers, and beyond the control of both the exporter and the buyer.

The policy does not cover losses due to the following risks:

- Commercial disputes including quality disputes raised by the buyer, unless the exporter obtains a decree from a competent court of law in the buyer's country in his favour.
- Causes inherent in the nature of the goods.
- Buyer's failure to obtain necessary import or exchange authorization from authorities in his country.
- Insolvency or default of any agent of the exporter or of the collecting bank.
- Loss or damage to goods which can be covered by general insurers.
- Exchange rate fluctuation.
- Failure or negligence on the part of the exporter to fulfil the terms of the export contract.

The Standard Policy is meant to cover all the shipments made by an exporter, on credit terms during the period of 24 months after the issue of the policy. In other words, an exporter is required to offer for the cover of the Policy each and every shipment that may be made by him in the next 24 months on DP (Documents Against Payments), DA (Documents Against Acceptance) or Open Delivery terms to all buyers other than his own associates.

An exporter may exclude shipments made against advance payment or those, which are supported by irrevocable Letters of Credit, which carry the confirmation of banks in India, since the exporter faces no risk in respect of such transactions. Exporters of the status of trading houses and above are allowed to exclude shipments of specified commodities or shipments to buyers in specified countries or any combination of these two, from the purview of the Standard Policies held by them.

Exporters holding Standard Policy may opt to get shipments against irrevocable Letter of Credit excluded from the scope of the policy. However, unless they are confirmed by banks in India, payment under irrevocable Letters of Credit (LC) is subject to political risks. Exporters are, therefore, well advised to get such shipments also covered under the policy. For such shipments, an exporter has option to obtain cover for either political risks only or for comprehensive risks, i.e., for all political risks and the risk of insolvency or default of the bank opening the irrevocable Letter of Credit. The comprehensive risk cover also provides indemnity to the exporter to the extent of 25% of the gross invoice value if the LC opening bank refuses payment on the ground of discrepancies in LC, which are not clearly attributable to the exporter. In either case, cover will be provided by ECGC only if the exporter agrees to get all the shipments made against irrevocable Letter of Credit covered under the policy. Cover will not be available for selected transactions.

Shipments to foreign buyers who are associates of the exporters, i.e. in whose business the exporter has a financial interest, are normally excluded from the policy. They can, however be, covered against political risks under the policy if an exporter so desires. Where both the exporter and the associate are public limited companies and where the exporter's share holding in the associate does not exceed 49%, cover can be provided against insolvency risks in addition to the political risks.

(2) Turnover Policies

Turnover policy is a variation of the standard policy for the benefit of large exporters who contribute not less than Rs. 10 lacs per annum towards premium. Therefore all the exporters who will pay a premium of Rs. 10 lacs in a year are entitled to avail of it. The turnover policy envisages projection of the export turnover of the exporter for a year and the initial determination of the premium payable on that basis, subject to adjustment at the end of the year based on actuals. The policy provides additional discount in premium with an added incentive for increasing the exports beyond the projected turnover and also offers simplified procedure for premium remittance and filing of shipment information. It also provides for higher discretionary credit limits on overseas buyers, based on the total premium paid by the exporter under the policy. The turnover policy is issued with a validity period of one year.

The holders of turnover policy need not submit monthly declarations of shipment. Instead, they have only to submit a statement of shipments made during the quarter in a prescribed format within 30 days of the end of the quarter. The basic premium rates applicable for the standard policy will apply to the turnover policy also. However, an exporter holding a standard policy opts for turnover policy, he will be entitled to an additional discount of 10% over and above the 'no claim bonus' which he is enjoying under the standard policy, subject to a minimum total discount of 20%. If an exporter not holding the standard policy avails of the turnover policy, he will be entitled to a discount of 20%. In case of no claims in future, the exporter will be entitled to further 'no claim bonus' and consequently total discount. Thus the total discount could go up to 60%.

The premium calculated on the projected turnover is payable in four quarterly instalments (grant of facility of payment of premium in monthly instalments will be considered on a case to case basis). At the end of the year, if the premium payable on the basis of the actual turnover is less than the premium paid on the basis of the projected turnover, the excess amount paid will be carried forward to the next policy period and could be adjusted in the premium for the first quarter of the renewed policy. In case the policy is not renewed, and if difference between premium paid and premium payable is more than 10%, the same will be refunded subject to marginal adjustments. If the premium payable on the basis of the actual turnover exceeds the projected premium by not more than 10%, the excess premium need not be paid. Thus an incentive is provided to the policyholder to increase his turnover. If it exceeds by more than 10%, only the excess of the premium over 10% needs to be paid

(3) Insurance Cover for Buyer's Credit and Line of Credit

Buyer's Credit is a credit extended by a bank in India to an overseas buyer enabling the buyer to pay for machinery and equipment that he may be importing from India for a specific project. A Line of Credit is a credit extended by a bank in India to an overseas bank, institution or government for the purpose of facilitating import of a variety of listed goods from India into the overseas country. A number of importers in the overseas country may be importing the goods under one Line of Credit. ECGC has evolved schemes to protect the lending banks from certain risks of non-payment. These covers take the form of an agreement between the lending bank and ECGC and are issued on a case to case basis. Credit terms and the length of the credit period should be in conformity with what is appropriate for the export of the relevant items. There should be adequate security for the repayments to be made by the borrower. Cover can be granted either for political risks or for comprehensive risks. Political risks covered under the scheme are:

- The occurrence of war between the country of the overseas party and India.
- The occurrence of war, hostilities, civil war, revolution, rebellion, insurrection or other disturbances in the country of overseas party.
- The operation of law or of an order, decree or regulation having the force of law which in circumstances outside the control of the lender and/or the overseas party, prevents, restricts or controls, the transfer of the sums due to the lender by the overseas party under the Financial Agreement.

If ECGC agrees to provide comprehensive risks cover, the risk of protracted default of the borrower to pay the amounts due under the loan agreement and insolvency of the borrower, where applicable, will be covered in addition to the political risks mentioned above. The premium rates applicable to comprehensive risk cover will naturally be higher than that for political risks cover. Normally ECGC covers up to 85% of the loss. The premium rates depend on the country to which exports are made and the period of repayment. At least 20% of the total amount of premium should be paid in advance. The balance amount of premium may be paid on a quarterly basis in proportion to the amount of credit disbursed.

(4) Specific Shipment Policies - Short Term (SSP-ST)

Specific Shipment Policies - Short Term (SSP-ST) provide cover to Indian exporters against commercial and political risks involved in export of goods on short-term credit not exceeding 180 days. Exporters can take cover under these policies for either a shipment or a few shipments to a buyer under a contract. These policies can be availed of by (i) exporters who do not hold SCR Policy and (ii) by exporters having SCR Policy, in respect of shipments permitted to be excluded from the purview of the SCR Policy.

Options available under the policy are:

(a) Specific Shipments (commercial and political risks) Policy - short-term

(b) Specific Shipments (political risks) Policy - short-term

(c) Specific Shipments (insolvency & default of L/C opening bank and political risks) Policy-short-term.

The risks covered under the above said policies are:

(i) Commercial risks: [For SSP-ST policies of the type (a) above]

- Insolvency of the buyer
- Failure of the buyer to make the payment due within a specified period, normally four months from the due date.
- Buyer's failure to accept the goods (subject to certain conditions).

(ii) Political risks: [For all the SSP-ST policies]

- Imposition of restrictions by the Government of the buyer's country or any Government action which may block or delay the transfer of payment made by the buyer;
- War, civil war, revolution or civil disturbances in the buyer's country;
- New import restrictions or cancellation of a valid import license;
- Interruption of voyage outside India resulting in payment of additional freight or insurance charges which cannot be recovered from the buyer;

(iii) Insolvency & default of LC opening bank: [For SSP-ST policies of the type (c) above]

- Insolvency of the L/C opening bank;
- Failure of the LC opening bank to make the payment due within a specified period, normally four months, from the due date;
- Commercial disputes including quality disputes raised by the buyer, unless the exporter obtains a decree from a competent court of law in the buyer's country in his favour;
- Causes inherent in the nature of goods;
- Buyer's failure to obtain necessary import or exchange authorization from authorities in his country;
- Insolvency or default of any agent of the exporter or of the collecting bank;
- Loss or damage to goods;
- Exchange rate fluctuation;
- Failure of the exporter to fulfil the terms of the export contract or negligence on his part.

(5) IT-enabled Services (Specific Customer) Policy

IT-enabled Services (specific customer) Policy is issued to cover the following commercial and political risks involved in rendering IT-enabled services to a particular customer:

Commercial risks:

- Insolvency of the customer.
- Failure of the customer to make the payment due within a specified period, normally four months from the due date.
- Buyer's failure to accept the services rendered (subject to certain conditions).

Bank risks:

- Bankruptcy of L/c opening bank
- Failure of L/c opening bank to make the payment due within a specified period, normally within four months from the due date (Non-payment due to discrepancies in the document will not be covered)

Political risks:

- Imposition of restrictions by the Government of the customer's country or any Government action which may block or delay the transfer of payment made by the customer;
- War, civil war, revolution or civil disturbances in the customer's country;
- New import restrictions or cancellation of a valid import license by authorities in the customer's country;
- Cancellation by the Government of India a legally valid and binding contract between the exporter and the customer.

(6) Buyer Exposure Policies

Presently, in the policies offered to exporters premium is charged on the export turnover, though the Corporation's exposure on each buyer is controlled through a system of approval of credit limits on the buyer for covering commercial risks. While this suits the small and medium exporters, many large exporters having large number of shipments have been complaining about the volume of returns to be filed under the policy necessitating the deployment of their resources for this purpose and also resulting in possible unintentional omissions or commissions in such reporting, which have an impact on the settlement of claims. There has been a demand for simplification of the procedures as well as for rationalization of the premium structure. Considering the requirements of such exporters, the Corporation has decided to introduce policies on which premium would be charged on the basis of the expected level of exposure.

Two types of Exposure policies are offered, viz,

(i) Exposure (Single Buyer) Policy – for covering the risks on a specified buyer

(ii) Exposure (Multi Buyer) Policy – for covering the risks on all buyers.

An exporter can choose to obtain exposure based cover on a selected buyer. The cover would be against commercial and political risks attached to the buyer for both non-LC and LC transactions. A separate Buyer Exposure Policy will be issued for each buyer covering all the exports to be made to the buyer during a period of twelve months. If the exporter has opted for commercial and political risks cover, failure of the LC opening bank in respect of exports against LC will also be covered, for the banks with World Rank (WR) up to 25,000 as per latest Banker's almanac. For covering any bank with ranking beyond that level, the exporter has to obtain specific approval from the branch, which issued the policy prior to making the shipment. For covering the political risks only, in respect of LC transactions or shipments to associates, Buyer Exposure policy with endorsement restricting the cover to political risks only with significantly less premium is offered. This policy can be availed by exporters holding Standard Policy in respect of any of their buyers. Shipments to the buyers covered under Buyer Exposure Policies would be excluded from the purview of the Standard Policy. Risks covered would be same as covered under the existing Buyer wise Policy.

The loss of coverage would be 90 percent for those who also hold our Standard Policies and at 80 percent for others. If it is mutually agreed between the Corporation and the policyholder, the Policy could provide for a higher share of loss to be retained by the insured with proportionate reduction of premium. The Policy would specify the loss limit up to which claim will be entertained due to any of the risks covered under the Policy in respect of shipments made to the buyer during the policy period. The claim amount payable shall be arrived at by applying the percentage of loss covered to the actual loss amount, subject to the loss limit.

(7) Consignment Exports Policy:

Economic liberalization and gradual removal of international barriers for trade and commerce are opening up various new avenues of export opportunities to Indian exporters of quality goods. One of the methods being increasingly adopted by Indian exporters is consignment exports where the goods are shipped and held in stock overseas ready for sale to overseas buyers, as and when orders are received. To protect the Indian Exporters from possible losses when selling goods to ultimate buyers, it was decided to introduce Consignment Policy Cover. There are two policies available for covering consignment export viz; Consignment Exports (Stock-holding Agent) and Consignment Exports (Global Entity Policy)

(8) Buyerwise Policies - Short Term (BP-ST):

Buyer wise Policies - Short Term (BP-ST) provide cover to Indian exporters against commercial and political risks involved in export of goods on short-term credit to a particular buyer. All shipments to the buyer in respect of whom the policy is issued will have to be covered (with a provision to permit exclusion of shipments under LC). These policies can be availed of by (i) exporters who do not hold SCR Policy and (ii) by exporters having SCR Policy, in case all the shipments to the buyer in question have been permitted to be excluded from the purview of the SCR Policy.

Different types of BP (ST)

(a) Buyer wise (commercial and political risks) Policy - short-term

(b) Buyer wise (political risks) Policy - short-term

(c) Buyer wise (insolvency & default of L/C opening bank and political risks) Policy-short-term.

The different risks covered under BP (ST)

(i) Commercial risks: [For BP-ST policies of the type (a) above]

- Insolvency of the buyer
- Failure of the buyer to make the payment due within a specified period, normally four months from the due date.
- Buyer's failure to accept the goods (subject to certain conditions).

(ii) Political risks: [For all the BP-ST policies]

- Imposition of restrictions by the Government of the buyer's country or any Government action which may block or delay the transfer of payment made by the buyer;
- War, civil war, revolution or civil disturbances in the buyer's country;
- New import restrictions or cancellation of a valid import license;
- Interruption of voyage outside India resulting in payment of additional freight or insurance charges which cannot be recovered from the buyer;

(iii) Insolvency and default of LC opening bank [For BP-ST policies of the type (c) above]

- Insolvency of the L/C opening bank;

- Failure of the LC opening bank to make the payment due within a specified period, normally four months from the due date;
- risks not covered under BP (ST)
- Commercial disputes including quality disputes raised by the buyer, unless the exporter obtains a decree from a competent court of law in the buyer's country in his favour.
- Causes inherent in the nature of goods;
- Buyer's failure to obtain necessary import or exchange authorization from authorities in his country;
- Insolvency or default of any agent of the exporter or of the collecting bank;
- Loss or damage to goods;
- Exchange rate fluctuation;

(9) Small Exporter's Policy:

The Small Exporter's Policy is basically the Standard Policy, incorporating certain improvements in terms of cover, in order to encourage small exporters to obtain and operate the policy. It is issued to exporters whose anticipated export turnover for the period of one year does not exceed Rs. 50 lacs.

Period of Policy: Small Exporter's Policy is issued for a period of 12 months, as against 24 months in the case of Standard Policy.

Minimum premium: Premium payable will be determined on the basis of projected exports on an annual basis subject to a minimum premium of Rs. 2000/- for the policy period.

No claim bonus in the premium rate is granted every year at the rate of 5% (as against once in two years for Standard Policy at the rate of 10%).

Declaration of shipments: Shipments need to be declared quarterly (instead of monthly as in the case of Standard Policy).

Declaration of overdue payments: Small exporters are required to submit monthly declarations of all payments remaining overdue by more than 60 days from the due date, as against 30 days in the case of exporters holding the Standard Policy.

Percentage of cover: For shipments covered under the Small Exporter's Policy ECGC will pay claims to the extent of 95% where the loss is due to commercial risks and 100% if the loss is caused by any of the political risks (Under the Standard Policy, the extent of cover is 90% for both commercial and political risks).

Waiting period for claims: The normal waiting period of 4 months under the Standard Policy has been halved in the case of claims arising under the Small Exporter's Policy.

Change in terms of payment of extension in credit period: In order to enable small exporters to deal with their buyers in a flexible manner, the following facilities are allowed: A small exporter may, without prior approval of ECGC convert a D/P bill into D-A bill, provided that he has already obtained suitable credit limit on the buyer on D/A terms. Where the value of this bill is not more than Rs.3 laks, conversion of D/P bill into D/A bill is permitted even if credit limit on the buyer has been obtained on D/P terms only, but only one claim can be considered during the policy period on account of losses arising from such conversions; A small exporter may, without the prior approval of ECGC extend the due date of payment of a D/A bill provided that a credit limit on the buyer on D/A terms is in force at the time of such extension. Resale of unaccepted goods: If, upon non-acceptance of goods by a buyer, the exporter sells the goods to an alternate buyer without obtaining prior approval of ECGC even when the loss exceeds 25% of the gross invoice value, ECGC may consider payment of claims up to an amount considered reasonable, provided that ECGC is satisfied that the exporter did his best under the circumstances to minimize the loss. In all other respects, the Small Exporter's Policy has the same features as the Standard Policy.

Guarantee to Banks

Timely and adequate credit facilities at the pre-shipment stage are essential for exporters to realize their full export potential. Exporters may not, however, be easily able to obtain such facilities from their bankers for several reasons, e.g. the exporter may be relatively new to export business, the extent of facilities needed by him may be out of proportion to the equity of the firms or the value of collateral offered by the exporter may be inadequate. The Packing Credit Guarantee of ECGC helps the exporter to obtain better and adequate facilities from their bankers. The Guarantees assure the banks that, in the event of an exporter failing to discharge his liabilities to the bank, ECGC would make good a major portion of the bank's loss. The bank is required to be co-insurer to the extent of the remaining loss.

Conclusion

Risks involved in export business have assumed large proportions today, due to various political and economic changes that are sweeping the world. Exporters require adequate cover to boot their exports. Since its inception ECGC as a catalyst in India's export, has come of age. As the opportunities and threats for Indian exporters rise with globalisation, ECGC role has become very crucial in the promotion of exports from the country its role in future is not merely of being a credit but of being a partner in India's export endeavours.

8

CRM for Life Insurance Industry

M. Thyagarajan, J. Udhayakumar

Introduction

As the Indian economy is quickly integrating with the global economy we are seeing a number of multinational companies begin their operations in India. This scenario unfolds the kind of competition that was not experienced by most of the Industries including Insurance. It is quiet evident from the success of these multinationals, that the key factor distinguishing them from others is the sophisticated customer service standards and practices that they meticulously adopt. Not to be left behind in the race, a number of Indian companies are moving forward and have identified the magic mantra – CRM.

CRM the acronym for Customer Relationship Management is a strategic business initiative, which goes beyond traditional selling and customer contact programs. It is an integration of technology with activities of employees and business associates to deliver faster, more customized service to customers. CRM is a method for long term management of customer relationships, which is backed by a defined and focussed business process. CRM solutions not only offer value to businesses, but importantly the main attribute " scalability", ensures that it can be implemented in various stages of increasing complexity and value. While total CRM solution is desirable, the insurance companies can also deploy the solutions at different stages in line with their growth and yet the same can be a part of the total solution.

Life Insurance and the need for CRM

Life Insurance is a service business, which is highly data dependent and sensitive.

The winners in this business are those who ensure customer delight. As competition opens up, this sector poses immense challenges and provides varied opportunities.

Listed below are some of these challenges and opportunities.

- The Low penetration of Insurance via a visa the huge insurable population
- The plethora of policies (in the case of some companies) and a few policies with many options and riders (in the case of most of the new insurers)
- The necessity to deliver policies and service them across wide and geographically spread locations
- The complexity of pre and post sales operations like generating product awareness, policy management, claims management and agency administration
- The necessity to control costs in marketing and administration
- Converting a one time transaction into a long term relationship

To Meet these Challenges the Life Insurer Must Implement the Following Processes

- Online linking of the various distribution channels upto post sales service which gives an edge over competition.

- Online help desks and communication assistance to respond to the demanding customer and his information requirements.
- Net working the various offices and transmission of various statistics and financial returns on a real time basis to enable prompt and efficient service as well as data integrity.
- Controlling costs and avoiding delays due to the large geographical spread of offices and population in a subcontinent like India

The following components of CRM would enable achievement of these Parameters

- **Networking**
- **Data warehousing**
- **Data mining**
- **E enabling**
- **Call centers**

Phased implementation in the above order or complete implementation and integration of all these components would result in highly effective customer centric approach, substantially improving the business bottom line and ensuring customer delight.

Let us look at the important features of each of these components and see how their implementation would impact the functioning of a Life Insurance organization.

Networking

Full-fledged Data ware housing and Data mining process can be accomplished only by having proper Networking in place. Networking is a process, which ensures the connecting of all the offices through delivery media such as leased lines, Internet, VSAT, and DSL lines. This will enable data capture and retrieval from different access points. As the communication infrastructure is growing day by day and the cost of communication is coming down, an efficient networking should no longer be difficult to implement.

Data Warehousing

In Life business, the data required to be captured is substantial from the proposal stage to settlement of claims. It is not only the capture and storage of data from various sources, locations and data bases but also retrieving the same in the desired output formats. The complex aspects of the business make this difficult because of the legacy of data, data integrity, and wide distribution of data and need for collating the entire data as per the requirements of the Insurer. Further the data is to be maintained throughout the life of the policy. It is also mandatory to comply with regulatory mechanisms, which stipulate the need for maintaining data for a specific period.

In the case of Life business Data warehousing typically captures different data including those of the policyholders and agents/advisors spread across geographic locations to one centralized database. It also enables more sophisticated analysis of various performance parameters such as business growth, claims settlement and profitability. The carefully collected information is finally consummated by the policyholders either through Internet, Call centers or Servicing offices.

Data Mining

Once Data warehousing is implemented, its offshoot Data mining enables a Life Insurer to utilize the data to achieve the essential objective of maximizing sales and ensuring customer delight. Data Mining entails looking for patterns in the customer data. The data for data mining can come from the insurer's transactional history of customers. It enables drawing correlation and patterns from easily accessible data on all the functional areas including the trends in customer preferences, payment of premium, queries from customers, performance of agents/ advisors. This not only simplifies but also puts an efficient process in place for the managers. Call centers greatly benefit from

Data warehousing and Data mining and quickly attend to the customer requirements. Data centers can be located at various places to provide support to the call centers and functional offices.

E-enabling

Internet is emerging as one of the key marketing and distribution channel with a vast potential, wide reach, and long term prospects. It creates a strong, powerful idea and is impacting people. It also ensures brand loyalty to be fostered by reflecting the organizations core values online, and enables quick and convenient transactions.

By e-enabling their key functions, Life Insurers provide greater visibility, rapid access to data and quick service to new prospects, policyholders and agents/advisors. Internet enables interactivity and interoperability by offering product information, comparative analysis, advisor/agent location, service corner, and premium payments for people across the country. The benefits are enormous as the prospects can access product information and other relevant details "Any Time, Any Where". The life of agents/advisors would become easier as the prospect is well informed and the time to close the transaction is extremely minimal. The Service corner helps the policyholders obtain information / status to most of their queries. Little value adds like auto responders for queries, risk profiling, investment and tax calculators, email alerts for premium payments, new product information, and gestures like birthday/anniversary wishes can be easily implemented enhancing the image of the organization and also bonding the ties with the customers.

Agents/Advisors can also be trained through e-learning modules and product information can be quickly disseminated. Agents can be quickly accessed on the net.

Call Centers

Finally successful Call centers are the benchmark for the total and proper deployment of customer relationship management. They help in providing "single point access that ensures "customer delight" the focal objective of a Life insurer. It is imperative that a well-planned and defined road map is worked out to open and operate call centers in all strategic locations. These will be the primary access points for all the policy holders/prospects to call for their queries and requirements. Tele marketing is also a major utility provided by Call centers.

Action Plan

Following are the suggested action points for the implementation of CRM solutions

- Finalization of the Technology strategy which is aligned with the Life insurers goals
- Stage wise plan with time lines
- Identification of a competent IT end to end solutions provider with a strong insurance domain competence, quality processes, and proven technology alliances
- Clear documentation of the requirements and ensuring adequate understanding of the business processes
- Enabling Wide area and Local area Net working
- Appropriate and cost effective networking support systems like, communication, hardware and uninterrupted power supply
- Identifying strategic locations for Data warehousing and Call centers.

Costs on CRM is Up

Insurance firms spend close to 12 percent of their IT budgets on CRM software and services. The cost includes operational CRM and spending on BI tools. If A spokesperson of an upcoming insurance firm adds, "Of our total IT budget, we are spending 14 percent on CRM applications." Industry pundits believe that insurance firms are looking for CRM initiatives with budgets ranging from Rs 50 lakh going right up to Rs 3 crore. The sector is busy compiling data on individuals, including their purchasing patterns and buying preferences of policies, pension plans and the like. In many cases, policy renewal marketing to existing customers remains an unsophisticated exercise, often amounting to little more than a request to renew, with no attempt at putting a value proposition before the customer. With a little help from CRM software, insurance firms can sell multiple insurance policies and pension plans to the same customer.

Using analytical CRM insurance companies

- Cross- and up-selling capability to provide market
- Opportunities within an existing customer database.
- Predictive capability to determine customer behaviour.
- Information regarding customer retention or attrition helps to determine the likelihood of policy lapses and helps to identify customers worth targeting for retention campaigns.
- Customer segmentation that leverages data to create accurate categories for use in marketing strategies.
- Analytics with campaign management functionality to help drive a more effective and efficient marketing campaign.

Conclusion

To conclude what else could be the right strategy than the "CRM Mantra" for it can revolutionize the business and customer service approach and ensure that the Life insurer is not only visible but is distinguished and sought after. There are several pain areas that new insurance firms face—acquiring new customers, retaining them, cross-selling products and controlling rising costs while providing comprehensive support. CRM helps connect a bank's high net worth customers with insurance firms.

9

Banc Assurance - A New Channel of Distribution of Insurance in the Global Scenario

Dr. R. Eswaran, Mrs. M. Vidhya

Banc assurance is seen by many to be a significant or even the primary channel. The banking and Insurance industry have changed rapidly in the changing and challenging economic environment throughout the globe. In the competitive and open environment each and every one wants to do better than others. And they know that if they are not able to provide better service they won't survive in the Industry. Insurance companies are also to be competitive by cutting cost and serving in the better way to customers. Now the time has come to choose and adopt appropriate distribution channel.

The insurance industry has indeed awakened to deregulated environment in which several private companies have partnered with multinational insurance companies. Despite a billion of population, India still has a low insurance percentage of 1.95 and it is in 51st position in world. Despite of the fact that India boosts a saving rate around 25%, less than 5% is spending on insurance. To streamline the saving in to insurance Banc assurance is the best channel to tackle four challenges facing the insurance industry :

- Product innovation
- Distribution
- Customer Service
- Investments

Meaning

Banc assurance, known as Alfinanze and most popular in Europe is the simplest way of distribution of insurance products through a bank distribution channel. It is basically selling insurance products and services by leveraging the vast customer base of a bank and fulfill the banking and insurance needs of the customers at the same time. It takes the various forms depending upon the demography, economic and legislative climate of the country, while demographic climate will determine the kinds of insurance products, economic climate will determine the trends in terms of turnover, market motives behind the activities are directed towards shares etc, legislative climate will decide the periphery within which bancassurance has to operate. The motives behind the bancassurance also differ. For banks it just acts as a means of product diversification and additional fee income; for insurance company it acts as a tool for increasing their market penetration and premium turnover and for customer it acts as a bonanza in terms of reduced price, high quality products and delivery to doorsteps. So every body is a winner here. It is a phenomenon where insurance products are offered through the distribution channels of the banking services along with a complete range of banking & investment products & services. In simple term we can say Bancassurance tries to exploit synergies between both the insurance companies and banks. In the simple term of insurance there are only three parties. The Bank, The insurer and the customer.

BENEFITS

Bancassurance is an important tool in the hands of bankers, insurers and customers to maximise their benefits at a time. As everybody is a winner in this system.

- **From the View Point of Bankers**

Bankers have power, existing structure to relate to the customers needs why bank will enter in this area the reasons behind it are given below:-

(i) In a situation of constant asset base the bank can increases Return on Assets (ROA) by increasing their income, by selling insurance products through their own channel. It can cover operating expenses and make operating expenses profitable by leveraging their distribution and processing capabilities.

(ii) The bankers have a branch network to make face to face contact with the customers and a great deal of trust over the customers. By leveraging the facilities, the bankers can guess the attitude and diverse needs of the customers and could change the face of insurance distribution to personal line insurance.

(iii) Banks enjoy significant brand awareness within their geographical region providing for a lower per lead cost when advertising through print, radio and television. The advantage of a bank over traditional distributors is the lower cost per sales lead made possible by their sizeable loyal customer base.

(iv) Banks have extensive experience in marketing to both existing customers and non-customers. They also use technology access multiple communication channels such as statement inserts, direct mail, a TMS, telemarketing etc for the improvement in transaction processing and customer service. European banks have more than doubled the conversion rates of insurance leads into sales and have increased sales productivity to a ratio which is more than enough to make bancassurance a highly profitable proposition.

- **From the View Point of Insurer**

(i) The insurer can increase their volume of business through banking distribution channel and gain better.

(ii) If can solve the difficulties arising out of price competition which has driven down the margins and increased the compensation demand of successful agents.

(iii) Through agents the insurer can only sell fewer and larger policies to a more up scale client. Mainly middleclass income holders who comprise the bulk of bank customers get very little attention. By using bank channel the insurer can capture much of it's under served market.

(iv) By cutting cost insurers can serve better to the customer in terms of lower premium rate and better risk coverage through product diversification.

- **From the Customers' View Point**:

Product innovation and distribution are directed towards the satisfaction of the needs of the customer. Bancassurance model assists customers in terms of reduced price, diversified products quality products, in time and doorstep service.

Strategies

The strategy for using the established, entrenched distribution network for one product to market other new products has long existed in the consumer goods sector. Thus the networks for soaps and detergents have been used by companies to distribute newly launched food products; the distribution channel for Radios has been used to market televisions and so on. Of course, the basic promise for this kind of cross selling is the fact that companies keep diversifying their product portfolios, using established 'incumbent' networks to promote and distribute new product lines. Banks, too, have in the recent past adopted this strategy both in India as well as internationally. They have moved away from the classical model of deposit taking and credit disbursal through their branch networks and have begun to offer a wide range of products and services like security broking facilities and mutual funds. This is the phenomenon of 'universal banking' that builds on the principle of leveraging existing networks to broaden portfolio offerings. Change in regulatory regimes has also facilitated this diversification. The famous Glass Steagall Act in the US that restrained bans from diversifying into related areas was effectively rendered obsolete by the late 1990s. This diversification of banking services has been driven by a number of factors, all of which have threatened bank profitability Growing disintermediation by corporate borrowers (direct borrowings by firms from the debt market for both working capital and term loans), better inventory practices that have reined in working capital needs and a liberalized external borrowing regime coupled with dwindling international rates have all eaten into 'fund incomes' of banks. In short, the margins or spreads that banks make between the costs of funds (deposits plus borrowings) and the returns on funds (interest earnings on loans).

Diversification

Banks have felt the need to offset these through growing fee incomes particularly from the retail side. To target the retail segment, banks have felt the need to offer a more diversified product range to appeal to a diverse range of risk profiles. On the other hand, stand-alone financial product providers (NBFCs, mutual funds etc.) have faced crippling distribution costs that in the face of growing competition, they have not been able to pass on as 'load' on this product. Thus as far as banks and other financial services providers are concerned, there has been a 'double coincidence' of needs that has led them to collaborate either through direct equity participation or ownership by banks or strategic alliances. One of the more recent examples of financial diversification is bancassurance', the term given to the distribution of insurance products through branches or other distribution channels of banks. The concept that originated in France now constitutes the dominant model in a number of European countries. In France 70 per cent of new business premiums come through this distribution channel, 69 per cent in Portugal, 63 per cent in Spain and so on. Projections by insurance giant Aviva peg the distribution share of bancassurance at 33 per cent by 2010, making it the single largest distribution channel. In Asia, the share of this network is small but growing rapidly. In China for instance, this accounts for more than 20 per cent of the urban market in insurance in 2003. In India the concept of bancassurance appears to be gaining ground quite rapidly both through commission based arrangements and joint ventures between banks and insurance companies.

Impact on Retail Customer

Retail saving choices is getting increasingly complex internationally and idea is no exception. There is growing need for more diver's instruments and avenues of investment. This coupled with need of integrated financial 'one stop shops' to reduce the transaction costs associated with diversification. Globally, insurance products are a major important savings and this is likely to be the case in India as well as insurance penetration gathers steam. The issue of building brand equity is critical for new entrants into the insurance market. However, tying up with a bank might provide counter-productive if this objective is to be achieved. A number of surveys in the European market have shown, for instance, that in bancassurance partnerships, it is the banks rather than the insurers brand that dominates and insurance brands often get stifled. The issue of integrating the bank's IT and other support systems also needs to be emphasized. If these are not dovetailed, the possibility of serious systems failure becomes real. Often this issue is relegated to the background and the obvious synergies between banks and insurers get more than their due emphasis.

Regulatory Perspective

From a regulatory perspective, bancassurance raises some key questions regarding anti-competitive behaviour. It is a basic tenet of competition law and regulation that the ownership of large networks is a significant barrier to entry. Thus insurers who tie up with ones with large networks could effectively keep out potential entrants. This might not have an immediate impact on the pricing of premium. The need to penetrate the untapped Indian market might keep premiums low at this state. However, over the medium to long term this could lead to monopoly power and high premiums. This is a regulatory issue that needs to be addressed as bancassurance gets under way in India either through the competition commission or through the insurance regulator's office. This is by no means an issue that is unique to bancassurance – the regulation of ATM networks and other payment systems in Europe has been a hotly debated issue. A possible solution is to have an arrangement by which all entrant insurers have access to bank networks. Another regulatory issue related to 'binding' or the phenomenon through which banks offer a consolidated package of products at a single rate. This often involves cross-subsidization within the package. Thus a bank could charge an artificially low premium for an insurance product and subsidize it through a relatively high charge on a credit card. This form of 'bundling' not only impedes transparency of pricing but could also lead to 'unfair' advantage for banks offering bancassurance vis-à-vis stand-alone insurers. This might warrant regulatory intervention. Thus, while bancassurance does provide an apparently viable model for product diversification by banks and a cost-effective distribution channel for insurers, there are some potential areas of conflict between the two that need to be ironed out. The success of the partnership between the two entities depends on the right model partnership. It is vital for this model to ensure that banks remain fully committed to promoting and distributing insurance products. This commitment has to come from both senior management in terms of strategic inputs and the operations staff who would provide the front end for these products. Prima facie, a formal collaboration between banks. There are costs associated with setting up a successful bancassurance network. The proper training of bank personnel to understand and market insurance schemes is vital to the success of these ventures. There is also a need to invest extensively in IT and other support systems that would provide an integrated 'back-end' for banking and insurance services Regulatory issues need to be addressed comprehensively and sorted out particularly with respect to competition and market structure problems. Given these changes, bancassurance and collaboration between banks and insurers has a long way to go in India.

Banc Assurance in India

Banc assurance in India is a very new concept, but if past gaining ground. In our country the banking and insurance sectors are regulated by two different entries. They are:

- Banking is fully governed by RBI and
- Insurance sector is by IRDA

And banc assurance being the combination of two sectors comes under the purview of both the regulators. Each of the regulators has given out detailed guidelines for banks getting into insurance sector.

Guidelines Given By RBI:

The Reserve Bank of India has given certain guidelines for banks entering into the insurance sector. They are as follows:

1. Any commercial bank will be allowed to undertake insurance business as the agent of insurance companies & this will be on fee basis with no-risk participation
2. The second guideline given by the RBI is that the joint ventures will be allowed for financial strong banks wishing to undertake insurance business with risk participation.
3. The third guideline is for banks which are not eligible for this joint venture option, an investment option of (1) up to 10% of the net worth of the bank or (2) Rs. 50 crores, Whichever is lower is available.

The bank that wants to enter in participates in the Insurance industry they have to follow the above guidelines given by the Reserve Bank of India.

Guidelines given by IRDA:

The Insurance regulatory development and Authority has given certain guidelines for the Bancassurance they are as follows:

(1) **Chief Insurance Executive**:

Each bank that sells insurance must have a chief Insurance Executive to handle all the insurance matters and activities.

(2) **Mandatory Training:**

All the people involved in selling the insurance should under-go mandatory training at an institute determined (authorized) by IRDA and pass the examination conducted by the authority.

(3) **Corporate Agents:**

Commercial banks, including co-operative banks and RRBs may become corporate agents for one insurance company.

4) Banks cannot become insurance brokers.

Issues for Regulation:

Certain regulatory barriers have slowed the development of Bancassurance in India down. Which have only recently been cleared with the passage of the insurance (amendment) Act 2002. Prior it was clearly an impractical necessity and had held up the implementation of Bancassurance in the country. As the current legislation places the: -

(1) Training and examination requirements:

Upon the corporate insurance executive within the corporate agency, this barrier has effectively been removed. Another regulatory change is published in recent publication of IRDA regulation relating to the (2) Licensing of Corporate agents

(2) Specified Person to Satisfy the Training and Examination:

According to new regulation of IRDA only the specific persons have to satisfy the training & examination requirement as insurance agent.

Exception:

A noticeable exception is that for the individuals who processing the Certified Associateship of Indian Institute of Banks (CAIIB) only 50 hours training rather than 100 hours.

Restrictive Feature:

A restrictive feature of Bancassurance regulation is that:

(1) They appear to constrain the corporate agents to receive only commission, the profit sharing arrangements would seen to be ruled out.

2) The products sold through bank channels / networks can be highly profitable and so such agreement with banks is highly beneficial for banks only.

IMPORTANT BANC ASSURANCE TIE-UP IN INDIA:

There is certain tie-up between the Insurance Company and banks are given at present days these tie-up are going well, running well and past in the field of bancassurance. The present status of bancassurance can be understood from the following display

Insurance Company	*Partner Banks (Total No. of Branches)*
ICICI Prudential	ICICI Bank, Bank of India (2,524), Citibank (15), Allahabad Bank, Federal Bank (120), South Indian Bank, Lord Krishna Bank, Punjab and Maharashtra Co-Operative Bank.
SBI Life	SBI (9,000), associate banks (4,000)
Birla Sunlife Insurance	Development Credit Bank (62), Deutsche Bank (3), Citibank (15), Bank of Rajasthan (348), Andhra Bank, Catholic Syrian Bank (329), Bank of Muscat (1)
ING Vysya Life	Vysya Bank (450)
Aviva Life Insurance	ABN Amro (12), Lakshmi Vilas Bank (212), American Express (6), Canara Bank (2,421)
Royal Sundaram Alliance	Standard Chartered (63), ABN Amro (12), American Express (6), Citibank (15)
United India Assurance	Indian Bank, South Indian Bank (372), Andhra Bank (1,018)
HDFC Standard Life	Union Bank, Indian Bank
Life Insurance Corporation	Corporation Bank (800), Central Bank (3,115), Bank of Punjab (20), Andhra Bank (1,018), Nedungadi Bank (150)
MetLife	Karnataka Bank (356), Dhanalaxmi Bank (153), j&k bank(150)

Issues to Be Kept in Mind While Tie-up:

The followings are certain issues that we have to keep in mind while tie-up with bank for Bancassurance purpose.

Do not depend upon traditional Method:

The tie-up needs to develop innovative products and services rather than depends upon the traditional tracks. The kind of products that the bank would be allowed to sell is another major issue. For example: - a complex unit-linked life insurance product is better sold through brokers & agents, while a standard term product or simple products like auto Insurance, home loan and accident Insurance cover can be handled by bank branches.

Clarity on operational activities:

There is need to be clarifying on the operational activities of Bancassurance that :-

(a) Who will do branding?

(b) Will the Insurance Company prefer to place a person at the branch of the bank? Or

(c) Will the bank branch train and keep its own people?

(d) Who will pay remuneration of above-mentioned people bank or Insurance Company or both in some ratio?

Required Good Training:

Even though the banks are in personal contact with its client, a high degree of active marketing skill is required to sell the insurance products. These can be possible through proper training only bancassurance and collaboration between banks and insurers has a long way to go in India.

Emerging Trends

Though banc assurance has traditionally targeted the mass market, bancassurers have begun to finely segment the market, which has resulted in tailor-made products for each segment. The quest for additional growth and the desire to market to specific client segments has in turn led some bancassurers to shift away from using a standardised, single channel sales approach to adopt a multiple channel distribution strategy. Some bancassurers are also beginning to focus exclusively on distribution.

In some markets, face-to-face contact is preferred, which tends to favour bancassurance development. Nevertheless, banks are starting to embrace direct marketing and Internet banking as tools to distribute insurance products. New and emerging channels are becoming increasingly competitive, due to the tangible cost benefits embedded in product pricing or through the appeal of convenience and innovation.

Finally, the marketing of more complex products has also gained ground in some countries, alongside a more dedicated focus on niche client segments and the distribution of non-life products. The drive for product diversification arises as bancassurers realise that over-reliance on certain products may lead to undue volatility in business income. Nevertheless, bancassurers have shown a willingness to expand their product range to include products beyond those related to bank products.

Strategic Challenges

These developments are expected to challenge traditional bancassurers in the following ways: The shift away from manufacturing to pure distribution requires banks to better align the incentives of different suppliers with their own. Increasing sales of non-life products, to the extent those risks are retained by the banks, require sophisticated products and risk management. The sale of non-life products should be weighted against the higher cost of servicing those policies. Banks will have to be prepared for possible disruptions to client relations arising from more frequent non-life insurance claims.

World's Perspective:

If we are looking around the world then we can see that European countries are doing better than others where hardly 20% of US banks are selling insurance in 1998 against 70% to 90% in many European countries. Market penetration of bancessurance in new life business in Europe ranges between 30% in UK to nearly 70% in France. Almost 100% banks in France are selling insurance products. In 1991 rationale

Nederland of Netherlands merged with Post Bank, the banking subsidiary of the post office to create the ING group a new dimension to the bancassurance is harnessing the databank of the post office as well. CNP, the largest independent insurance company in France has developed its products distribution through post offices. The mergers of Winterthur, the largest Swiss insurance company, with Credit Suisse and Citibank with Travelers group have resulted in some of the largest financial conglomerates in the world. Despite the phenomenal success of bancassurance in Europe, properly and casualty products have not made much inroads. In Spain, Belgium, Germany and France where more than 50% of all new life premium is generated by bancassurance, only about 6% P and C business comes from banks in Spain, 5% in Belgium, 4% in France and Italy. A recent study try Boston consulting Group and Bank Administrative Institute in USA claims that if bank made a major commitment to insurance and a more narrowly targeted commitment to investors within 5 years they could increase retail revenues by nearly 50%.

It further states that

- Banks could capture 10% to 15% of the total US insurance and investment market by selling products to 20% of their existing customers.
- Banks existing infrastructure enables them to operate at expense level that is 30% to 50% lower than those of traditional insurers.
- Banc assurance's bank branch based sales system sales 3 to 5 times as many insurance policies as a conventional insurance sales and distribution force.
- By simplifying banc assurance products each bank office bank employees can quintuple managing policies compared to traditional insurers.

Conclusion:

With the opening up of insurance sector and with so many players entering the Indian Insurance Industry it is required by

Insurance Companies to come up with well established infrastructure facilities with good call centre service to attract and provide information to customer regarding different good policies and their premium pay scheme. The life Insurance Industry in India has been progressing at a rapid growth since opening up of the sector. The size of country, a diverse set of people combined with problems of connectivity in rural areas, makes insurance selling in India is a very difficult task. Life Insurance Companies require good distribution strength and tremendous manpower to reach out such a huge customer base. Where legislation has allowed bancassurance had mostly been a phenomenal success and although slow to gain pace, is now taking of across Asia, especially now that banks are starting to become more diverse financial institution and the concept of universal banking is being adopted.

In the field of bancassurance banks will bring a customer database, leverage their name, recognition and reputation of both local and regional levels. If they are using personal contact with customers and non-customers then only they can success in the field of bancassurance.But the proper implementation of bancassurance is still facing so many hurdles because of poor manpower management, lack of call centers and no personal contact with customers, inadequate incentives to agents and unfullfilment of other essential requirements. Finally we can say that the bancassurance would mostly depend on how well insurers and bankers understanding is with each other and how they are capturing the opportunity and how they are providing better service to their customers. Let us you all pay more attention towards the policies and enjoy the service provide by banks and Insurance Companies by the mode of Banc assurance.

References

1. Economic Times (Delhi),
2. Financial Express (Delhi),

3. Business Standard (Delhi),
4. Business Economy.
5. Banking Review,
6. Annual Report of RBI.

10

The Role of Private Players in Insurance Sector

Dr. S. Kalaiselvi

Introduction:

Ever since the privatization of the Insurance sector in India in 2000, the industry has been witnessing the birth of numerous private players, mostly joint ventures between foreign insurance giants and Indian diversified conglomerates. With well-crafted products and benefits, each one is trying to make an inroad into the huge untapped market. The expansion of the State-as-insurer has played a major role in the long-term growth of the public sector, but we are probably reaching the turning point. Because of its manifold failures, the State-as-insurer is facing crisis all around the world, with exploding expenditures. This will probably induce a shift in the private–public frontier, which makes it much more important than in the past to regulate the insurance industry efficiently. Coming back to the failures of the State-as-insurer, we should underline the role played by this flawed hypothesis that sets market logic and private interest against public interest.

By providing financial protection against the risk of dying too soon, life insurance became the biggest financial industry of the last century. Providing financial protection against the new risk of not dying soon enough may well become the current century's major and most profitable financial industry. Obviously the fear of longevity compounded by a state of helplessness in the area of financial security causes instability in the social firmament. People are now re-working their priorities and planning for their future. In such a context it is very reasonable and sensible if a proper pension regime develops. "The last decade of the previous century accentuated the break-up of accepted social obligations in this country viz. that the successor generation takes care of the predecessor generation and non sustained efforts need be built to look for individual help lines, be they in the form of insurance or health care and most particularly pension" (IRDA Report).

The Insurance and Risk Management Industries

The insurance and risk management industries are typically considered to have little interest in energy issues, other than those associated with large energy supply systems. The historical involvement of these industries in the development and deployment of familiar loss-prevention technologies such as automobile air bags, fire prevention/suppression systems, and anti-theft devices, evidences a tradition of mediating and facilitating the use of technology to improve safety and otherwise reduce the likelihood of losses. Through an examination of the connection between risk management and energy technology, it has been identified nearly 80 examples of energy-efficient and renewable energy technologies that offer loss-prevention benefits (such as improved fire safety). Approaches in the categories of: information, education, and demonstration; financial incentives; specialized policies and insurance products; direct investment; customer services and inspections; codes, standards, and policies; research and development; in-house energy management; and an emerging concept informally known as "carbon insurance" were identified. While most companies have made only a modest effort to position themselves in the "green" marketplace, a few have comprehensive environmental programs that include energy efficiency and renewable energy activities.

Public Policy and Private Sector Provision of Health Services

Public sector policies often try to extend access and redirect public resources, depending on private sector actions. These strategies focus on reducing demand, improving efficiency, and generating increased revenues in the public sector. In order to provide incentives for efficiency, acquire capital, and redirect limited public resources to public priorities, there must be an expanded role for the private market in the provision of health services. This presents opportunities to improve the focus of resources on high-priority health activities in the public sector and to make more effective and efficient use of the resources of the private sector. While the overall set of options available to policy makers can be identified, what is an effective strategy in one country may be neither appropriate nor feasible in another. The challenge to policy research is not to identify what works, but rather to understand the conditions that make a policy effective in some settings but not in others. The objective is not to prescribe the actions to take but to understand the factors that create the current experience in a specific setting.

The public sector is the dominant financier of health care in most OECD countries. But in the last two decades the extent of private finance has increased in most of these countries, and private finance now accounts for around a quarter of all health care finance. On the delivery side, the dominance of the public sector is much less strong and mixed public and private provision is common. Many recent reforms in health care have sought to increase the role for the private sector in health care provision.

It seems likely that reforms that increase the role for the private sector in financing health care will increase health care expenditure. High shares of private finance in the overall financing of health care are accompanied by higher costs, and systems which have high shares of public finance appear to have been better at cost containment. But lower cost does not necessarily mean better health care. The higher expenditure that accompanies private finance may in part reflect lower access costs and higher quality. Systems that rely heavily on private finance for health care tend to be less progressive than those that use public finance. Marginal increase in private finance will necessarily lead to the evolution of the public sector into a 'poor service for the poor' is not strongly supported by empirical evidence. High levels of private finance do not appear to be associated with later lower growth of public finance. And while those who buy supplementary private finance in systems where individuals have public cover are less supportive of spending on public services, the evolution of their attitudes is not necessarily very different from that of users of the public system.

Recent Trends in the Private Role in Finance and Delivery

Health care financing throughout the OECD is dominated by the public sector. Only in the US is health care predominantly privately financed. However in recent years against the backdrop of a concern with cost containment there has been a trend for the share of government finance to fall. In 16 out of the 24 countries, the public share of total expenditure fell 1980-94.

Finance for public health care is raised by a mixture of general taxation, social insurance (payroll tax) contributions and local tax. Examples of systems in which general taxation dominates are the UK and Denmark. An example of a country that uses earmarked social insurance contributions is the Netherlands. Private finance is usually raised by insurance premiums and/or out of pocket payments. Private insurance can be used to provide supplementary cover to public cover where those covered are offered no tax breaks or initial cover for those without comprehensive public cover or cover against public sector co-payments levied on prescription medicines, dental care etc. Out of pocket payments can be predominantly co-payments with the third party usually paying the major share of the bill or can amount to substantial use of the private sector on a fee-paying basis. While the public sector plays a key role in finance, the provision (i.e. supply) of health care varies widely in terms of a public-private mix. In the OECD delivery spans from being nearly 100 percent in the public sector to being substantially the role of the private sector. Even where finance is predominantly social insurance or tax based, countries may use mainly private providers. Canada, for example, has predominantly public finance but private providers.

Increasing the Role for the Private Sector in Finance

A higher share of public financing in total health care financing is associated with lower nominal health care expenditures as a percent of GDP. Globerman and Vining (1998) found that the simple correlation between the share of public financing and health care expenditure as a percent of GDP in 1992 was -0.41. In effect this indicates a higher public share in health care expenditure supports a lower share of health care expenditure in GDP. This implies that public insurers are able to control health care expenditures better than private insurers. It is worth noting that countries with mainly private providers, such as the US, the Netherlands and Switzerland, are amongst those with the highest levels of health care expenditure in GDP.

Attitudes and Relationship Between Private Finance and Public Sector

The dynamics of the relationship between private financing and the evolution of the public system turn on the relationship between the quality of the public sector, use of the public and private sector, and political support for the public sector. Thus the private finance will lead to a downward spiral towards a 'poor service for the poor' depends upon the premise that support for public sector financing is negatively associated with private demand and the demand for a privately financed alternative is affected by the quality of the public sector.

There are several possible relationships between support for public finance and use of private health care. Users of private health care services may be less supportive of public services than others on ideological grounds or because they simply see little personal return from public services they do not use. This suggests use of the public or private sector may affect attitudes. Empirical evidence from the UK suggests that those who use the private sector are in general less supportive of public financing of health care. There is evidence from the UK that the quality of the NHS is associated with use of the private sector: longer waiting lists have been found to be linked with higher levels of demand for private medical insurance though not with use of the private sector.

Therefore there is a relationship between an increase in private finance and a subsequent erosion of support for the public sector, and so lower future levels (or slower growth) of public expenditure on health care. It is found no association between lower relative growth of public finance in health care and past levels of public expenditure in the OECD. It may be suggested that increasing private finance will not necessarily erode support for the public sector.

The Impact of Private Health Care Financing on Equity

Demand for health care is income elastic. Therefore in systems in which the private sector is either a supplement to or an alternative to public care, it would be expected that richer individuals use more private care. Evidence from the UK where the private sector care is used both to top-up NHS care and as an alternative to NHS care indicates this to be broadly true.

While systems that rely heavily on private finance for health care tend to be less progressive than those that use public finance are, the impact on progressively of an expansion of private finance will depend on the form of that expansion. Allowing richer individuals to 'opt-out' of contributions to public insurance is likely to decrease the progressivism of a given financing system. On the other hand, an expansion of supplementary private finance, where individuals cannot 'opt out' of taxes for the public sector but buy additional private cover, will not be more regressive, as those individuals who buy the supplementary private finance will essentially be paying twice for their health care. While there is a clear relationship between equity in the finance of health care and the share of public finance, there is no clear relationship between the mix in finance and equity in the delivery of health care within a single country.

Role of The Private Sector Delivery

The overall level of private sector delivery has raised little. The real growth in private health care delivery has been in niche markets. In Sweden, where only 1% of the populations are covered by private insurance, 25% of coronary bypass surgery in 1988 was performed in the private sector. This trend may account for the sizeable proportion of private beds in Sweden. In addition there is growing interest in private health insurance market, especially for small businesses.

Health services in New Zealand are all contracted by the Health Funding Authority who may purchase them from private or public providers. In reality an increase in the role for private providers has only been seen in the area of elective surgery. Rankin (1998) found that in 1993, 31% of all surgical operations were performed in private hospitals in New Zealand. However evidence shows while private participation has grown in a number of areas the overall level is less than expected. Scott (1998) found that over 92/93-95/96 total inpatient discharges and day patient discharges from the private sector increased by 5.0% and 6.1% per annum respectively. The elective nature of the work of medical specialists in their private capacity has not supported the development of large acute capability in the private sector. In part, this is due to lower unit costs for professional services in the public sector relative to those offered in the private sector. Economics of scale also prohibit duplication of such high cost care in both sectors. It appears that public and private insurance and provision arrangements appear to be compliments, not alternatives. Similarly, in the UK a significant area of growth of private sector delivery has been elective surgery. Private health insurance is mainly for cover of procedures of this type. Laing (1996) estimated that the private sector share of UK hospital based health care increased from 7.5% in 1984 to 20% in 1995. However there has been little increase in the use of the private sector for publicly funded acute care. The real development has been in private delivery of non-acute long term care. In 1995 long term care for the mentally ill and mentally handicapped was predominantly delivered by the private sector but predominantly publicly funded.

Conclusion

In terms of underwriting, on one scenario, the economic cost of weather losses could reach over 1 trillion USD in a single year by 2040. The impacts will be worse in developing countries. The private sector needs to work with the public sector, as part of a "triple dividend" approach that coordinates adaptation, disaster management and sustainable economic development. For asset management the indirect impacts are key. Greenhouse gas emissions have to drop by 60 per cent by 2050, which means transforming the energy economy. Finance for renewable will reach 100 billion USD a year soon. Political uncertainty is a serious blockage to market forces, and the re-evaluation of assets and project returns is happening too slowly. Finally, insurers have a duty as ubiquitous players in the economy and society to help to shape climate policies in a responsible and effective way.

References

1. Burchard, T. and Propper, C. (1999) Does the UK have a private welfare class? University of Bristol, Centre for Market and Public Organization; Working paper 98/006
2. Feldstein, M. (1974) 'Social Security, Induced Retirement, and Aggregate Capital Accumulation', Journal of Political Economy LXXXII, pp. 905-926
3. Globerman, S. and Vining, A. (1998) 'A Policy Perspective On "Mixed" Health Care Financial Systems Of Business and Economics', Journal Of Risk And Insurance 65(1), pp. 57-80
4. Hall, J. and Preston, I. (1998) 'Public and Private Choice in UK Health Insurance', Institute for Fiscal Studies Working Paper Series, W98/19
5. Propper, C. and Soderlund, N. (1998) 'Competition in the NHS internal market: An overview of its effects on Hospital prices and Costs', Health Economics 7, pp. 187-197
6. Rankin, D. (1998) 'The Role of the Private Sector In Health Service Delivery', Health Care Review On-line: Private/Public Sector issues in the Provision of health Care in New Zealand.
7. Saltman, R.B. and Figueras, J. (1998) 'Analyzing the Evidence on European Health Care Reforms', Health Affairs 17(2), pp. 85-108
8. The Icfai Journal of Management Research, Vol. 5, No. 10, pp. 7-17, October 2006
9. The Geneva Papers, Volume 33, Number 1, January 2008 , pp. 71-90(20)

11

Role of MLM in Insurance Sector

S. Lakshmi

Multi-Level Marketing (MLM)

Multi-level marketing is an efficient method to distribute products or services to the consumer. It is a marketing method, and each marketer is an independent distributor, not an employee in a company. Each distributor has his/her own business. Let us examine the mathematics of a downline. Say I am at the top and I recruit 5 people. Each of those 5 people recruits 5 more. The new 5 then recruit 5 more.

Multi-Level Marketing in Insurance Sector

Multi-level marketing in insurance is selling a policy (services) directly to a prosperous consumer by a corporate agent by registering his name in an insurance company.

MLM Model

In India, the direct selling industry is estimated to be around worth of Rs. 2, 400 crores. With the entry of reputed players like Hindustan Lever Network (a HLL co.), the seriousness in the industry is getting more and more.

Multi Level Marketing also known as Network marketing or Matrix Marketing is business form in which company sells product directly to customers through reference. In this references and direct marketing is used to sell product. Its business model is like this that company uses independent salespeople (distributor) to sell the product by forming a distributor chain in down-line, which also helps in expanding customer base.

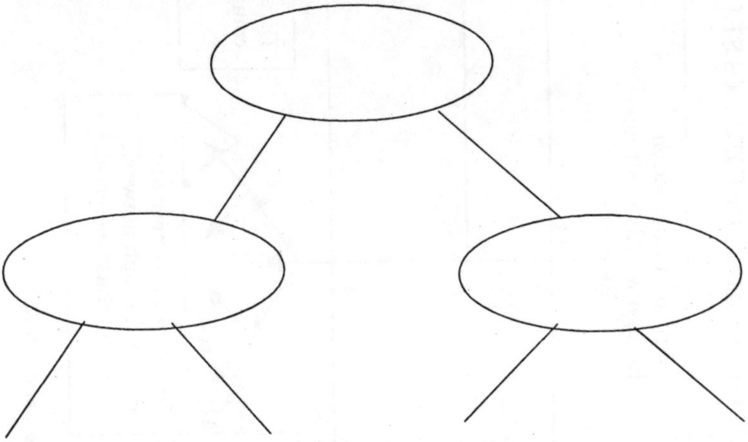

Various compensation plans like unleveled plans, binary plans are used by firms now-a- days for MLM. There are many firms which uses MLM to sell their product. Some of them are Amway, Medicare, Angel etc. Most networking firms deals in physical goods initially but due to its advantages it is now also used by, websites services, educational courses etc. Max New York Life is one such firm which is using MLM model in Insurance sector. Amway which has made MLM famous at least in India is also now entering into Insurance sector by using MLM model. MLM is also used by websites particularly job sites. Reffster.com is a reference based recruitment firm which offers cash for candidates' successful recommendation.

MODEL OF INSURANCE AND OTHER PRODUCTS SELLING USING MLM

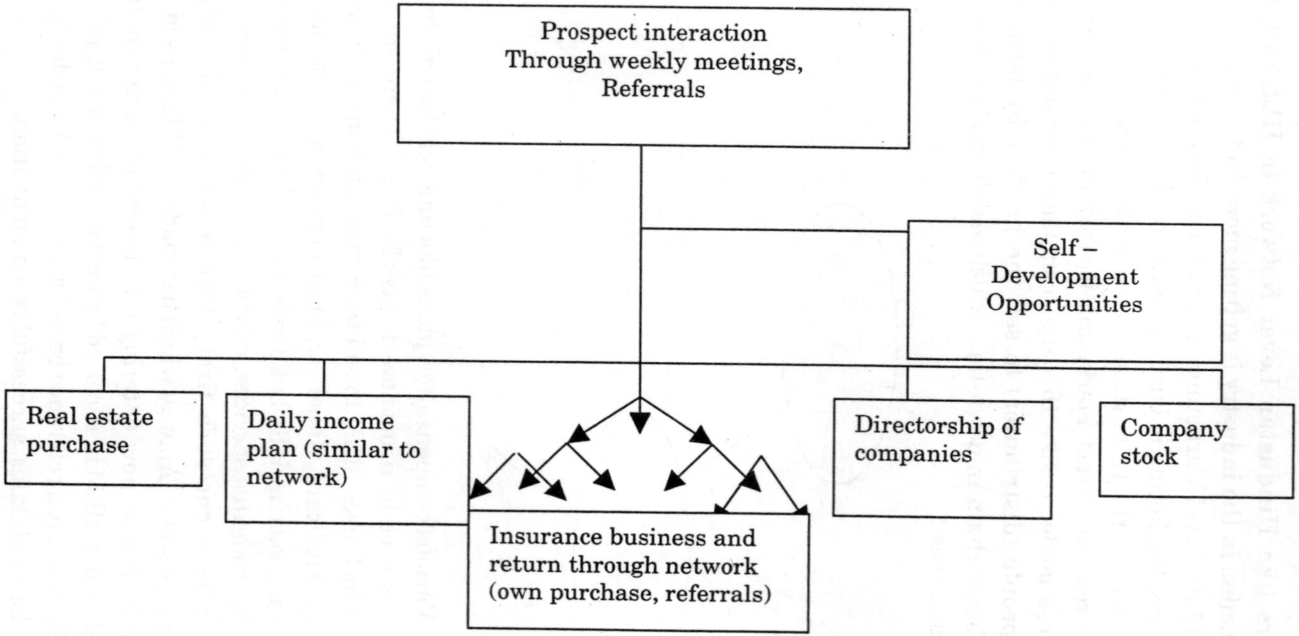

Model of insurance and other products selling using MLM

MLM is particularly useful for small firms as it provides a cheaper and effective way to promote and sell product. MLM also offers an easy way to sell product for distributors, as it is easy to sell to whom one knows rather than selling to unknown. MLM due to its huge potential is now commonly used. However image of MLM has been tarnished by similar schemes such as pyramid scheme which is illegal. MLM is also often as 'get rich overnight' opportunity, which is not so as it requires a lot of hard work. Also there is always a risk associated with MLM that it may destroy personal relationship.

Still the future of MLM is very good as MLM firms are growing and expanding in rural areas also.

Parties Involved in MLM in Insurance Sector

- **MLM Company or Corporate Agent or Direct Agent**
  Those company carryout to sell the product of insurance companies is called as multi-level marketing company.
- **Agent**
  Agent is to sell the product of insurance companies to customer by the Multi-level marketing company.
- **Customer/Policyholder/Insured**
  Customer is to buy the insurance policy under the chain of multi-level marketing.
- **MLM Companies Involved in Insurance Sector**
  NR Insurance India Ltd in case of LIC (it is not now at present)
  Team Life Care Insurance India Ltd in case of Bajaj Alliance insurance

Role of MLM in Insurance

Multi Level Marketing (MLM) is embracing more and more arenas today. Insurance business is just one among them. Selling insurance policies, traditionally, is considered as a de-motivating and dragging job. Well, not until you discover the power of MLM to boost policy sales. With the competition heating up in the insurance sector, companies are looking for innovative methods to spread the message and garner maximum business in shorter time. Many local MLM companies like NR Insurance India Ltd in case of LIC and Team Life Care Insurance India Ltd in case of Bajaj alliance insurance having quite large spread in the market are joining hands with leading insurance brands to promote their products along with an assortment of their own products. Insurance sector makes available long term debt for the economic development of the country. At the same time, the MLM route provides employment opportunities to lakhs of people and enhances their social status. The MLM members also get tremendous opportunity to develop themselves personally. This multiple role of MLM companies can be looked at as a social contribution and these companies or cooperatives are emerging as a development oriented social movement. It is just be a policyholder, bring policyholders. MLM can play an increasing role by creating jobs and mobilizing long term funds. MLM plays vital role in insurance sector by making quality products and innovations, employment generation, social contribution, product reachable etc. MLM was introduced in insurance sector nearly in 2004. After introducing it in MLM, LIC has earned tremendous profit.

Result of Oral Interview

Oral interview was conducted to a member of MLM Company by the candidate are given below.

For the question "what is the role of MLM in insurance sector and what do you think about the MLM in insurance sector" actually he is a LIC agent. He said that

- MLM is usually not relevant to insurance companies because of commission is stopped after buying the policy.
- Even LIC stopped the NRI offers from insurance package.
- Order issued by MLM is one and it is not implemented the operation that is another one.
- Even though policyholder does not receive the benefit, he can not stop the payment of premium.

- The benefit is vested in the hands of corporate agent or agent. But to the agent, it is of great loss.
- Corporate agent has only huge profit with the advent of MLM in insurance sector.
- Since the NRI can be benefited at high level, he can do the investment.
- Customers are expecting much benefit but he can not earn.
- In the initial stage, he can get but while the years are passing the benefits are downward and stopped.
- For getting the benefit in the greatest manner small activities are sacrificed by them.
- MLM is the fraud to deceive the member.
- According to IRDA act MLM should not be adopted in practice.

A Case Study Relating to MLM in Insurance Sector

In Tamilnadu, under NR life insurance company **shanmugam** is recruited as a member of the company in **attur**. He recruited **pandian** as a member of it. Earlier shanmugam received commission like mobile, car like. Commission is now stopped. And pandian also received commission by cheque in the first time only. He is also not receiving the commission now. It is actually favour for corporate agent and insurance company not for members of MLM.

Positives of MLM In Insurance Sector

Positives of MLM in insurance sectors are the following

- Employment generation
- Mobilizing long term funds
- Improving quality of life of people
- Promotion expenses on advertising, channel margins etc are distributed among the members as incentives.
- It provides competitive advantages.
- MLM works on the concept of time leverage i.e, it saves time.

- It gives more benefit to insurance sector and corporate agent such as NR Insurance India Ltd in case of LIC, TLC Insurance India Ltd in case of Bajaj alliance.
- After introducing MLM in insurance sector, product (policy) comes into a quality and innovation.
- A person buying insurance is getting tax saving benefits as per the rules. An average tax payer can save 20% of the premiums for renewals also.
- He is offered a valued gift like a mobile phone or a car or a bundled offer for insurance plus a few other products priced very low (below MRP).
- The person becomes a member of a MLM chain and eligible to pursue the MLM business as a part time income generating opportunity. He automatically becomes part of a large distribution network and can recommend a host of products to his friends/relatives/associates. These are commonly purchased products from popular dealerships in his town. Whenever a purchase is made by another person recommended by him, he earns an incentive.
- Corporate agent also offers annual incentives in the form of lowering the premium amount to their member.
- Down-line network method inviting, unemployed, part time employed, housewives, NRIs, VRS persons offering an opportunity to earn part-time.
- Conventional marketing may become slow or stagnated over a period of time.

Negatives of MLM in Insurance Sector

The negatives of role of MLM in insurance sector are

- Successful personal selling based on referrals. If sales person is successful in generating referrals from each customer. This will have a multiplication effect otherwise; it will have in a large time.
- MLM is the trick for corporate agent who will stop the commission after buying a product by policyholder and policyholder who will continue their premium regularly.

- We can select our product which is liked most by us in outside. But in MLM, we can select the product which is only provided by them. It is a hindrance of policyholder's freedom
- Problem with the MLM business model (which is legal) is that it is hard to distinguish from a pyramid scheme that is iilegal.
- In reality and generally only the people at the top of the pyramid stand a chance of making any serious money. The rest will pay their joining fee to find that there is no market for their products and be faced with trying to either enroll new recruits or lose their joining fee.
- Even though member can not afford to pay premium, members thought that they will afford as they are getting commission after receiving policy. Their thinking is totally spoiled later i.e. commission is stopped.

Suggestions

- First of all, we have to see the company. Whether it is right one.
- We have to balance the price about sales price and market price. Then we may buy a policy which is suitable for us.
- The more reputed companies in MLM like Amway, Medicare, Oriflamme, Tupperware, Quantum, RMP, Good ways, Placement services etc. are conducting weekly meetings of members and prospective members to explain the business plan, demonstrate products, recognize the achievers etc. Like that, for LIC, NR insurance India Ltd may be conducted the same and for Bajaj alliance insurance, TLC insurance India Ltd can do that.
- Shortsighted approach results in shortsighted results. Member should avoid short sight about future course of action of possibilities of income, availability of members etc.
- Separate law should be established relating to MLM like US and other developed countries. And law relating to control of price, quality should be established.

- Members must not join under network by selling their house, pledging their jewels etc.
- If they have sufficient time and need of money, they may join under MLM plan.
- According to IRDA act MLM in insurance is prohibited. Hence people should be aware of it and follow the rules.

Conclusion

Even though the role of MLM in insurance sector has lot of advantages and its benefits provided to people, insurance company and country, it also has number of shortcomings such as commission will be stopped by the agent at a particular point of time, deceiving the policyholder, misleading the middle class people, not considering the affordability of people, getting more amount for entrance fees when joining as a member of MLM etc. But according to the candidate, MLM in insurance sector is better because of networks with membership numbers in a few lakhs are providing employment opportunity for unemployed youth and other sections of society, with the recent changing in laws relating to contract employment, part-time employment etc., many enterprising youth may embrace it as a source of second income, by mobilizing large amount of funds through insurance sales, they indirectly help the economic progress of the country also. If MLM is used in a proper manner, it will reduce the commission of brokers or agent like wholesaler, retailer and avoid advertising charges and distributing charges and it will give tremendous development in insurance sector. By that, its fund will largely be used in social contribution. And also consider the Insurance regulatory development authority norms as regarding become a member of MLM company.

Sources:

- Websites: google.com
  Wikipedia.com
  MLMwatch.com.org

- Magazines
- A. sreekumar "a study on Multi-Level Marketing (MLM), as a potential tool for socio-economic development"

12

Life Insurance Corporation - The Leader on the Backfoot

Dr. T. Nagananthini

Yogakshema Vahamyaham, the famous words from Lord Krishna's discourses at Kurukshetra, is the catchphrase. LIC has convincingly used all these years in its monopoly avatar as the sole life insurer. Your welfare is our responsibility is what LIC proclaims through its catchphrase. Ever since the life insurance industry was nationalized in 1956 and the Life Insurance Corporation (LIC) born on September I, 1956, the monopoly grew in size and stature with every passing decade. From 57 hundred thousand policies in operation in 1957 to some 985 hundred thousand by the end of year 2002-2003, the LIC has come a long way. It is India's largest life insurance company. Offers over 50 plans to cover your life at various stages. Have over 12 million policy holders and over 9 lakh agents. It has underwritten more than 120 million policies. Has a life fund to the tune of Rs 2,270,090 million (as on 31st March 2002), Has 2,048 branch offices (all computerised) of which, over 1,500 are networked. However, this more than seventeen-fold increase is still miniscule if it takes into account the fact that insurance on life in India is still 20 per cent of the estimated potential. Nevertheless LIC has grown considerably in several years.

But liberalization is here, and so are the competitors. With the insurance sector deregulated, private players with strong financial muscle from India and beyond have entered the market: The wheel seems to have come a full circle. The monopoly status of LIC is being threatened. The insurance giant is now a player rather than the player in the life segment as was the case prior to nationalization in 1956. LIC now has to worry about its own 'yogakshema'. To borrow the catchphrase from their competitor AVIV A they need to think about exercising 'Kal Par Control' as they are slowly losing market share to other entrants.

Liberalization

The first step towards liberalization can be said to have been initiated in 1993 when the then Government headed by the Prime Minister P.V. Narasimha Rao set up the Malhotra Committee under the chairmanship of insurance secretary and RBI governor R.N. Malhotra. The frame of reference of this committee was to evaluate the Indian insurance industry and recommend its future direction. The committee submitted its report in 1994 and thereafter it was some six years later that the next step of implementing its recommendation was taken.

The committee had recommended structural and regulatory changes to suit a newly liberalized regime. One recommendation was to bring down the government stakes in the insurance companies to 50 per cent and the private companies with a minimum paid up capital of Rs. 100 crore to be allowed entry in the industry. There were other recommendations relating to structural changes but the significant one was opening the industry to foreign players in collaboration with domestic companies.

The recommendation related to regulatory change was that the insurance act be changed and a regulatory body was set up to act independently and given the responsibility of carrying out the reforms in the insurance sector. Once the Insurance Regulatory And Development Authority (IRDA) act was passed, IRDA was formed in the year 2000. The authority promulgated regulations covering various activities of the insurance companies, both in public and private sectors. The idea was to regulate the conduct of insurance business in the best interests of various stakeholders. IRDA was vested with the power to register the old and the new insurance companies, which was mandatory for carrying out business in India.

The insurance industry in India is now open and the new entrants have already started capturing the market share of the LIC. One estimate is that the LIC has lost some 13 per cent already and the contenders are adopting such an aggressive marketing strategy that may soon give the former a run for their money. With government no longer sympathetic to the state owned corporation, LIC has to fend for itself. Naturally, their much-trumpeted punch line 'We Know India Better' will not be enough, they need to 'Understand India Better'. Just knowing has its own limitations under the given circumstances.

Historical Perspective

Although the concept of insurance is a development of the recent past, the story of insurance is perhaps as old as mankind itself. Its beginning can be traced back to almost 6000 years with the evolution of village and community life by ARYANS. Evidence of insurance is available in crude form of maritime contracts made by Babylonians, Rhodians and Greeks about the middle of the third millennium Be. However, the early story of insurance is hidden in the mists of antiquity. The earliest available reference to some form of insurance is found in the codes of Hammurabi and Manu. The term 'Yogakshema' is used in the Rig-Veda suggesting that some form of community insurance was practiced by Aryans in India over 3000 years ago.

The early development of insurance was spasmodic and was restricted mostly to fields other than life. Scientific life assurance is a heritage from England, where the first life policy providing temporary cover for a period of twelve months was issued as early as 1583 AD. The development of mortality table was a landmark in the history of life assurance. With this development life assurance acquired a scientific character. The early history of modem insurance in India is somewhat obscure. The earliest references are traceable to the days of the East India Company when the policies on the life of its officers were issued. A few British companies, which attempted to underwrite business on the lives of Indians, came to grief or amalgamated with others. The failure of two British companies 'The European' and 'The Albert' in the year 1870 had adversely affected many people in this country.

The first organized effort to establish a life assurance office was made in 1870 with the formation of 'Bombay Mutual Life Assurance Society'. It was first Indian insurance company and its creation is of more importance if it takes into account the fact that it was the first life insurance company to treat Indian lives on par with that of the foreigners. The Swadeshi movement of 1905 provided impetus of the formation and mushrooming of several insurance companies. A further impetus in it was witnessed during the Second World War when inflationary pressure tended to swell the volume of business written in the country.

From then onwards Indian insurance business continuously progressed and every passing year witnessed a slow but steady rise in the per capita insurance in the country. The first attempt to regulate insurance business in India was with the enactment of legislation-Life Insurance Companies Act of 1921. However, the first comprehensive legislation to govern both Life and Non Life business was the insurance act of 1938. Simultaneously the development of insurance under the authority of superintendent of insurance was established. This act was extensively amended in year 1950. Following this, publishing of an insurance year book (Blue Book) by the controller of insurance every year and giving information relating to the progress of life and other type of insurance business in India become a mandatory obligation.

Formation of LIC

By the year 1955, approximately 170 insurance companies and about 80 provident societies has been registered for transacting life insurance business in India. A few of these were foreign companies with their head office outside India. In addition to these insurers a large number of other insurers who had registered themselves for transaction of life assurance business had either gone into liquidation or had been taken over by the existing insurers. From a study conducted at about that time it was found that the concept of trusteeship which should have been the cornerstone of life insurance was entirely lacking and most management had no appreciation of the clear and vital distinction that existed between trust money and those belonging to stock companies owned by shareholders.

Therefore, it become necessary to nationalize Insurance business with a view to-

- Provide 100 per cent security to policy holders
- Ensure use of the fund for national building activities
- Avoid wasteful effort in competition
- Save the dividend paid to the shareholders of insurance companies
- Avoiding of certain undesirable practices adopted by some insurance companies
- Speeding up of insurance business in rural areas.

The first step in this direction was taken on January 19, 1956 by promulgation of an ordinance vesting the management and control of life insurance business in India in the Central Government. On this occasion, the then finance minister Sir C.D. Deshmukh in his broadcast to the nation said-

"The nationalization of life insurance will be another milestone on the road the country has chosen in order to reach its goal of a socialistic pattern of society. In the implementation of second five year plan it is bound to give material assistance to the lives of millions in the rural areas. It will introduce a new sense of awareness building, for the future in the spirit of clam confidence which insurance alone can give. It is a measure conceived in a genuine spirit of service to the people. It will be for the people to respond, confound the doubter's and make it a resounding success."

Thus, the life insurance industry was nationalized in the year 1956 and the "LIFE INSURANCE CORPORATION OF INDIA" came into existence on the 1st day of September 1956. To remember this historic event insurance week is celebrated from 1 to 7th September every year thereafter. The objectives of nationalization were defined as conducting the business with utmost economy in true sense trusteeship, to charge premium no higher than narrated by strict actuarial consideration, and to invest the fund for obtaining maximum yield consistent with safety of capital and render prompt and efficient services to the policy holders, etc.

The mission given to LIC at that time can be summarized as-

- Providing protection of insurance to people in every nook and corner of the country
- Mobilizing savings for the development of country
- Responding to customer sensitivity.

Consequent to that, tracing the development of life insurance industry is nothing but wading through the progress of LIC itself.

Life Insurance Products and the LIC

Life insurance products usually veer around two basic elements-Risk cover (benefit payable in the event of death) and Savings (benefit payable in the event of survival). However, in

India, life insurance policies have often been viewed as a means of tax saving, particularly for the salaried class. In fact, every year a large section of LIC customers anxiously wait for the. Annual budgetary exercise of the Government to find out what is there in store for them in terms of 'tax incentives in LIC policies. Thus we can say that plans of life insurance are combinations of all three elements, i.e. risk cover, savings and tax incentives.

Generally, the following types of plans are available-

- Term Life-Here the sum assured is payable in the event of death during the term. Since only death risk is covered, premium is low and contract is simple.
- Whole life insurance-Here the risk covered is for the entire life of the policy holder and the policy money plus the bonus are payable to the nominee or the beneficiary only on death of the policy holder.
- Endowment type plans-These policies cover risks for a specified period at the end of which the sum assured is paid back to the policy holder along with the bonuses etc.
- Combination of whole life and endowment type plans.
- Children's assurance plans-These are deferred assurance plans providing risk cover on life of the child after it has attained 18 years of age.
- Annuity and pension plans-In these plans when a person purchases a life insurance contract, he agrees to make a series of payments (premiums) to the insurer and in return the insurer agrees to pay a specified sum to the beneficiaries. A pension is also an annuity. When annuity is provided by an employer to the employees or their dependents in consideration of the service rendered, it is generally called pension.

LIC and New Challenges

As things stand today, LIC is still on strong footing vis-à-vis its competitors. However, to retain its market leader status the LIC needs to acquire competitiveness. With new contenders entering the fray there is need to act more market savvy. Rather than getting bogged down by competition the LIC needs to see the challenge as an opportunity. Insurance in India was largely misconstrued as an investment or a tax saving device rather than a security hedge. In fact, insurance agents were promoting policies on life as instruments of returns and tax saving. Insurance consciousness as such was largely missing from the market.

The new entrants with their aggressive penetration strategies are at least contributing to the cause of LIC by creating insurance consciousness in the minds of a wide cross section of consumers. Privileged by its monopoly status LIC did not bother much about creating an insurance consciousness, as its objective was to insure anyhow that was happening. This complacency now has to go and LIC must opt for marketing insurance as insurance. Furthermore, India is utterly underinsured, not only in comparison to other countries but also in relation to its own needs.

The scenario is that only around 20 per cent of the population has any insurance cover worth its name. Moreover, such a cover meets only 25 per cent of their needed and affordable insurance cover. If we take a look at the per capita insurance premium in India it is a measly $4 against $964 for the US and $3817 for Japan. As a percentage of GDP insurance premium is 1.3 for India against that of 7.3 for the US and 10.10 for Japan. The obvious conclusion that needs to be drawn is that 'Sky is the limit'. LIC has to dare and dare seriously.

The insurance consciousness is creating the market is evident from the fact that there was a spurt in business underwritten in March 2004 at Rs. 5,670.07 crore and the life insurance industry underwrote first year premium of Rs. 18,710.15 crore during the fiscal 2003-2004, recording a growth of 10.4 per cent over the previous year. In policy terms the insurers exhibited a growth of 12.83 per cent with 286.27 hundred thousand policies.

Private insurers increased their shares of premium to 12.96 per cent as against 5.66 per cent in the year 2002-03. Individually, all the private insurers increased their market share in comparison to the previous year. Moreover, the private insurers recorded 153 per cent growth in terms of first year premium underwritten by them. Cumulatively the 12 private players (Allianz Bajaj, ING Vyasa, AMP Sanmar, SBI Life Insurance, TATA-AIG, HDFC Standard, ICICI-Prudential, Birla Sunlife, Aviva, OM Kotak, Max Newyork Life and Met Life) underwrote premium of Rs. 2425.46 crore.

LIC underwrote premium of Rs. 16,284.68 crore during the year under reporting. The market share for LIC in the year 2003-04 was 87.04 per cent. In terms of number of policies, LIC contributed 94.21 per cent.

However, LIC needs to worry about the fact that the new entrants have increased their share four folds in just two years during 2002-03. In the first quarter of 2003-04, this share of new players grew further to 11 per cent. No mean performance given the fact that the new players are still in the process of finding their feet. If the trend continues the LIC needs to take guard and prepare for strike.

What Needs to Be Done

In order that LIC is able to retain its numerous undo positions some strategic rethinking is required. LIC with its wide reach and deep penetration has to concentrate on utilizing its potential and brand equity. With over 2000 branches and 9 hundred thousand agents LIC could perform well than what they have. The latest figures show that life premiums have grown 62 per cent in May over April 2004 and the industry underwrote a premium of Rs. 1427.27 crore during the month of May 2004. Taking the cumulative premium underwritten to 2304.52 crore, the share of LIC in this was 83.27 per cent. This was less than the percentage share of 86.99 attained for the corresponding period during the previous year. It is interesting to note that most of the new players increased their market share over the year 2003-04.

As far as policies are concerned the market share of the new players and the LIC were 9.04 per cent and 90.96 per cent against 5.79 per cent and 94.21 per cent respectively for the year 2003-04. Thus the trend is not encouraging as far as LIC is concerned. And herein comes the question of thinking anew and coming up with some effective strategies to outsmart the competitors.

The following are some dimensions that LIC needs to look into-

Creating New Markets

Given the brand equity, visibility, credibility and wide reach the LIC enjoys, tapping unexplored markets will not be difficult. The vast and under explored rural market is a case in point. Only LIC can tap the rural market effectively by using its huge sales force. The insurance industry is one of the fastest growing industries in the country, and is growing at a rate of 26% per annum. The outcome of liberalization over a period of five years has been positive in terms of the premium underwritten and the annual growth rate. Private life insurers have captured 26% of the market share. While banc assurance being in its nascent stage has made little progress in improving penetration of insurance business, the proposed government's move to withdraw the guarantee of the 16 crore policies of LIC of India may prove to be a hurdle for the growth of the insurance business in the coming years. With more than 60% of the rural people uncovered, the role of private insurance players becomes all the more significant in the innovative global market.

Competition in the Markets

The life insurance industry has entered a new phase, with the Insurance Regulatory and Development Authority (IRDA) granting registration certificates to new life-insurers, enabling them to set up shop soon. In the next few weeks, close to a dozen companies are expected to get their Registration Certificates. The market is also expecting select public sector banks to get clearance — notably, the SBI is poised to set up a life insurance subsidiary with a start-up capital of Rs 250 crore. All eyes will be focused not only on the early take-off of new life insurance ventures but also on the ability of the giant Life Insurance Corporation (LIC) to face the emerging pressure. The delay in ushering in competition gave the major adequate time to gear up to the challenges of competition. Among the earliest strategies adopted by LIC was a three-pronged effort to galvanize the entire organization.

The immediate task of 'upgrading the marketing skills' of its fledging mammoth marketing team was to be initiated. Also, it was felt that as the entire organization would need to be energized, 'human resource development' and renewed emphasis on 'training efforts' for all levels was to be put in place. To respond to the customers with speed and quality of service, the adoption of greater use of technology support for the operating unit was taken up. For a mighty organization to accept the need to improve the overall efficiency, manage growth and develop a mindset to accept change was indeed an onerous task.

In terms of numbers, LIC can boast of a well-spread marketing setup. With a network of over 2,300 operating units, the life insurance products are marketed with the help of over 20,000 development officers overseeing more than 600,000 agents. Ten per cent or more of the agents are 'direct' and 'independent'. The challenge really is the level of professionalism of the sales force. The new business growth of an insurer is directly related to the productivity level of agents. For fiscal 1999-00, 1.69 crore new policies were sold (average sale per agent 28 policies). The new business premium was Rs 4393 crore — the best effort — yet much short of what could have been achieved even if 50 per cent of the field-force had been activated and utilized. The total premium income amounted to Rs 27,850 crore.

The financial strength and clout of LIC is attributable to the total life fund, put at an impressive Rs 1, 54,043 crore at end-March 2000. What, however, needs to be reviewed is whether more could have been mobilized. After all, the organization was in the unique position of being the only life insurer for over four decades. It had a Government guarantee, a brand image. The national economy supported insurance, particularly in the 1990s by providing new opportunities. The market presented a resurgent economy, with GDP growth showing an impressive and respectable level of 7 per cent for a number of years.

Opportunities in the LIC Market

To express in clear terms the future opportunities for the life insurance business, a look at the compatibility of Lick's business results with the economic indices is relevant:

- The margin of GDP growth rate in the 1990s showed an increase of 10.60 per cent over the 1980s, yet the margin in the total premium growth rate in the 1990s over the 1980s was + 2.85.
- GDP grew from Rs 6,30,and Rs 772 crore in 1992-93 to Rs 15,83,604 crore in 1998-99. Life premium grew from Rs 7,987 crore (1.26 per cent to GDP) in 1992-93 to Rs 22,806 crore (1.44 per cent to GDP) in 1998-99.
- The growth pattern witnessed in non-bank deposits in the 1970s, 1980s, and 1990s was 37.90 per cent, 20.20 per cent, and 49.50 per cent respectively. The rate of growth achieved by life insurance fund for the same period was 16.10 per cent, 19.20 per cent, and 20.30 per cent respectively.

There could be several parameters for judging the performance of a financial institution. What really needs to be understood and appreciated is that the performance assessment is to be linked with the factors supporting economic growth. The life insurance industry needs to act to accelerate economic growth. It has to spearhead a marketing initiative to help expand the industry's role in the country's overall economic growth.

Countries such as South Africa, South Korea, and Japan procure a total life premium exceeding 10 per cent of the GDP. The LIC may have to accept a paradigm shift in its efforts if it is serious to retain the leadership of life insurance industry for several years and assume the challenge for massive growth levels of the life insurance premium. What are the expectations from the LIC as it makes its moves towards strategic changes in its marketing setup, approach, and attitude? Changes cannot happen merely by changing structure, systems — a big task in itself — but in ushering in 'new thinking' that encourages changes. LIC has a reservoir of marketing strength. If genuine change is to come about, the following must happen:

- Radical steps to improve to quality of agents recruited, as better agents alone can bring in better business. The retention of agents will have to be a priority for sustained business growth. The exit to recruitment ratio has to change dramatically.
- The IRDA regulations on agents' recruitment, qualification and training make the task easier for LIC. It need not be pushed around to recruit at any cost as it is to be more closely monitored by the regulator.*Overdue emphasis on number of sales per agent need to make way for better customer-oriented sales. It is a matter of concern for any insurer that 35-40 per cent sales are of such low values that there is every possibility of their going out of the books.
- Training efforts for the marketing team need to focus on development of marketing skills and a professional approach. Genuine marketing efforts would lead to the creation of demand for the company's products, its distribution and services for customers who purchase the products. Skill development would lead to trained, experienced, representatives in the market. Customers

would be encouraged to retain their life insurance policies and use the valuable life insurance protection and savings.

- Renewed efforts to streamline marketing on a more scientific line. All agents cannot sell all products. Market research leading to a pointed support system for each agent would help. A lot needs to be done in relating technology to real growth in business, product development customers' services and market awareness.
- 'Face-to-face' sales efforts would be the main stay for LIC's marketing thrust. Yet the organisation needs to make conscious efforts to enlarge the profile of distribution channels to build a real marketing environment. LIC had attempted to enlarge the distribution channels by involving cooperatives and panchayats in its market areas. More need to be done.

Improved Customer Service

In any organization customer service should be given top priority. Organization's market share and profits can get affected by the quality of customer service, more so in the case of a service providing organization. LIC being a service providing company offering invisible and intangible products, evaluating the performance is quite difficult. Customer satisfaction is dependent on the factors like the advantages he perceives as accruing from the policy, the way the policy is presented to him and the expectations regarding the services from the agent who is the conduit between the company and the customer.

Furthermore, since the contract runs for a very long period, sometimes few decades, customer must be convinced about the credibility of the service the agent is going to offer. With competitors entering in the market this has become all the more important for LIC. In fact, to maintain the quality of the service and retain the customer LIC needs to work harder. To do it successfully LIC must focus its attention on the following points-

(i) Service at the branch-While there is a lot of effort to train agents, LIC has given little attention to improve the services at the various branches. As a result customers often feel pain at the 'careless' attitude of the branch staff. Since LIC is represented by these people, the corporation also must take serious steps to train its branch staff and make them more customers friendly. LIC should also initiate steps to strengthen their information-based connectivity between different branches so that customers can deposit their premium at any of the branches.

(ii) Simplified policy documents-In an insurance contract the clauses must be simple and easy to understand. In India, policyholders usually do not read the policy documents for the simple reason that the way the clauses are framed therein they do not make sense to the average reader. New players are introducing the free look-in period. Whatever be the 'free' part of it, the policyholder is being made to go through the clauses or the policy conditions and to this extent alone, it is a great achievement. In this regard LIC should think and prove its leader's position in the market.

(iii) Right insurance-The problem of both the insurers and the insured that is confronting the whole industry, is that the distributor (the agent or the broker) is not honest in communicating a product to the prospect. Little attention is given to the proponent's needs and the risk profile and more to personal interest, whether in the form of high commission or achievement of high targets. These acts of cleverness do not go a long way. More so, in a business like insurance where credibility and trust are essential ingredients for success one possible solution to this problem could be having in place a better motivational system that takes care of both material and non material needs of the agents who would propel them to look at the long-term perspective rather than the short-term interests like an immediate high rate of commission.

(iv) Trained agents-It would be helpful for the LIC to have trained and educated agents who can explain the nuances of the proposed contract to the prospect and do the job of the primary underwriter. It can increase the satisfaction level of the insurer and lead to higher retention ratio. Hitherto, agents were working like sales persons interested in selling the product anyhow. It is time they switch over to the marketing concept focusing more on identifying customer needs and satisfying those needs, which benefits both the customer and the society at large.

It is obvious that with the customer having a wider menu to choose from customer service benchmarks are improving. The reason is very simple-if you don't hold the customer tight he will slip away to some other suitor. For the companies also, it is beneficial in the sense that there are others sharing the responsibility of increasing awareness, initiating policy changes. Insurers are now forced to recognize customers' needs, exploit new opportunities and risk in venturing into newer market areas.

But on the other hand the industry has now to deal with customers who know what they want and are more demanding in terms of better service and speedier responses. With the advent of new distribution channels and payment mechanisms, customer awareness is expected to improve further forcing the industry to become more customers friendly. The dynamic interaction is certainly leading to a win-win for both the parties.

The Life Insurance Corporation of India needs to welcome competition with open arms and treat it as, an opportunity rather than a threat. The ultimate objective of reforms is to increase insurance-density and insurance penetration levels by designing more tailor made products for customers, both individuals and institutions. LIC now needs to use its reach and visibility to penetrate deeper into the Indian market. With a wide network to distribute LIC needs further customization of insurance products.

The challenge for the LIC is three-fold creating the need where it is not there, changing the need into their want and turning the want into demand which they must be able to satisfy. LIC needs to rebuild trust with the public and to deliver sustainable, affordable and understandable products. An agent is a link between the insurer and the insured so that the policyholder treats him as a representative of LIC. In the absence of the positive role expected from these agents, the policyholders may be deprived of the services that they expect and gets dissatisfaction. The agents must learn to satisfy their policyholders in contract that can retain customers' interest in their policy and also in the agents.

(v) Informed customers-While some new products have been introduced in the market, information related to them is not being communicated completely thereby putting the customer in a quandary. When a new policy is being introduced in the market it sounds as if it is a competitive product rather than a genuine useful product for customer. The LIC must make sure that its products and their implications are properly understood by the customers.

Improved Distribution Channels

As the agent network was not found to be good enough to retain its market in the competitive scenario, LIC must now stress on alternate distribution channels to increase its penetration. Since its competitors are already sharing the market with high growth rate, LIC needs to spread its reach through various strategic means. Efforts have already started through banc assurance and corporate agency tie-ups. In this connection LIC appointed Help age India as its corporate agent. LIC has banc assurance ties with eight banks including Corporation bank, Oriental Bank of Commerce and Indian

Overseas Bank, apart from tie-ups with 30 brokers and 130 corporate agents.

LIC has decided to set up a separate 'special business unit' for alternate distribution channels to ensure that 5 per cent of its new business (about Rs. 80 crore) comes from banks, corporate agents and NGOs. Its subsidiary LIC Housing Finance will approach the European market to raise $50 million through GDR in the next couple of months. It has appointed Kotak Securities and CLSA as its merchant bankers for the purpose.

With the declaration of the IRDA Act, 1999, the Insurance Act, 1938, the basic backbone of insurance, stands revised. Thus, according to sections 32B and 32C of the IRDA Act it has been made obligatory for life and non-life insurers to undertake a certain percentage of business in the rural market. The rural and the social sector have been defined in the Act and LIC can take a cue from this and aggressively go for these sectors. This is one area in which LIC can take a big lead over its competitors. In fact, even the MNCs today have realized the potential of the rural markets and are targeting them.

Highlights of the rural market ;

- Around two-third of the rural population lives in villages.
- Sixty per cent of the villages have the population less than 1000.
- Around a quarter of the rural population is below the poverty line.
- Around 75 per cent of the rural households fall in low and lower middle income group.
- The literacy rate is less than 40 per cent.

Any strategy to tap the rural market must take into account these ground realities. As such while targeting the rural market the four P's of the marketing mix, viz. product, price, place and promotion need to be designed accordingly. Initial efforts at entering the rural market will not get duly rewarded but once the idea of insurance gets going the benefits will be easy to come. And as far as the rural markets are concerned LIC definitely is in a better position to charm the rural customers than its competitors.

But going for the rural market is not the only option for the LIC. There is a huge segment in the existing urban market that offers a big opportunity. Insurance on life hitherto has largely been focusing on the breadwinner of the family, the idea being to provide succor to the family members in times of distress. Targeting the housewife segment can be an intelligent strategy. However, the idea has to be sold. Insurance cover can be packaged as a gift to someone you love and care for. The middle and high-income group can definitely be brought into the net. There can be other niches as well that can be carved out.

Innovative Product Line

The customer of today is having more to choose in terms of policy instruments as new players have come up with innovative product line. Naturally, the policies issued by LIC need to be seen in this light and suitable steps taken to customize the products. Hitherto, when challengers were not there LIC could get a way with whatever products it had to offer. The customer had no inkling as to what insurance could offer by way of products. Obviously, he was satisfied with whatever he could get. Entry of new players has changed all this.

As the new players are coming up with their innovative products the customers' expectations are rising. Even though LIC is the market leader, it still needs to change its product mix to suit customer needs. Further it can carve out a niche for itself with the help of these innovative product lines. In fact LIC has already started launching these products with a view to targeting new markets. Its latest plan for the disabled child Jeevan Adhar (Whole Life) and Jeevan Vishwas (Endowment) is an indication that LIC is thinking in terms of innovating its product line in order to take competition head on.

India's Life Insurance Market Set a Boom

- Wealthier, aging Indians will help transform the country's largely untapped life insurance market into one of the world's fastest growing over the next five years.
- Life insurance is already the most popular financial product among Indians because of the tax benefits and income protection it offers in a country where there is no social security.
- But with household earnings accelerating in the fast-growing economy, the life insurance income premiums market could double from 40 billion dollars to 80 billion or even 100 billion dollars by 2012.
- All factors are in place for the Indian life insurance industry to blossom into one of the fastest-growing financial services markets in the world.
- At the size of the market we're talking about and potential the only one with similar potential is China. The next five years will be very exciting.
- Key to insurers' enthusiasm about India is its increasing affluence, aging population and low penetration of insurance coverage at a time when the market in industrialised countries is relatively saturated.
- The potential in the country of 1.1 billion people can be seen from the fact the ratio of life insurance premiums to GDP — a common measure for penetration — is 4.1 per cent, far lower than developed market levels of 6-9 per cent.
- This will change as India sees strongly accelerating household income and a more favourable demographic profile over the next two decades.
- Household disposable income is seen rising by 5.3 per cent annually, much more than the 3.6 per cent annual growth over the past two decades.
- With increased GDP growth there will be more income for consumers to put into life insurance, the life insurance

industry could witness a rise in insurance sector premiums to between 5.1 and 6.2 per cent of GDP in 2012 from 4.1 per cent.

- Demand for pension cover is also seen raising, with 113 million Indians expected to be over 60 by 2016, a figure seen swelling to 179 million by 2026. There is an untapped opportunity in pensions where life insurance players have no meaningful presence.
- Just 10 to 11 per cent of India's working population is covered by formal old-age social security schemes. There are currently close to 30 public and private firms in India's insurance market with state-owned Life Insurance Corp of India (LIC) still holding a stranglehold of over 70 per cent.
- But private players have moved aggressively, chasing for business after being allowed to compete with LIC in 2000. And overseas insurers have raced into the market despite rules limiting foreign direct investment in domestic insurers to 26 per cent.
- The global bank HSBC Holdings signed a deal for an insurance venture with two state-run Indian banks, gaining access to over 40 million customers. HSBC will hold a 26-percent stake — the maximum allowed to overseas insurance partners — while India's Bangalore-based Canara Bank will take 51 percent. The rest will be held by Oriental Bank of Commerce.
- Oriental Bank chairman Alok Mishra was upbeat about prospects, calling life insurance penetration rates in India. The Congress government has been seeking to raise the FDI cap to 49 percent as part of economic reform but its communist allies fiercely oppose such a step.

Conclusion

Insurance after globalization has brighter future. The economic status of people is changing. So many new government policies and economic reforms are impetus for insurance sector. The firmament of economic growth is vast and never ending but the insurance as a bird have to fly. No doubt insurance market after globalization is "A flying bird"! The insurance industry in India has witnessed a sea-change ever since it was opened up to private players in 1999. The liberalization transformed the industry's outlook towards the huge Indian market. The sudden rise in the number of players has brought about innovation in product development and distribution channels. The Indian customer thus has a whole new range of insurance products to choose from. There is choice for every societal segment.

Previously insurance meant merely obtaining a policy on life through the ubiquitous agent. The horizon has widened today offering coverage to health and wealth as well. Competition amongst insurers has brought a new trend-to attain as well as retain customers by all means. This has brought about some unethical practices in the business, which is not a healthy sign. But these aberrations apart, competition has definitely proved to be a better bargain for the customer in terms of quality of service. Competition is an essential ingredient of open markets. LIC's competitive strength can be seen only in a large market share, low-cost operations, ability to differentiate in the market by adopting flexible strategies, and developing special capabilities and competencies. The future will witness tremendous challenges. Changes in technology, biology, medicine, social values, demography, environment and international relations will impact the insurance markets. The Indian insurance market is going to be extremely dynamic in the wake of an emerging stronger economy. LIC's growth and strengths in the new competitive environment would depend on whether it adopts the dictum of a distinguished American insurance agent, who once commented that "the people who succeed in this world are the people who get up and find the circumstances they want - and if they can't find them, they make them."

13

Marketing Mix Components of Life Insurance Corporation of India

Dr. B. Baskaran

Introduction:

The Insurance Industry plays a very significant role in the emergence of powerful, self-reliant and prosperous India. This concept is very necessary for the growth of any developing country. India is no exception. Whether property or life it is subject to risk. Insurance is the scientific innovation of mankind to avoid risk in human life and property. In fact insurance support is the only input, provides sustenance for the growth of people. Life Insurance is one of the most popular forms of insurance and has acquired a leading position all over the world. Life Insurance occupies an important place among the other forms of insurance, because it provides protection to the human life.

Historically insurance is almost as old as large scale economic activity. Insurance, as a facilitating function has become an inseparable part of modern business. It is almost certain that in the absence of risk-bearing and risk-taking agency, modern business would come to a grinding halt. There is no area into which insurance has not entered into. Life Insurance, Marine Insurance, Fire Insurance, Fidelity. Guarantee Insurance, Workmen's Compensation Insurance etc., are all very common. It has extended to more and newer areas on a commercial basis. Today it is possible to insure a musician's voice, an athlete's limbs, a surgeon's hands, part of an actress' anatomy, a travel from one place to another.

Life Insurance is one of the most common forms of Insurance and has acquired a leading position all over the world in providing economic security to the people.

Marketing of Life Insurance Services

Marketing mix components like product, price, place and promotion for the LIC is briefly discussed hereunder

The basic principles and functions of marketing are applicable to all industries and insurance industry is no exception. The usual method of blindly applying the basic marketing principle will not help marketing of life insurance. Life insurance selling is really tough. No individual will willingly go in for insurance and that is why it is customary to say, in the insurance parlance, insurance is never bought, it has always to be sold. Life insurance is not considered a necessity even by educated and security conscious class in our society. This is why insurance market is virtually untapped in many pockets or segments in the society even in developed countries.

Product Mix

A product is anything that can be offered to a market for attention, acquisition, use or consumption that might satisfy a want or need. It includes physical objects, services, persons, places, organisations and ideas. A product mix (also called assortment) is the set of all product line and items that a particular seller offers for sale to the buyers.

The policies of LIC are evolved on the basis of the product mix strategies, (Family protection, need for insured and his family, old age needs) .In order to fulfil different needs mentioned above, some policies are evolved such as educational annuity policy, marriage endowment policy, money back policy, Janaraksha policy, Jeevan mitra policy, Jeevan Anand , Jeevan saati policy, Bima Sandesh policy, Jeevan Shree, New Bima Gold etc.

To look after the family at old age, certain policies are introduced such as Jeevan Akshay policy, Bhavishya Jeevan policy, Jeevan Dhara Policy etc. From this, it could be understood that the product development strategy of LIC primarily centered on the family protection. LIC was not considered from the point of view of investment. Now, the product development of LIC is also considering the investment point of view in mind. The bonus to the insured is offered to fulfil the above said investment objective. Previously, bonus was declared once in two years. Since 1985, annual bonus is declared. Increase in percentage of bonus every year declared by LIC is a proof to fulfil the investment objective.

Price Mix

The purpose of life insurance is to cover the risk of human life. For covering such risk, an amount is collected by the insurer from the insured as a consideration for the insurance contract, which is known as premium. In other words, premium is the price of insurance. Fixing the premium is called "ratting". Premium is fixed on the basis of risk covered. Pricing is an important decision for any organisation. Insurance companies are not exception to this. The successes of marketing of life insurance services are also dependent on the price of the policy. Retaining the sales of the policy, expansion of sales, entering into new market etc., are possible mainly on the basis of good pricing decision. Therefore, pricing decision is significant with reference to LIC.

As pointed out earlier, the premium is fixed on the basis of risk. Higher is the risk the more will be the premium. Each and every proposal should be evaluated to determine the amount of risk for calculation of premium. Theoretically at least, all the persons should be charged different premiums, but it is not practicable to charge so many premiums in relation to number of accounts. Therefore, for practical purpose the risks are classified and premiums are determined according to human life expectations and life tables. The risks, are measured or evaluated for fixation of premium depending on the value and cost of service

For any product, price is determined by taking into various considerations such as demand, supply, cost of production, profit margin, etc., To insurance service, as a product, the above said considerations are applicable. The insurance company is offering a number of policies to suit to the requirements of different economic groups. Insurance company is modifying different economic groups. Insurance company is modifying different categories of policies in order to meet the changes in the demand side. Pricing strategies are effective tool used by the insurance company for attracting more number of people under the insurance coverage. One of the strategies adopted by the LIC is to arrive at a final price is the price adjustment strategy. There are different pricing strategy such as geographical pricing, etc., Discount is the strategy used by LIC in certain categories of policies. Hence, it would be worth mentioning about discount strategy of the LIC.

Place Mix

Channels normally described a forward movement of products. Channel distribution for service is usually simpler and more direct than industrial and consumer goods. This is due to the intangibility of services. In other words, shorter channels are used for service marketing. The marketer of the service is often less concerned with storage, transportation and inventory control because these are not required. But, he faces the problem of making their output available and accessible to target population. Generally, marketing intermediaries like agents or brokers are used by firms. LIC is no exception to this. In the case of life insurance, its policies are marketed through zones, divisions, branches, development officers and agents. Usually the targets fixed for zones and divisional offices are implemented by the branch offices. Branch offices reach the target with the help of Development Officers of the respective branch. In turn, the Development Officers fix individual target for agents, who are working under them.

From this it could be understood that development officers and agents are the important functionaries in selling of life insurance services. Therefore, it would be relevant to explain in detail about their role in the of marketing. As mentioned earlier, Development Officer fixes target and he is instrumental in reaching the individual target of the agents.

Promotion Mix

The last phase of marketing of life insurance services is the sales promotional efforts. "Promotion is the function of informing, persuading and influencing the consumer's purchase decision". Promotional strategy is closely related to the process of communication – the transmission of a message from the company to the user. The components of promotional mix are personal selling and non-personal selling (including advertising, sales promotion and public relations). Personal selling and advertising are the most significant elements, usually accounting for the bulk of a service organisation. Insurance organisation is no exception. Personal selling is made through Development Officers and agents. This part consists of non-personal selling, publicity at the branch office premises, wall painting, advertisement through newspaper, television, radio, participation in local festival are some of the non-personal selling method adopted by the LIC.

At the grass root level, the branch office plays an important role in spreading the message of LIC. It has contact with the public and the policy holders, through agents. In notice board at branch office are displayed details of loans paid, maturity claims paid, and death claims paid. This information, in the notice board of LIC gives an idea to the policy holders about the performance of the concerned branch. In practice, this notice board information may not be considered as effective as of other promotional media. Better clientele, at various levels in the branch, from manager to subordinate staff may prove an effective sales promotional method, mainly to retain the existing customer.

Advertisement is another technique used by the LIC at various levels. Advertisements through newspapers, magazines, journals etc., are regularly and repeatedly given by the LIC. Television and Radio are also extensively used media. Besides, wall-paintings are also used for publicity programmes. LIC also participate in all local festivals like Shandy Day, Temple Kumbabishekams, etc. where LIC arranges to take height and weight of the people who participated in the festivals by the LIC volunteers, at free of cost. While giving the height and weight card, they also distribute the LIC pamphlets. Distribution of pamphlet is also done in all the local temple festivals with the help of agents and development officers.

14

Health Insurance – An Overview

Dr. B. Sekar

Introduction:

We are in a country where we have the proverb "HEALTH IS WEALTH". But many people in India are not aware of the health problems prevailing in the country. Today is a situation where numerous diseases even not named properly is prevailing in our country. Our country comprises mostly of villages and rural people, who don't have enough economic facilities, and are not aware of the Health Schemes available in our country – both in public and private sector. While the health care sector in India is improving, it is still far behind the goal of "Health for All". We have to take a lot of steps in improving the health care of our country. A large share of GDP is being spent on the health of the Indian population. The primary health-care is looked after by the state right from the earlier days. The policy maintains eloquent silence on the role of the private sector health care delivery. Nevertheless, the private and voluntary sectors have developed to meet the increasing demand for medical care services. The medical care infrastructure in India is a very large network and the government runs a multi-tiered, partially integrated medical care system. The private and voluntary sector is largely fragmented and dominated by the nursing home and dispensaries.

On the supply side, only a few investor-owned hospitals have come up, and foreign alliances have increased, private health insurers are entering the market and information technology is being used extensively by providers to improve the reach of their services. As the government is not able to meet with the needs of the people, the entry of the private sector is positively skewed.

Prospects of Health Care in India

The move towards higher quality is evident in the Indian healthcare-sector. But the word quality has different connotations with different people. Over the last 50 years India has achieved a lot in terms of health improvement. But still India is lagging behind when compared to fast developing countries such a China, Vietnam and Sri Lanka in health indicators. The government funded health care system has always remained a major concern in case of the quality and the access of services. As a result private health market has grown very rapidly in India. This private sector helps in bridging the gap between what the government offers and the need of the people. But a thing of higher concern is the cost of the health care that has become very expensive now-a-days. It is not affordable to a large segment of population. Somehow or other new options are to be found out to manage such problems.

The new economic policy and liberalization process followed by the Government of India since 1991 has paved a way for privatization of insurance sector in the country. Health insurance is now poised for a fundamental change in its approach and management. The IRDA bill passed in the Indian Parliament is important in the beginning of changes as it is significant in the health sector. The privatization of insurance and constitution of IRDA has envisaged improving the performance of the insurance sector in the states.

Health insurance is different from the other segments of insurance business and is more complex because of serious conflicts arising out of adverse selection, moral hazard, and information gap problems. The IRDA should have a significant role to play regarding this in regulation of this sector and it should take the responsibility to minimize the consequences of this change.

The government health infrastructure of India has developed a large in the past 50 years with more than 150 medical colleges, 450 district hospitals, 3000 community health centers, 20,000 Primary Health care centers and 1,30,000 Sub-health centers. Other than this we have a number of private and NGO health facilities and practitioners through out the country. For the past 50 years health department has improved a lot in our country. Death rate and Infant mortality rate has reduced considerably and life expectancy has increased from 31 to 63 years. But still there are some challenges like life expectancy 4 years below world average, communicable disease, negligence of women's health care, environmental degradation etc. Out of the 6% expenditure of the country, 4.25% is of the private funding and the remaining 1.75% is from the government.

Indian health financing scene raises a number of challenges like

- Increasing health care costs
- High financial burden on poor eroding their incomes
- Increasing burden of new diseases and health risks and
- Neglect of preventive and primary care and public health functions due to under funding of the government health care.

Health Insurance in India

Health Insurance in a very narrow sense means, individual or group purchases in advance, the health coverage by paying a fee called "premium". But it can be also defined in a broad sense by including all financing arrangements where consumers can avoid or reduce their expenditures at time of use of the services. The health insurance existing in India covers a very wide spectrum of arrangements and hence the latter-broader interpretation of health insurance will be more appropriate. Though health insurance is a very well developed concept in many countries, it is a new concept in India.

Types of Health Coverage in India

There are various types of health coverages in India. It can be divided based on the ownership of the existing health insurance schemes as:

- Government or State-based systems
- Market-based systems (private and voluntary)
- Employer provided insurance schemes and
- Member organization (NGO/co-operative)

Mediclaim Scheme

Mediclaim scheme was the first health insurance scheme introduced by the government in 1986. It is reimbursement based insurance for hospitalization. It does not cover outpatient treatments. Initially there was category wise ceilings like medicine, room charges, operation charges etc., and later on when the policies were revised such ceilings were removed and total reimbursements were allowed within the limit of the policy amount. The upper limit for the policy coverage was also increased to 5 lakhs against accidental and sickness hospitalizations during the policy period as per the latest guide lines of the GIC which is offered by all the four subsidiaries of the GIC. According to a recent statistical study, out of the one billion population of India, only two million people are covered by this mediclaim. There are several reasons for the unpopularity of this scheme. The main reason may be that the subsidiaries of the GIC who are an expertise in dealing with non-life insurance are not expertise in marketing health insurance and so this scheme is not popular.

Mediclaim has provided with a model for health insurance for the middle class and the rich. It covers hospitalization costs, which could be catastrophic. But given that the premium is on higher side it remains limited to the middle class and the urban tax paying segment of the population.

There are also problems and negative unintended consequences of this scheme. They are

- reported fraud and manipulation by clients and providers
- monitoring systems are weak
- a chance of pushing up the prices of services in the private sector owing to payment without limit.

There are various health insurance schemes which are prevailing in India. Some of them are discussed in the following paragraphs.

Employee State Insurance (ESI) Scheme

Under the ESI Act, 1948, ESI Scheme provides protection to employees against loss of wages due to inability to work due to sickness, maternity, disability and death due to employment injury. It also provides medical care to employees and their family members without fee for service. It was implemented for the first time in India at two centers namely Delhi and Kanpur simultaneously in February 1952, and it covered about 1.2 lakhs employees. Presently the scheme is spread over 22 states and Union territories across India covering 91 lakhs employees and more than 350 lakhs beneficiaries. The Act compulsorily covers: (a) all power using non-seasonal factories employing 10 or more people; (b) all non-power using factories employing 20 or more employees and (c) service establishments like shops, hotels, restaurants, cinema, road transport and news papers are covered.

The financing of the scheme is done by Employees State Insurance Corporation (ESIC) which is made up of contributions from: (a) employees who contribute at the rate of 1.75 per cent of their wages (if daily wage is Rs.25 or less, his contribution is waived); (b) employers who contribute at the rate of 4. 75 per cent of total wage bills of their employees to contribution on behalf and for employees having daily wage of Rs. 25 or less; and (c) State Governments contributes 12.5 per cent of total shareable expenditure worked out by prescribed ceiling on expenditure which is Rs. 600 per insured person per annum and expenditure incurred outside/over and above the prescribed limit.

The delivery of medical care is through service (direct) system and/or panel (indirect) system. It provides allopathic medical care, but medical care by other systems like ayurvedic and homeopathy in the states is also provided as per the state government decision. The medical care consists of preventive, promotive, curative and rehabilitative types of services provided by the scheme through its own network or through arrangements with reputed government or private institutions by concept of proper referral system and regionalization.

Even though the scheme is formulated well there are many problem areas in managing this scheme. Some of the problems are:

- large number of employers try to avoid being covered under the scheme,
- a large number of posts of medical staff remains vacant because of high turnover and lengthy recruitment procedures,
- there is duality of control,
- rising costs and technological advancement in super speciality treatment,
- management information system is not satisfactory.
- there is low utilization of the hospitals
- workers are not satisfied with the services they get.
- the access to services is a problem in rural area.

Health Insurance for Poor by NGOs

With 70 per cent of population in India living in rural areas and 95 per cent of work-force working in unorganized sectors, and disproportionately large percentage of these populations living below poverty line, there is strong need to develop social security mechanisms for this segment of population. This need for security is further increased because the poor are the most vulnerable for ill health, accidents, death, desertion, social disruptions such as riots, loss of housing, job and other means of livelihood. There are some efforts in this direction of providing social security to the poor by a few NGOs. The most prominent among them is that of Self-Employed Women's Association (SEWA). The other scheme by government insurance companies developed to focus on poor is called Jan Arogya Bima Policy which was introduced in 1995 and covers expenditure up to Rs. 5000 for a premium of Rs. 70 per annum.

It is estimated that about 5 million people are covered under various NGO insurance schemes. There is need in India to promote these schemes as they address the needs of the poor. Over the last few years in India small and big NGO's like Tribhuvandas, SEWA, ACCORD etc. have implemented the insurance schemes. Many of these schemes are designed to meet the needs of the poorer segments of the community. They have developed several innovations such as

- mechanism of monitoring the performance,
- pricing of various services,
- integration of various risks in one single product,
- linking of insurance schemes with savings,
- coverage of many services not included in market based schemes such as maternity services, transportation, coverage of risks such as from riots, floods etc.

Some NGOs have developed special linkages with public health systems, private facilities and also accessed resources through insurance companies.

SEWA's Health Insurance and Social Security Schemes for the Poor

Poor women are the most vulnerable sections of a developing society. SEWA - a membership based women workers' trade union, has developed an initiative to protect the poor women from financial burdens arising out of high medical costs and other risks. Each member has option to join the programme by paying Rs. 60 per annum and it provides limited cover for risks arising out of sickness, maternity needs, accidents, floods and riots, widowhood etc. The scheme is also linked with saving scheme. Members have the option to either deposit Rs. 500 in SEWA Bank and interest on this deposit will cover the annual premium or pay annual premium of Rs. 60. The scheme has 30,000 members and is expected to grow to 50000.

Other NGO health insurance schemes

Over the last several years there have been efforts to develop health insurance by various small NGOs. Some of the prominent among them have been ACCORD in Karnataka, Tribhuvandas foundation, Aga Khan Health Services, India (AKHSI) and Nav-sarjan in Gujarat, and Sewagram medical college Maharashtra. ACCORD works with tribal population in forested areas of Karnataka, AKHSI works with Ismaili population in North Gujarat, Tribhuvandas Foundation works in villages of Kheda district where there are strong milk producing unions of Amul Dairy Cooperative, Nav-sarjan works with schedule castes in 2000 villages of Gujarat. Ranson (1999) has reviewed NGO efforts in India in this field. There are some common features of NGO schemes. The coverage of these schemes varies and most use their own health workers to provide primary care and have tied up with a hospital to provide secondary care.

With the liberalization of insurance and entry of private companies in this business it is very important that specific interventions are developed which focus on increasing the consumer awareness about insurance products. One of the major challenges after privatization of insurance would be how to develop such mechanisms, which help making consumers aware about the various intricacies of insurance plans. As of now information, knowledge and awareness of existing insurance plans is very limited. With Consumer Protection Act coming in force it has become easy for aggrieved consumers to complain and seek redressal for their problems. Consumer organizations such as CERC of Ahmedabad have been helping consumers to get due justice in disputes with the insurance companies. Their experience would be varying valuable in guiding development of health insurance plans that are transparent and just. Many a times the insurance claims are rejected due to some small technical reasons. This leads to disputes. Most of the time the conditions and various points included in insurance policy contracts is not negotiable and these are binding on consumers. There is no analysis on what fair practice is and what unfair practice is. Given that insurance companies are large and almost monopoly setting the consumers is treated as secondary and they do not have opportunity to negotiate the terms and conditions of a contract. Many times insurance companies do not strictly follow the conditions in all cases and this create confusion and disputes.

The most important area of dispute and unfair treatment is the knowledge and implications of pre-existing conditions.

Impact of Health Insurance on Structure and Quality of Private Provision

The experiences in liberalizing the private health insurance suggest that it has undesirable effects on the costs of health care. The costs of care generally go up. Given the present system of fee for service and current scenario of health infrastructure in private sector, the development of insurance will need improvements in quality and change in structure. The new investments to improve quality will result into high cost and therefore increase in prices of insurance products. There would be developments in the direction of exploring options of managed care, which would help in reducing the costs.

Role of Regulators

The government has established Insurance Regulatory and Development Authority (IRDA) which is the statutory body for regulation of the whole insurance industry. They would be granting licenses to private companies and will regulate the insurance business. As the health insurance is in its very early phase, the role of IRDA will be very crucial. They have to ensure that the sector develops rapidly and the benefit of the insurance goes to the consumers. But it has to guard against the ill effects of private insurance. The main danger in the health insurance business we see is that the private companies will cover the risk of middle class who can afford to pay high premiums. Unregulated reimbursement of medical costs by the insurance companies will push up the prices of private care. So a large section of India's population who are not insured will be at a relative disadvantage as they will, in future, have to pay much more for the private care. Thus checking increase in the costs of medical care will be very important role of the IRDA. Secondly, IRDA will need to evolve mechanisms by which it puts some kind of statue in place that private insurance companies do not skim the market by focusing on rich and upper- class clients and in the process neglect a major section of India's population.

Thirdly the regulators should also encourage NGOs, Co-operatives and other collectives to enter into the health insurance business and develop products for the poor as well as for the middle class employed in the services sector such as education, transportation, retailing etc and the self employed.

Conclusion

India has limited experience of health insurance. Given that government has liberalized the insurance industry, health insurance is going to develop rapidly in future. The challenge is to see that it benefits the poor and the weak in terms of better coverage and health services at lower costs without the negative aspects of cost increase and over use of procedures and technology in provision of health care. The experience from other places suggest that if health insurance is left to the private market it will only cover those which have substantial ability to pay leaving out the poor and making them more vulnerable. Hence India should proactively make efforts to develop Social Health Insurance. Given that India does not have large organized sector employment the only option for such social health insurance is to develop it through co-operatives, associations and unions. The existing health insurance programmes such as ESIS and Mediclaim also need substantial reforms to make them more efficient and socially useful. Government should catalyze and guide development of such social health insurance in India. Researchers and donors should support such development.

References

- Gumber A., Kulkarni V. 2000. Health Insurance for Informal Sector: Case Study of Gujarat. Economic and Political Weekly, Sep. 30.
- Dholakia R. Economic reforms: Implications for Health Insurance. Presentation at One day workshop on 'Health Insurance in India'. Indian Institute of Management, Ahmedabad. Oct. 30, 1999.
- Ellis RP., Alam M, Gupta I. 1996 Health Insurance in India: Prognosis and Prospectus.
- Boston University: Boston and Institute of Economic Growth: Delhi. December 18.
- IIM A 1999. Indian Institute of Management, Ahmedabad. Report of the one day workshop on 'Health Insurance in India'. Oct. 30, 1999.

- IIMA 2000. Indian Institute of Management, Ahmedabad. Report on Conference on Health Insurance, March 18-19, 2000 and three Technical Workshops on March 15-17, 2000.
- Naylor CD, Jha P, Woods J, and Shariff A, 1999. A Fine Balance: Some Options for Private and Public Health Care in Urban India. The World Bank: Washington DC. May, 1999.
- Ranson MK. 1999 The Consequences of Health Insurance for the Informal Sector: Two Non-Governmental, Non-Profit Schemes in Gujarat. London School of Hygiene and Tropical Medicine; Dept. of Public Health and Policy, Health Policy Unit. May 13, 1999. (Unpublished).
- Satia J, Mavalankar D, Bhat R, Progress and Challenges of Health Sector: A Balance Sheet, Indian Institute of Management, Ahmedabad October 1999 Working Paper 99-10-08
- Shah M. 1999. Consumer perspective on health insurance. Presentation at One day workshop on 'Health Insurance in India'. Indian Institute of Management, Ahmedabad. Oct. 30, 1999.
- Srivastava DC 1999. Details of Various Medical Insurance Schemes Being Marketed by the Insurance Industry in India. New Delhi.

15

Marketing of Micro Insurance

Ms. N. Deepa, Ms. S. Thenmozhi

Introduction :

Today, the promise of providing social security to all is not being fulfilled in India. Instead, in many developing countries, social exclusion is on the rise. Only 20% of world population enjoys adequate social protection. Ironically the poor, who are the most in need of social protection, are the excluded ones. Rural population has to face many risks and hardships. Low income households are vulnerable to risks and economic shocks. One way for the poor to protect themselves is through insurance. Life insurance in rural households is viewed as a means to save money to meet long term family goals, such as buying a piece of land or meeting the cost of daughter's marriage. Unlike in urban areas, where the purchase of insurance is influenced by tax considerations, rural buyers tend to view life insurance as a reliable and essential form of saving. Rural customers are bound to prefer endowment and anticipated endowment products with policy terms of 25 years and beyond.

Considering the preference of rural households for saving-oriented life cover, the insurance regulator IRDA has requested companies to devise "innovative savings products for the rural market", rather than confining themselves to offering pure term insurance cover to fulfill rural business quotas. By helping low-income households manage risks, Micro Insurance can assist them to maintain a sense of financial confidence even in the face of significant vulnerability.

Meaning of Micro Insurance

Micro Insurance refers to insurance for low income people differing from traditional insurance in general by the modest premium and benefit packages. Micro Insurance covers risks of lives, crops, huts, livestock and tools at an affordable cost. We can say that it is protection of poor people and their families against specific perils like death, illness, wealthier catastrophes, etc., in principle micro insurance works like any typical insurance business. Currently 74% of micro insurance schemes operate in 4 southern states in India with Tamil Nadu accounting for over 23% of the market pie.

The draft paper prepared by the Consultative Group to Assist the Poor (CGAP) working group on micro-insurance defines micro-insurance as "the protection of low income households against specific perils in exchange for premium payments proportionate to the likelihood and cost of the risk involved." The paper deliberates on the key roles to be played by all stakeholders – insurers, regulator and the Government. The working group also agrees that the cost of such cover should be affordable.

Micro Insurance and Normal Insurance

There are several things that differentiate it from normal insurance. First it is group insurance that can cover thousands of customers under one contract. For example in India, Allianz covers 42000 customers under one contract. Second, Micro

Insurance requires an intermediary between the customer and the insurance company. Preferably this intermediary is a Non-Governmental Organization (NGO) or Microfinance Institution for example a rural bank that can handle the whole distribution and most of the administration process. Micro Insurance is a risk transfer device characterized by low premiums and low coverage limits, and designed for low-income people not served by typical social or commercial insurance schemes. It requires different design, different distribution strategies and it also requires active involvement of an intermediate agency representing the target community.

Need for Micro Insurance

Insurance functions on the concept of risk pooling, and likewise, regardless of its small unit size and its activities at the level of single communities, so does micro insurance. Poverty is not just a state of deprivation but has latent vulnerability. Micro insurance should, therefore, provide greater economic and psychological security to the poor as it reduces exposure to multiple risks and cushions the impact of a disaster. There is an overwhelming demand for social protection among the poor. Micro insurance in conjunction with micro savings and micro credit could, therefore, go a long way in keeping this segment away from the poverty trap and would truly be an integral component of financial inclusion. Micro insurance links multiple small units into larger structures, creating networks that enhance both insurance functions and support structures for improved governance.

There is a huge population that still needs to be tapped by the insurance companies. If we look at the total population of India and compare it with the rural population we find out that it is a huge proportion of the total population. It is low focus area for the general insurance company and subsidiaries. Therefore there is low penetration. The recognition of need for social security mechanisms for this group is increasing amongst all stakeholders. It is, in this context that micro insurance is becoming a significant tool to address the risks of the poor households and is perceived as part of the social security package. It also well for protection of wealth created out of banks micro lending which will contribute towards the business growth of banks in the long run. Banks' clients while enjoying all other financial services will greatly benefit from access to insurance services also, which is a basic and bare minimum for the community to fall back upon to protect against losses arising out of damage to assets, shelter and livelihood.

Many of the micro insurance products cover the risks holistically and can still be affordable to the community. It is said that a poor family can pay up to 6% to 8% of its annual income as premium which mean approximately INR 42 per month as premium to cover all its risks. Before extending micro insurance to the poor two most important points that need to be kept in mind by the companies and these are:

- the flexibility in premium payments by the insured and
- the second one being there is the difference between the micro insurance provided by the micro finance institutions and non micro finance institutions.

Main Players in Micro Insurance

The main player's involved in micro insurance in Indian market is:

- Insurance Companies
- Micro Financial Institutions
- Non – Governmental Organizations (NGOs)
- Banking Institutions
- Central / State Governments
- Co-operative Society
- Village Council (Panchayat Samitis)
- Employer's organizations
- Health providers and Various other third parties related to Health Insurance.

Micro Insurance Products

Micro insurance, like regular insurance, may be offered for a wide variety of risks. These include both health risks (illness, injury or death) and property risks (damage or loss). A wide micro insurance product exist to address those risks, including crop insurance livestock / cattle insurance, insurance for theft or fire, health insurance, term life insurance, death insurance, disability insurance, insurance for natural disasters, etc.

Product wise Estimated Demand for Micro Insurance

Micro Insurance Products	*Potential Size of Demand in number*	*Market size / demand for services in INR crores*	*Basis of calculation*
Crop Insurance	35 million (30%)	105	1 acre as an average
Cattle Insurance	34 million (20%)	136,000	35 as annual premium
Hut Insurance	20 million (10%)	3000	INR 15 per hut as premium
Life Insurance	100 million (50%)	100,000	INR 100 premium per family
Health Insurance	20 million (10%)	80,000	INR 400 premium per family
Micro property (asset) Insurance	20 million (10%)	2,000	INR 10 premium per household

Addressing Differing Perspectives in Micro-insurance

As already indicated, there are contrasting perspectives which have traditionally impeded the growth of this sector globally. The same is true of the Indian experience also. The competing perspectives of the insured, viz., need, affordability

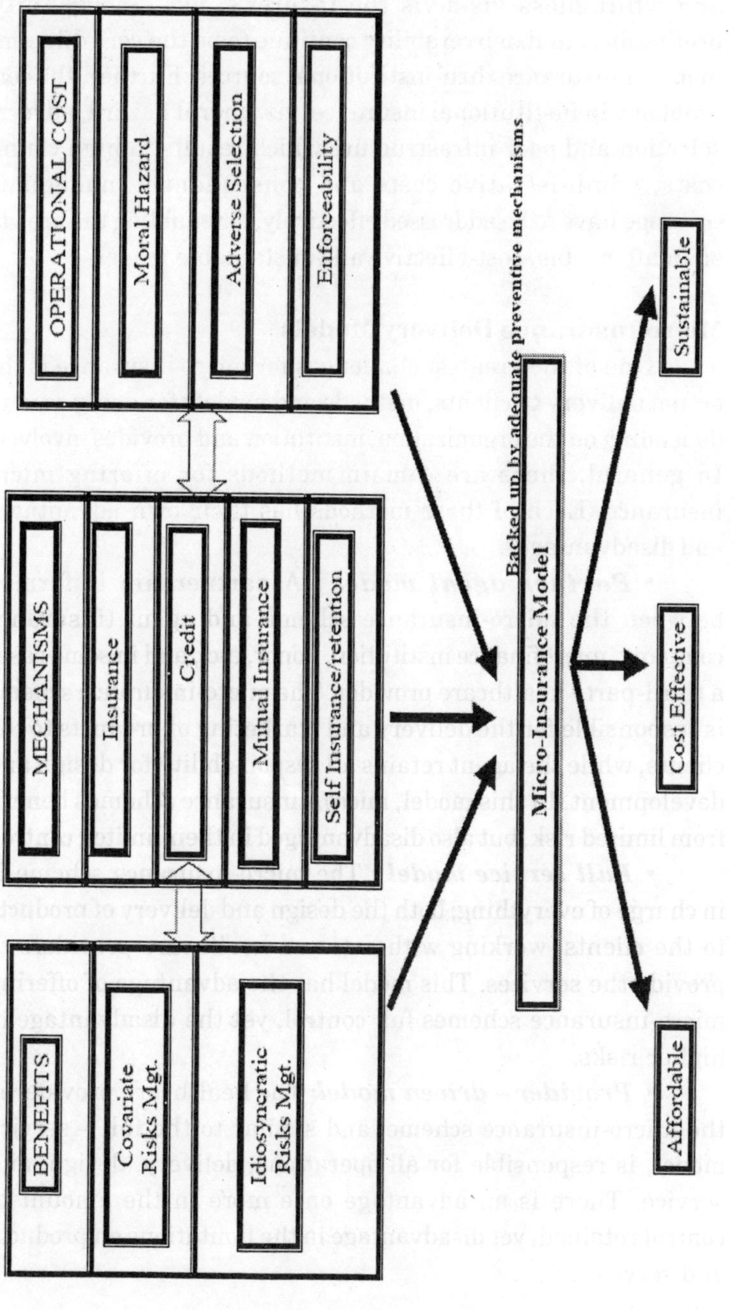
BENEFITS
Covariate Risks Mgt.
Idiosyncratic Risks Mgt.
MECHANISMS
Insurance
Credit
Mutual Insurance
Self Insurance/retention
OPERATIONAL COST
Moral Hazard
Adverse Selection
Enforceability
Backed up by adequate preventive mechanisms
Micro-Insurance Model
Affordable
Cost Effective
Sustainable

and willingness vis-à-vis the insurer's, viz., insurability, profitability and deliverability continue to be the core dilemma in micro-insurance thru' institutional sources. Further, the core problems in institutional insurance, viz., moral hazard, adverse selection and poor infrastructure which results in high claims costs, administrative costs and consequently inadequate coverage have to be addressed effectively, for enabling the growth of an affordable, cost-effective and sustainable model.

Micro Insurance Delivery Models

One of the greatest challenges for micro insurance is the actual delivery to clients, methods and models for doing so vary depending on the organization, institution and provides involved. In general, there are 4 main methods for offering micro insurance. Each of these methods has their own advantages and disadvantages.

- ***Partner agent model :*** A partnership is formed between the micro-insurance scheme and agent (insurance company, microfinance institution, donor, etc), and in some cases a third-party healthcare provider. The micro-insurance scheme is responsible for the delivery and marketing of products to the clients, while the agent retains all responsibility for design and development. In this model, micro – insurance schemes benefit from limited risk, but also disadvantaged in their limited control.
- ***Full service model :*** The micro-insurance scheme is in charge of everything; both the design and delivery of products to the clients, working with external healthcare providers to provide the services. This model has the advantage of offering micro-insurance schemes full control, yet the disadvantage of higher risks.
- ***Provider – driven model:*** The healthcare provider is the micro-insurance scheme, and similar to the full – service model, is responsible for all operations, delivery, design, and service. There is an advantage once more in the amount of control retained, yet disadvantage in the limitations on products and services.

• ***Community – based / mutual model*** **:** The policy holders or clients are in charge, managing and owning the operations, and working with external healthcare providers to offer services. This model is advantageous for its ability to design and market products more easily and effectively, yet is disadvantaged by its small size and scope of operations.

Marketing of Micro Insurance

Micro finance is the most important socio-economic development of our times. Due to the economic circumstances the poor had no bank facilities for the long time. But with the concept of micro credit coming in picture it has been proved that the poor can become credit worthy if they form small groups. Micro credit in India started in big way in the 1990s. In the late 1990s, numerous agencies involved in micro credit operations in India started adding other financial services, including micro insurance to its micro credit operations. The importance of micro finance can be seen from the fact that, in spite of the fact that there are many banks in the country but still poor people specially in the rural areas by-passed the formal banking procedure and formed their own groups for micro finance activities.

It's been seen that most of the companies don't get involved in the micro insurance because they feel that poor would not be able to afford and also the margin being involved. There had been many possible solutions given to the government and IRDA to make these companies involved in the micro insurance. One of the suggestions may be imposing tax on these companies if they don't cater to this section of the society. But there are many companies who have taken this obligation by IRDA in positive spirit and have made genuine attempt to cater to this segment of the society. There had been many companies who have not stick to the idea that there are very few margins in the rural section of the society and they have actually taken out ways to cater to these people and have also been able to make huge margins.

The problem lies there being enough potential in this segment but still there is no push on the part of the insurance companies to provide insurance to this segment of the people. It is also indicated that the micro insurance initiatives can definitely alter the picture of low insurance penetration in rural areas in India and immediate future but obviously there are **certain challenges** to be overcome to achieve sustained and scalable micro insurance models.

A study commissioned by the **United Nations Development Programme (UNDP)** titled "Building Security for the Poor - Potential and Prospects for Micro insurance in India" states that 90% of the Indian population - some 950 million people - are not covered by insurance and signify an untapped market of nearly US$2 billion. This enormous "missing market" is ready for customized life and non-life insurance, but first, serious mismatches between the needs of the insured and the insurers must be overcome, putting priorities against profits. The UNDP report has analyzed **six key issues** pertinent to the growth of the micro-insurance industry in India, capturing the concerns of different stakeholders as indicated below :

- There are specific reasons for low demand for insurance in spite of intense need. Suppliers have their own concerns which help to explain why there have been so little efforts at market development. Consequently, the rural market is characterized by limited and inappropriate services, inadequate information and capacity gaps.
- There are challenges in product design, which has resulted in a mismatch between needs and standard products on offer. Efforts at product development / diversification have been limited.
- Pricing, including willingness to pay and the availability of subsidies, influence the market. In the absence of a historical data base on claims, premium calculations are based on remote macro aggregates and overcautious margins. Building and sharing claims histories can help

in aligning pricing decisions with actuarial calculations, thereby reducing prices.

- Difficulty in distribution is one of the most cited reasons for absence of rural insurance. The high costs of penetrating rural markets, combined with underutilization of available distribution channels, hinder the growth of rural insurance services. This adds to costs, both, managerial and financial. Like inclusive credit, inclusive insurance is expected to be a "low ticket" business, requiring volumes for viability.
- Cumbersome and inappropriate procedures inhibit the development of this sector.
- Contrasting perspectives of the insured and the insurers, lead to low customization of products and low demand for what is available.

The UNDP report further states that micro-insurance solutions should, therefore, attempt at addressing key issues that will improve customer satisfaction (demand-supply gaps, appropriate products and pricing), provide distribution efficiencies for better outreach and remove procedural hassles facilitating easier renewals and claim settlements. With a view to reduce costs, the report has also suggested that the premia payable on micro-insurance be exempted from payment of service tax, which will also enable greater penetration in rural markets.

Before launching any product, need based analysis is done. Naturally we cannot sell wedding insurance in the rural sector of the economy. Because their needs are very different from the needs of the urban people who are rich and can afford. Therefore first important thing to be done by any company launching micro – insurance product must do the need based analysis.

Strategies for Success of Micro Insurance Products

Various parameters need to be considered while marketing various life insurance products in rural section. Following aspects need to be considered:

• **Increasing the need for insurance**. This can be done by educating the target group about the need for insurance and not only that the benefits for the same should also be stated to the people. This can be done by marketing about the benefits of these products by the agents from the individual agencies themselves by meeting one-by-one all the people in the area assigned to them. Or else they can hold a large crowd in one group and explain the need and benefit of not only life insurance but also of the general insurance.

• **Ease of process**. If we look at the insurance process followed by the insurance companies in our country we find out many flaws in the insurance process. So, for the population of the country this is not well educated and is skeptical about the insurance as such. It's better for the companies dealing in micro-insurance that they should focus on the ease of the process like subscription, renewal and claim settlement.

• **Product promotion.** One common mistake done by the insurance companies that they are not able to know the need for the rural poor and that is why most of the products launched by such companies are failure. Focus should be on the promotion of the agriculture pump set and cattle insurance among the owners And also there is a need to promote health and personal accident policies. Focus should also be on the policy holders and lapsers of the policy.

• **Pricing strategies.** Lower premiums would be preferable. And there should also be flexibility in the payment of the premium because we all know that the rural poor are able to earn their earning on the seasonal basis. So it is preferable to charge premium instead of yearly but on quarterly or monthly or seasonal basis.

• **Channels of the sale**. Channels used for the sale of the insurance policies should be banks, co-operative societies, and sarpanch. Why these channels?- only because of the personal feeling which the villagers enjoy with the sarpanch and these co-operative societies and also the factor of trust is involved in it.

• **Participative information dissemination.** Small groups of the farmers and the villagers should be called for the meetings at the melas, co-operative society's meet, and the farmers meet and there they all should be made aware about the new kind of the insurance products available to them and also told about the existing products if they are not aware about them they could come to know of them.

• **Need for the health insurance products as riders of the life policies.**

Health insurance products should be more often developed so that they are able to meet the needs of the customers. "Health insurance has a great potential in the country but remains highly untapped. According to some estimates only 3% of India's population is covered under some form of voluntary health insurance schemes". This segment needs regulator's focused attention for its development.

• **Sustained expansion of the market size.** Our metro areas and the large urban markets would saturate in 3-5 years time. For sustained expansion of the market size, it is critical to introduce simple products and distribute them in semi urban and rural markets.

Certain Bima yojanas have already started doing their work in the better way. Examples are : Sankat Haran Bima Yojana (launched long back in Sep, 2001 by ITGI). It covered 5.5 crores of farmers across the country. Not only this – it had also increased visibility, familiarity, and accessibility of insurance.

Recommendations

• **Leveraging Existing Network for Micro-Insurance**

It would be difficult for the insurers to establish a vast network for distribution of micro-insurance products. They need to utilize existing Government organizations, banks, MFIs, NGOs and SHGs to increase the outreach of micro insurance to the poor. The advantages of these entities are that they find greater acceptability among the financially excluded, and with a better understanding of their needs are well equipped to advise them on the choice of products. In India with a vast rural population characterized by challenges and complexities, it makes sense to latch on to an existing mechanism operating in these segments to lower costs and to help the insurer to leverage on the faith already generated by the entity. Hence it would be prudent to choose a partner-agent model for delivery where the insurer underwrites the risk and the distribution is handled by an existing intermediary. This model keeps the cost of insurance attractive enough for the poor to enter and remain in its fold even while addressing the concern of the insurers about the low returns of micro-insurance.

- **Linking Micro-credit with Micro-insurance**

It is becoming increasingly clear that micro-insurance needs a further push and guidance from the Regulator as well as the Government. The Committee concurs with the view that offering micro credit without micro-insurance is bad financial behaviour, as it is the poor who suffer on account of such bad product design. There is, therefore, a need to emphasize linking of micro credit with micro-insurance. Linking micro-insurance with micro-finance makes good business sense. Further, as it helps in bringing down the inherent risk cost of lending, the Committee feels that NABARD should be regularly involved in issues relating to rural and micro insurance to leverage on its experience of being a catalyst in the field of micro-credit.

Implementation Strategy for Micro-Insurance

Keeping in view the various issues, the Committee has identified five major areas for formulation of strategies for effective implementation of micro-insurance programmes. These are explained in the following paragraphs:

- **Human Resource Requirement and Training**

As indicated earlier, the UNDP report states that there is a huge untapped market – of around 950 million people and nearly US$ 2 billion – for insurance in India. IRDA may consider putting in place an appropriate institutional structure for deciding on service packages including premia and formulating strategies for effective promotion of micro insurance. There is also a felt need for development, of both fulltime and part-time staff, thru' effective training in insurance marketing and servicing concepts.

- **Operations and Systems**

To address the requirements of the huge market potential available, appropriate systems should be evolved for tracking client information, either manually or using technology. While a technology platform may take time for setting up, in the long-run, the same will be cost-effective and reliable. Similarly, the procedures for premium payments, claims and other services should be formalized along with increased customization of products to stimulate demand.

- **Development of Adequate Feedback Mechanism**

Keeping in view the diverse nature of market requirements, suitable mechanisms to collect market intelligence, collating and interpretation of the same, in a formally structured manner, is important for product development and process refinement. Insurance companies should go beyond devising new products to improving their processes for building awareness, marketing enrollment, premium collection, claim settlement and renewal. For this they need use innovative channels such as business correspondents, SHGs, NGOs and MFIs as also cooperatives and mutual associations. Further, the use of technology such as mobile phones and ATMs for premium collection should be encouraged to keep transaction costs low.

- **Development of Data Base**

High costs of penetration and acquisition often leads to higher pricing of products, thereby impacting client outreach and market depth. Building up historical data base on risk profiles, claims, settlement ratios, etc., will facilitate in better pricing of products, based on actual rather than presumed risks. Besides enabling cost reduction, warehousing of such data will make the market more transparent for entry of more operators. The IRDA and the Government should help in provision of data such as human mortality and morbidity, weather parameters and livestock mortality/morbidity, on a timely, large sample and regular basis. This will lead to finer pricing on actuarial basis and eventually cut costs of insurance.

- **Consumer Education, Marketing and Grievance Handling**

  The micro-insurance sector is unique in the sense that there is an ongoing challenge to explain the concept and benefits to the insured. Creating awareness thru' use of pictorial posters, local folk arts and street theatres might be useful to explain the mechanisms of insurance. Local community-based organizations could organize premium collections, as they have better access to the local people. To make it more acceptable to the people, micro-insurance products, apart from covering only risks, should also provide an opportunity for providing long term savings (endowment).

IRDA's Regulations on Micro-Insurance

Building on the recommendations of the consultative group, IRDA notified Micro-Insurance Regulations on 10th November 2005 with the following key features to promote and regulate micro-insurance products. The regulations focus on the direction, design and delivery of the products :

- A tie-up between life and non life insurance players for integration of product to address risks to the individual, his family, his assets and habitat.
- Monitoring product design through "file and use".

- Breakthrough in distribution channels with inclusion of NGOs, SHGs, MFIs and PACS to provide micro-insurance, with appropriate compensation for their services
- Enlarged servicing activities entrusted to micro-insurance agents,
- Issue of policy documents in simple vernacular language.

Currently the IRDA regulations do not favor composite insurance (i.e., life and non-life insurances by the same company) and also limit the agency tie-up to one life and one non-life insurer. However, in recognition of the uniqueness of micro insurance, these regulations enable life and non-life companies to tie-up for offering a combined policy in rural areas. Further, the IRDA has allowed insurers to issue policies with a maximum cover of Rs. 50,000 for general and life insurance under these regulations. The regulations have also eased the norms for entry of agents relating to training and pre-recruitment examination.

Role of Banks in Marketing of Micro Insurance

Banks and post offices offer good retail chains for delivering micro – insurances services. It is also interesting to know from the last years experience that micro credit share of the non – southern states has increased to nearly 50% an opportunity that can be used by banks for layering the micro insurance initiative over the current micro credit initiative. Though post offices and phone booths in India offer a huge retail canvass like books, the specialization that insurance required in terms of financial intermediaries can be best done by banks than other retails due to their familiarity with insurance business as most of them are already part of Banc assurance models or part of joint ventures with the insurance industry. Banks need to play the big brother attitude in synergising the consortium and perhaps lead the consortium for capitalizing their presence more as complementing opportunity to take retail outreach to new scale.

Banc assurance is selling insurance policies through banks. In return, banks get commission from the insurance companies based on the volume of business premium sold. Under insurance regulations, banks can tie up with only one insurance company. For private insurers banc assurance accounts for significant portion of their business with new opportunities in insurance and micro insurance, banks are interested in setting up joint ventures with big players to make a firm into the insurance sector. Banks shall need to smartly use the NGO channels to augment the outreach of micro insurance. The shareholders turn out to be a captive market for the banks. With adequate financial support to the participating NGOs to cover their costs, micro insurance throws up a huge outreach canvas for the banks in India.

Bank -wise tie up with Insurance Companies

Bank	*Insurance Company*
Canara Bank	Aviva Life
Bank of India	ICICI Prudential
Oriental Bank of Commerce	LIC
Yes Bank	Max New York Ltd

Some of the banks have reportedly expressed their intent of having their own joint ventures in partnership with some foreign insurance players. This move is expected to outreach and bring a new paradigm in the business profile of insurance as an industry besides inducing competition. Banks need to see a real time business opportunity in Micro insurance and though the supervisory agencies like RBI and IRDA can coordinate in the beginning to have certain portion of their business to come from Micro insurance, pretty much like priority sector obligation unless banks realize this area as a business opportunity, Micro insurance cannot be integrated into their business plans.

Conclusion

Many insurance schemes for the poor being experimented with across the country covering security primarily for crop, property, assets and health hazards for the under privileged population and the time has come to scale up the pilot schemes to much larger populations with the active support of the governmental and non – governmental infrastructure that is available. At the root of the success will lay the ability to utilize the meager paying capacity of the poor to romp up a respective and quality scheme to remove the frequent health risk being faced by the poor and to prevent further deterioration of their well being. In simple terms, the success of rural insurance business in India centers around innovative product design, increasing penetration, finding effective and low cost distribution channels, education, access and affordability. These requirements may appear daunting, but new approaches are likely to pay dividends to insurers in the long run as the rural economy benefits from the growth being witnessed in the rest of India.

References

1. Insurance Chronicle Vol III, No XI, November. 2003 "Indian Insurance Industry- A Fresh Aroma".
2. The Insurance Times, Vol XXVI, No.4 April 2008 "Micro Insurance in India" Anabil Bhattacharya, Manager, National Insurance Co., Ltd., Mumbai.
3. The Insurance Times, Vol XXVIII, No.1 January 2006 IRDA's "Micro Insurance Regulations".
4. Insurance Chronicle Vol VI, No XII, December 2003, "Insuring Rural India".
5. Insurance Chronicle Vol VII, No VI, June 2007, "Extending Micro-Health Insurance Scheme to Lower Middle Class".
6. The Insurance Times, Vol XXVIII, No.5 May 2008 "Micro Insurance in India" Anabil Bhattacharya, Manager, National Insurance Co., Ltd., Mum.
7. The Indian Banker,Vol II, No 10, October 2007 "Micro Insurance- New business opportunity for banks in India".
8. Web Address:

- www.google.com
- www.yahoo.com
- www.rediff.com

16

LIC and Rural Life Insurance Market in India: Opportunities and Challenges

Dr. A. Selveraj, Shinie Poulose

Introduction:

Insurances are similar to banks and capital markets as they serve the needs of business units and private households in financial intermediation. The availability of insurance services is essential for the stability of the economy and can make the business participants accept aggravated risks. By accepting claims, insurance companies also have to pool premiums and form reserve funds. So insurance companies are playing an important role by enhancing internal cash flow at the assured and creating large amount of assets played on the capital market and hence may contribute to economic growth. Well developed financial markets have a significant positive impact on total factor productivity, which translates into higher long growth. The objective of this article is to analyze the role of Life Insurance Corporation of India in the economic development by exploring the rural market.

The Indian life insurance market is growing faster than most developed markets. India, along with other Asian economies like South Korea and Japan, has a double-digit growth figure in the life industry. The public-sector Life Insurance Corporation of India (LIC) is still the dominant force in the market, but its market share is slowly and steadily eroding. From being a monopoly for close to 45 years the corporation is today facing the greatest challenge of its existence from the private sector which today has a combined market share of slightly over 25% of India's life insurance market.

The Indian life insurance market can be divided into urban and rural markets. These two segments are diverse in nature and have distinguished characteristics. The economic growth of the two has not been the same. A wide disparity exists between the per capita income and literacy rate, among other things, in these two sectors. The ratio of rural Indian population is very high and it has growing insurance needs. From insurance perspective, it shows that rural population has low reach and the urban markets are rapidly getting saturated, so that the future growth potential lies in the rural areas.

There has been a tremendous change in the financial services arena across the world in last few years commoditization; globalization, deregulation, and rapid technological advancements are the sweeping changes that have changed the market scenario of financial services industry. While integrating the Indian economy with global economy of India initiated liberalization, which has opened up the insurance sector to the private insurance sector for the main objectives to provide better coverage to the Indian citizens and augment the flow of long-term financial resources to finance the growth of infrastructure. This has laid a great responsibility on the sector to ensure a very fast growth so that India can come to the level of the developed countries of the world in the penetration of insurance.

The Indian life insurance market has significant potential on account of low insurance penetration combined with low expenditure on life insurance. In spite of insurance reforms paving the way for private participation, the insurance sector is still under-Penetrated. India accounts for 16% of the world population, but only accounts for 1.68% of the world life insurance market in the year 2006.Insurance penetration or premium volume as a share of a country's GDP for the year 2005 stood at 2.53% and accounted 4.1% of GDP in 2006-07, which shows an upward movement from 1.2% in 1999-2000. This growth rate happens to be far better than its counterpart china, where insurance business accounts for only 1.75 of the GDP. However, this status quo is set to change and the level of penetration will tend to rise as income increases.

Even now, the Indian insurance customer views life insurance product as a means to perk up finances and avail tax benefits. The non-life coverage is largely considered unnecessary and waste of money. Even essential insurance products like health insurance are perceived similarly. However, the increase in per capita income together with the rising middle-class populace is said to double the insurance market in the next five to six years. Some of the customer segments which show tremendous potential and opportunity to the insurers are: the up-market or modern, traditional and rural and semi-educated segments. Against this background, this paper highlights the growth of insurance in individual policy, role of LIC in rural insurance, and reasons for the slow growth of LIC in rural India. The present study is based on secondary data.

New Business Performance-Number of Policies

LIC, the monolithic organization, has its insurance business in India as well as outside India. But the outside business of LIC is highly negligible as compared to the business in India. The new business performance of LIC in terms of policies (individual insurance) marketed both in India and outside India for a period of 11 years from 1996-97 to 2006-07 is gathered from Journal of Insurance Chronicle and LIC Annual Reports.

TABLE-1

No. of LIC Policies Marketed Under New Business Individual Insurance (Excluding Annuities)

(No. of policies)

Year	*In India (Rs in crs)*	*Out of India*	*Total*	*Annual Growth In India(%)*	*Annual Growth out of India(%)*
1996-97	1,22,68,476 (99.89%)	12,296 (0.11%)	1,22,80,772 (100%)		
1997-98	1,33,11,294 (99.89%)	13,904 (0.10%)	1,33,25,198 (100%)	8.50	13.07
1998-99	1,48,43,687 (99.90%)	13,356 (0.10%)	1,48,57,043 (100%)	12.49	(-)4.46
1999-00	1,69,76,782 (99.93%)	12,648 (6.07%)	1,69,89,430 (100%)	17.39	(-)5.75
2000-01	1,96,56,663 (99.95%)	76,911 (0.05%)	1,96,64,574 (100%)	21.84	(-)38.52
2001-02	2,24,91,304 (99.95%)	8,695 (0.05%)	2,24,99,999 (100%)	23.11	6.38
2002-03	2,42,68,416 (99.94%)	10,359 (0.06%)	2,42,78,775 (100%)	14.49	13.53

(Contd.)

(Contd. Table 1)

Year	In India (Rs in crs)	Out of India	Total	Annual Growth In India(%)	Annual Growth out of India(%)
2003-04	2,66,26381 (99.56%)	11,562 (0.04%)	2,64,67,882 (100%)	19.22	9.78
2004-05	2,35,41,685 (99.94%)	13,807 (0.06%)	2,25,50,859 (100%)	(-)25.14	18.26
2005-06	4,88,27,027 (99.95%)	13,370 (0.04%)	4,88,40,327 (100%)	206.40	(-)3.55
2006-07	3,81,86,384 (99.94)	12,059 (0.06%)	2,09,98,443 (100%)	86.73	(-)10.66
2007-08 (projected)	4,88,76,488 (99.97%)	12,583 (0.03%)	4,88,89,071 (100%)	87.13	4.26
2008-09 (projected)	5,59,37,106 (99.98%)	12,316 (0.02%)	5,59,49,422 (100%)	57.55	(-)2.17
2009-10 (projected)	6,40,17,690 (99.98%)	12,055 (0.02%)	6,40,29,745 (100%)	65.86	(-)2.12
2010-11 (projected)	7,32,65,581 (99.98%)	11,800 (0.02%)	7,32,77,381 (100%)	75.37	(-)2.07

Source : LIC Annual report.

It is felt that growth rate of LIC performance is in satisfactory level. To know its growth, compound growth rate (straight line method) has been used. Trend has been calculated by using the following formula. Y=a+bx. Findings are shown in Table-1.

Table.1 shows that, the number of policies marketed in India during1996-97 was 122.68lakhs, which account for 99.89% while the number of policies marketed outside India was a meager 12,296 policies, which constitute 0.11% only. Almost all, the same trend has been observed until 2003-04 with negligible variation. The number of policies marketed in India is the highest at 99.95% in 2000-01 and 2001-02 while it is relatively the lowest at 99.89% in 1996-97 and 1997-98 and the annual growth rate fluctuated between a low of 14.49% in 2002-03 and a high of 2.11% in 2000-01.

The number of policies marketed outside India has increased continuously to 13,904 in 1997-98 from 12,296 in 1996-97. Since then the policies marketed outside India declined for three years and reached a low of 7,911 in 2000-01. From 2000-01 onwards, an increase is noted in the policies marketed and finally stood at 11,562. The annual growth rate of policies fluctuated between a low of (-) 37.45% in 2000-01 and a high of 19.14% in 2002-03.

On the whole, the volume and value of business in India is far higher than that of the volume and value of business outside India. Mention should be made here that the relatively low annual growth rate of policies marketed in India in 2002-03 could be attributed to various factors. The withdrawal of tax benefits on single premium bonds in 2002-03, the imposition of 5% service tax on premium payments made (subsequently withdrawn)the fall of interest rates and the resultant withdrawal of guaranteed return policies and also the drought situation in the country during 2002-03 had adversely affected the business of LIC. The favorable investment climate with most of the economic indicators showing upward trend such as growth of GDP, per capita income, higher disposable income coupled with increased awareness of insurance has resulted in improved business performance of the insurance industry during 2004-05. The year 2004-05 was characterized by spurt in the growth rate of 422% in linked business. Non linked business stagnated with marginal growth rate of 0.3%. There was a shift in the preference of insuring public from non-linked to linked business in view of fall in the interest rates resulting in lower yield on non –linked products and this trend was continued till 2006-07.Further Table-1 shows that growth rate for LIC in India during the year 2007-08 would be Rs.4,88,76,488.In total this would be Rs.4,88,89,071.

Role of LIC in the Rural Insurance

LIC has been able to establish itself as a vibrant organization playing an important role in the lives of people in the hundreds and thousands of hamlets dotting the rural landscape of the country. Its proclamation therefore that "we know India better" is not without substance. LIC can also lay claim, more than any organization, to be deriving its strength and inspiration from the trust, corers of its policyholders in rural areas have reposed in it. Having recognized immense insurance potential, the LIC has concentrated on the rural sector. During 2003-04, of the 264.56 lakh policies marketed as many as 62.20 lakh Policies are marketed in the rural sector. LIC has also taken a number of measures to Professionalize the rural career agents and as on March 31,204 there are as many as 53,037 rural career agents. Further the promotional expenditure of LIC, which stood at Rs.3, 791.13 lakh in 1999-2000. rose to high of Rs. 9,659.66 lakh in 2003-04. In the rural areas, along the dusty roads, LIC is painting the walls and adopting folklores so as to market insurance plans to rural customers like never before. The new players, on the other hand, have not paid much attention to tap the rural market. In fact, they focused only on meeting the regulatory requirements rather than improving the business in rural areas. Table -2 shows the details of rural new business of LIC.

TABLE-2
Rural New Business of LIC

Year	*No. of Policies (in lakhs)*	*Sum assured (Rs in crores)*	*Annual Growth Percentage*	
			Policies	*Sum Assured*
1996-97	60.33	24,278.73	-	-
1997-98	68.40	27,550.69	13.37	13.48
1998-99	81.23	35,372.94	21.22	32.22
1999-00	97.0	44,168.19	25.15	36.23
2000-01	109.20	59,676.42	20.22	63.88
2001-02	37.02	25,461.94	-119.65	-140.92
2002-03	45.23	23,574.69	13.60	-7.77
2003-04	62.20	35,651.99	28.13	49.74
2004-05	55.03	46,037.01	11.88	42.77
2005-06	NA	NA	NA	NA
2006-07	88.50	68497.21	-	-

NA: Not Available

Source:LIC Annual report.

Table 2- shows that the rural business of LIC has increased from Rs.24, 278.73 cr under 60.33 lakh policies in 1996-97 to Rs 59, 676.42 cr under 109.20 lakh policies in 2000-01.But in 2001-02, the number of policies as well as the sum assured declined heavily and reached a low of Rs. 25, 461.94cr under 37.02 lakh policies. In the succeeding year, viz, 2002-03, though number of policies increased considerably to 45.23 lakhs, the sum assured declined to Rs. 23,574.69 cr. However, in 2003-04 the number of policies marketed and sum assured under rural new business increased significantly. In 2004-05 the number of policies sold was declined to 55.03 lakhs, but there was an increase in the sum assured. There was a significant improvement in both the number of policies marketed and the sum assured during the year 2006-07.

Reasons for the Slow Growth of Life Insurance in Rural India

The above analysis shows that growths of LIC in rural areas are not up to mark. Of course, this might be due to various reasons. Although, it is felt that the following may be reasons for the slow growth in rural area.

(1) Heterogeneity of Rural Population

The heterogeneity of rural population poses a big challenge to the steady growth of insurance. As rural India is widely dispersed over six hundred thousand odd villages, the customer base is so heterogeneous regarding its employment, income, and family size that around understanding of savings is not easily available. This lack of understanding will reflect in the product design, pricing, and frequency of premium payment.

(2) Disparities in Rural Savings and Investments

The disparities in rural savings and investments hinder the rapid growth of life insurance. The National Council of Applied Economic Research (NCAER) data on rural house household income distribution suggest that the top 4% of the households earn about 15 of the household income and the bottom 50% of the population saves about 3% of overall domestic savings. The typical rural informal sector deploys about 68% of its savings in physical assets, farm, business, housing, and gold. As a result, the rural folk are not left with sufficient savings to invest in life insurance.

(3) Dearth of Effective Intermediary Personnel

The dearth of effective intermediary personnel in rural areas precludes the progress of life insurance. The existing system of training, testing, and confirmation of agents are so loosely administered that a high proportion of insurance agents continues as mere spotters without adequate knowledge and professional competence.

(4) Lack of Efficient Distribution Channels

The lack of efficient and reliable distribution channels in rural areas is yet another factor that affects the growth of life insurance. Another area of challenge in dealing with distribution and operational channels is the need to provide sale literature, publicity materials, and proposal forms in local language to attract rural customers. An early difficulty in completing proposal documentation in rural areas is the possibility of lack of age proof for which practical solutions are to be found. There is also a need for proper accounting and banking arrangements to pool the collections.

(5) Insufficient Infrastructure

The insufficient infrastructure in rural areas in term of both manpower and material proves itself a stumbling block to the steady progress of life insurance, coming as it does in the way of effective policy servicing. The insurers are expected to introduce and maintain measures of quick mobility in delivery system so that insurance problems can be attended to without much delay.

(6) Problem of Illiteracy

The problem of illiteracy of the rural masses in rural areas is another critical problem that precludes the growth of insurance in the rural sector. So, there is a desperate need to make the rural masses literate at least up to a certain reasonable level before launching any rural insurance information dissemination programme. And it will be a Herculean task to conduct adult education classes in rural areas to enlighten the illiterate masses on the importance of life insurance.

Suggestion and Conclusion

On the basis of this study, the following suggestions are offered:

(a) There must be necessary to have innovative solutions to develop an efficient delivery system.

(b) By using all possible ways it is necessary to identify the potent rural needs.

(c) It is necessary to spread an insurance culture through group meetings, radio features, and cultural events like folk dances, songs, play lets, puppet shows etc.

(d) It must be necessary to take effective steps to have efficient distribution channels such as banks and micro finance institutions, panchayats, internet and e-commerce and promote non- traditional intermediary for better penetration.

(e) Steps must be taken to introduce the innovative products to meet the needs of rural customers.

In the competitive era if the above suggestive measures have been seriously considered by the policy makers, it will help the Life Insurance Corporation of India to recover its rural market potential in near future.

Conclusion

There are, therefore, immense possibilities and exciting times for selling life insurance in the now opened Indian market. The rural market is vibrant, dynamic and growing and unlike in the metros and cities, the selling of life insurance in rural areas requires great mobility and arduous effort. Competition in rural areas tends to be 'kinder and gentler' than in urban areas, which can easily be termed cut throat. The generally smaller policy amounts in rural areas would be more than offset by the higher volume potential in these areas in contrast with urban areas. The need now is to harness the full potential and explore the rural market.

References

1. www.licindia.com
2. www.insurancenetworking.com

3. www.datamonitor.com
4. www.irdaindia.org
5. LIC annual report .
6. Insurance Chronicle.

Footnotes

1. Samuel. B. Sekar "Indian Insurance Industry poised for growth" June 2008, Insurance Chronicle. pp- 40-45.

17

Insurance Industry and Use of Technology

N. Sumathi, J. Jayashree

Insurance industry worldwide is facing the challenges of deregulation, consolidation and convergence of financial services. An in-depth understanding and insight into their working can transform this challenge into an unprecedented opportunity. The intellectual capital in insurance has become so rich that we have been promptly recognized as consultants by State Insurance Company of Mauritius (SICOM) and entrusted consultancy job for formulating IT Strategy Plan in their businesses of Life, General, Pension, Actuary, Marketing, Legal and Compliance and other areas. The quality of our consultancy and coverage was so matured that they appreciated our services and they are now going for its implementation.

The aim of such consultancy is to elaborate the plans to support their business needs with the ultimate goal of making it a leading financial service provider in its business domain. The objectives of such consultancys are manifold and scopes of activities are described here:

- Analysis of potential impacts of various IT systems on operating efficiency
- Business Analysis with ROI for future years
- Economic Value Addition analysis with respect of each category of business
- Exploring the use of Internet and Portals for greater business opportunity
- Identification of appropriate quantitative indicators to measure the productivity gain with the implementation of IT systems, for example, analysis of figures in the existing Balance Score Card, Key Performance Indicator and how improvements can be augmented through appropriate deployment of IT
- Identification of right tool for strong and efficient Corporate Governance
- Development of Business Continuity and Disaster Recovery Plan
- Training and Development Plans for operations and management staff
- Development of Knowledge Bank for streamlining enterprise information repository

It In Insurance

Information technology is changing the way of insurance adjusters work, by reducing the paper shuffle and allowing them to work more efficiently at the site of a claim.

In Summary:

- Mobile technology untethers insurance adjusters from the office and allows them to work more efficiently at the site of a claim.
- Digital scanning and electronic distribution save time and effort.

- The lack of standardization between law and insurance firms can cause headaches.

Imagine two standard file cabinets loaded with documents—the insurance claims for a group of Louisiana properties damaged by Hurricane Katrina—and then imagine what it would take to fax or copy and mail each one. For one insurance adjuster who recently wrapped up multiple Katrina-related claims, technology means being able to electronically distribute scanned documents in a matter of seconds.

"Technology was absolutely vital. Without it, we wouldn't have been able to make timely submissions. We would have been constantly photocopying and transferring paper, which takes a long time, as opposed to being able to scan it one time, select it, and send it electronically. It also was going to multiple persons in multiple places. We saved an awful lot of trees," says Stephen R. Figlin, CEO of Stephen R. Figlin & Associates, a public adjuster in Philadelphia.

Figlin's experience is one example of how information technology is changing the job for insurance adjusters. There are an estimated 263,000 adjusters in the U.S., according to the U.S. Department of Labour. They help to determine the benefit for a covered loss, and may work on staff for insurance companies, as independent contractors for insurers, or as public adjusters representing property owners. The job can involve climbing through buildings ravaged by fire or flood or examining a car after an accident, photographing the damage, and estimating the cost of repairs.

Technology in Insurance

The insurance business in India is growing at a rapid pace. As in all industries, adapting and responding to change has become the key to competing in this market and the speed of deployment of products and strategy is critical to drive home the advantages of innovation. Technology has become an integral part of strategic initiatives as it touches all facets of the organization, from product development to customer experience. Another big differentiator is the service levels that the organization could provide to the customer along with new product offerings which have revolutionized the insurance options available to the customer. This, along with the speed of technological development, the desire to drive greater efficiency through business processes, and the need to have compliance with new regulatory regimes, has made I.T. strategy play a critical role in supporting business.

For new players, the need to establish and grow brought in the need to look beyond the boundaries of the industry and geography to explore best practices and to find ways of tapping technology to achieve higher efficiencies and sharpen the competitive edge. Before we touch upon technology and see how it fits into insurance, let us look at the structure of an insurance business, its components and the factors which impact the business.

The entities influencing and contributing to the business can be classified as (a) Environmental factors (b) External facing Entities (c) Core business functions (d) Support functions (e) Strategy and Management Intelligence. Environmental factors such as the Regulatory authority, Government, Economy, Market and the country's demographics. Externally connected entities constitute the Sales and Distribution channel; Partners; Customers and shareholders. Core business functions are Operations, Service, Investments, Actuarial, and Claims etc. These are supported by functions such as HR, Finance, IT, Process and others. Business intelligence and corporate planning functions empower the senior management to device strategies to accomplish its objectives. The first level automation need covers the Core Business Functions i.e. the business critical ones which revolves around the policy life cycle and the direct entities attached to it. Thus having a solid platform for policy administration is critical to the organization's success. It is important to have the functionalities desired by the business and at the same time conform to standards and comply with security and IT policies. Technology can address all these requirements. Core business functions such as Underwriting and Claims can be supported by an automated underwriting and rules engine which can provide the advantage of faster turn around times and process control.

A total solution for underwriting and new business processing for life insurers can help reduce policy assurance from weeks to days. As is evident from these examples, technology fits into the special needs of the insurance industry and provides a rapid return on investment by reducing operating costs. A rapidly growing business requires a strong Policy Administration System that can handle large business volumes and facilitates batch timings for daily transactions. The external facing entities can be supported by technology through various means. A flexible and parameterized channel management system will allow the business to easily configure and manage Distribution Channel Partners and the front line sales agencies. A strong channel system can give insights into the partner performance; strengths and weaknesses; segmentation; and support decision making for being competitive in the market. This in turn will lead to higher and better quality sales and keep the costs down by eliminating cost overheads by termination of unproductive channel entities and focusing more on productive and potential ones. Recent trends have also shown a shift towards convergence in financial services, in which captive channel entities sell investment products and traditional banking products; and the banking industry also sells insurance.

This convergence has driven insurance companies to assess and update their overall information technology strategies, so that they can provide sustainable competitive differentiation in terms of speed, flexibility, and effective communication with policyholders and business partners. Technology also enhances the efficiencies of support functions and binds them closely with the core business. One of the common objectives of the industry is to keep the costs within the budgeted limits, and efficient IT systems that can generate useful MIS is integral to attaining this objective. Reducing spend overflows requires process efficiencies across the organization which requires automation of the business processes of functions such as HR, Finance, Training, Investments, Marketing, IT, Product development etc.

The industry can use technology to interact with the external environment. It has woken up to the need for B2B and B2C automation. Self service modules on the website both for channel partners and for customers are examples of the same. Shareholder or parent company's MIS or the regulatory business to business integrations all call for having a strong technology focus. For the senior management and strategists, information and analytics are of paramount importance. The analytical systems are fit to transform the company's capacity to make the most of the existing information within the organization.

Using this tremendous amount of data, the analytic systems can provide insight from concrete information. The information can then be turned into knowledge and that knowledge turned into actionable plans; and therein lays the essence of business intelligence. As the management team must have insight to each and every part of the business, technology can be exploited to provide a clear view through the implementation of a stable and reliable information systems framework. The information needs of the organization can be categorized under Operational, Tactical, Analytical, Strategic and Decision Support heads. While it is possible to hit the base applications for the information requirement through standard reporting tools, it alone cannot form the best architecture for scalability, performance and capability for complex analytics.

This is where an ODS and a Warehouse come into picture. While the ODS caters to the operational data requirements and also supports the Operational and tactical reports, a Warehouse comes as a platform for high end analytics and data mining to support cross sell and up sell. It can also act as the base for a campaign management solution and provide a single point view of the organizations performance. Technology support to business at different levels and across applications requires that the organization have a strong infrastructure that acts as a foundation for growth, scalability and reach. The Network architecture; Data center, hardware and peripherals management; Server management; Security infrastructure; DR and BCP setup; Facilities management, Helpdesk etc are the main constituents of the IT backbone. We have seen above that the various business functions are touched by technology in one way or the other, but a question remains: How to strategically use technology to derive business value beyond its bare function automation fulfillment. Though it is easy to figure out basic automation needs and to establish a fitment of technology in supporting each of the entities listed above, it takes a lot of thought and planning to device the best possible architecture and technology mix for the organization. Building an IT strategy for an insurance company should take into consideration the fitments and the integration of various components. On the one hand there are the Core Insurance Systems while on the other, there are a lot of satellite systems catering to various non core business functions. These constitute the functionalities required to run the business covering policy admin, accounting, sales commercials, channel management, servicing and transactions management etc. The two pillars for success of a technology implementation can be attributed as Functionality and Performance. Any technology implementation should cater to both equally. Thus an equal focus on technologies to improve on performance is required. The below mentioned systems are some but not all areas where technology can be leveraged in the insurance industry.

Technology in Life Insurance

In the present day environment, business propositions and technological interventions are inseparable. Technology, which at one point of time was only an appendage to business, became business enabler in due course of time; and has now become business driver, leading to Business Process Re-Engineering. This can't be more true for any other business than insurance.

Insurance industry deals with the probability of happening of events. For its ability to accurately assess the probability, there is huge dependence upon the ability to collect a large data base over the years, spread over large geographical and demographic sections, store it in easily accessible forms with the ability to access this data base at a fast pace; and draw upon conclusions and complete different models with slight variations in the parameters. Comparing the results of different models and thereby developing different kinds of products at a cost which enables the insurance industry to sustain its business, therefore, requires intervention of modern day technology Information technology is an industry which deals with large scale data collection, warehousing, mining and generation of end results. By virtue of high speed of the present day processors, it has the potential to respond to the needs of business at a very fast pace. With the advancement in telecommunication, both terrestrial and satellite based, there is a vast improvement in the speed, reliability, uptime and distortion free linking up of offices and people from across the country/countries.

This advancement in technology means access to the central data bases from distributed networks and offices at the speed of thought. Insurance industry needs advanced technology for business sustainability; and its demands fuel technological advancement and applications. Because of the nature of the insurance industry and the abilities of IT/telecom industries; there is synergy for the two industries to flourish together and then the insurance industries can initiate re-engineering of business processes for providing better services to the customers, having a business model which ensures their viability and bringing out different, complex kinds of products which meet the needs of the customers. The mix and match of different kinds of technologies enables the industry to put in a proper business model. We will try to have further insight into the areas wherein technology can be utilized and to what extent.

IT in General Insurance

The customer expectations have reached an all time high. The opening up of the market has brought in competition in the market; and the customer decides the price of the product and service level offered. The position tends to get critical with the detariffed regime lying ahead. The insurance companies need to go in for a paradigm shift in the way insurance business is transacted. Customer retention, profitability, increasing the customer base and increasing the value of the product offered are the mantras for sustained presence in the market and maintaining the lead. This is where IT has a major role to play. When one can buy anything from air ticket to pizzas online at a place and time of his convenience why can't one buy insurance online? Why waste time visiting the office of insurance company unless the asset to be insured is a 20-year-old motorcycle. The customer has already started to draw a comparison of service levels offered in other areas like private banking with those offered by his insurance company.

We need to change the way the business is being done. The method of transacting business has to change. The IT intervention should be carefully deployed to achieve the desired effect. It should benefit all those concerned namely the customer, the underwriter, and various intermediaries; and accrue benefits for the future.

Internet Business Models in the Insurance Sector

Online Marketing

Virtually all insurance companies have website. In the simplest case the website is used only for product information. In more sophisticated cases insurers use their website as an additional channel for online sales of traditional products or of specialized internet products. Some insurers operate only on the internet without agencies or agents.

Online Portals

On portals web visitor can choose between many companies offering similar or supplementary products. For example in financial services. Thematic portals are websites linked to specific events which may make purchase of an insurance policy necessary – for example weddings, parenthood and retirement.

Online Market Places

Online market places also called aggregators or navigators help to identify suitable insurance offers- either by brokers or by independent comparisons.

Online Risk Markets

Online risk markets are mainly to be found in the business to business market. They act as - between trading partners-usually insurers, reinsurers and corporate clients –seeking to swap large risk.

Online Reverse Auctions

The internet may also be used by clients to call for tender from insurance companies. An example could be an automobile association using a reverse auction to find the most favorable car insurance for its members.

Conclusion

Technology is playing a vital role in the conduct of business, irrespective of the size of its operations and the line of activity. It provides managements with vital data and information; and enables them to take crucial decisions based on reliable data. It needs no emphasis that the role of technology is much more critical in such classes of business where the need for information base is vital for its success. Insurance is one such class of business; and especially as it deals with vast numbers, a proper database is absolutely essential for its success in the long run. Acquisition of technology is a high cost proposition. Further, by its very nature, technology suffers from an inherent disadvantage of becoming obsolescent very soon. Hence, it is a very crucial decision for the managements to invest in new technology. The method of transacting business has to change. The IT intervention should be carefully deployed to achieve the desired effect. Comparing the results of different models and thereby developing different kinds of products at a cost which enables the insurance industry to sustain its business, therefore, requires intervention of modern day technology.

References

1. 1. Tripathy & Pal "Insurance theory and Practice", Prentice-Hall of Indian Private Limited, 2005.
2. Dr.P.K.Gupta "Insurance and Risk Management", Himalaya Publishing House, 2005.
3. Life insurance corporation of India Annual Report 2003-04 to 2004-2005.
4. Mishra "insurance principles and practices" S.Chand Ltd., New Delhi.
5. IRDA Journal, April 2006.

Web Sites

1. www.licindia.com.
2. www.irdaindia.org.

18

Health Insurance Awareness

M. Karthigai Priya

Every asset is expected to last for a certain period of time during which it will perform. After that, the benefit may not be available. There is a life-time for a machine in a factory or a cow or motor car. None of them will last for ever. The owner is aware of this and he can so manage his affairs that by the end of that period or life-time, a substitute is made available. Thus, he makes sure that the value or income is not lost. However, the asset may get lost earlier. An accident or some other unfortunate event may destroy it or make it non – functional. In that case, the owner and those deriving benefits there from, would be deprived of the benefit and the planned substitute would not have been ready. There is an adverse or unpleasant situation. Insurance is a mechanism that helps to reduce the effect of such adverse situations.

The term Health Insurance is generally used to describe a form of insurance that pay for medical expenses. It is sometimes used more broadly to include Insurance covering disability or long-term nursing or custodial care needs. It may be provided through a government- sponsored social insurance program, or from private insurance companies. It may be purchased on a group basis (e.g.,) by a firm to cover its employees) or purchased by individual consumers. In each case, the covered groups or individuals pay premiums or taxes to help protect themselves from high or unexpected healthcare expenses. Similar benefits paying for medical expenses may also be provided through social welfare programs funded by the government. Health insurance works by estimating the overall risk of healthcare expenses and developing a routine finance structure (Such as a monthly premium or annual tax) that will ensure that money is available to pay for the healthcare benefits specified in the insurance agreement. The benefit is administered by a central organization, most often either a government agency or private of not-for-profit entity operating a health plan.

History and Evolution

The concept of health insurance was proposed in 1694 by Hugh the Elder Chamberlen from the Peter Chamberlen family. In the late 19th Century, "Accident Insurance" began to be available, which operated much like modern disability insurance. This payment model continued until the start of the 20th century in some jurisdictions (like California), Where all laws regulating health insurance actually referred to disability insurance. Accident insurance was first offered in the United States by the Franklin Health Assurance company of Massachsetts. This firm, founded in 1850, offered insurance against injuries arising from railroad and steamboat accidents. Sixty organizations were offering accident insurance is the US by 1866, but the industry consolidated rapidly soon thereafter. While there were earlier experiments, the origins of sickness coverage in the US effectively date from 1890. The first employer- sponsored group disability policy was issued in 1911.

Before the development of medical expenses insurance, patients were expected to pay all other health care costs out of their own pockets, under what is known as the fee-for-service business model. During the middle to late 20th Century, traditional disability insurance evolved into modern health insurance programs. Today most comprehensive private health insurance programs cover the cost of routine, preventive, and emergency health care procedures, and also most prescription drugs, but this was not always the case.

Hospital and medical expense policies were introduced during the first half of the 20th Century. During the 1920s, individual hospitals began offering services to individuals on a pre-paid basis, eventually leading to the development of Blue Cross organizations. The predecessors of today's Health Maintenance Organizations (HMOs) originated beginning in 1929, through the 1930s and on during World War II.

How it Works

A health insurance policy is a contract between an insurance company and an individual. The contract can be renewable annually or monthly. The type and amount of health care costs that will be covered by the health plan are specified in advance, in the member contract or Evidence of Coverage booklet. The individual policy – holder's payment obligations may take several forms.

Premium

The amount, the Policy – holder pays to the health plan each month to purchase health coverage.

Deductible

The amount that the policy –holder must pay out-of-pocket before that health plan pays its share. For example, a policy – holder might have to pay a $500 deductible per year, before any of their health care is covered by the health plan. It may take several doctors' visits or prescription refills before the policy – holder reaches the deductible and the health plan starts to pay for care.

Co-payment

The amount that the policy-holder must pay out of pocket before the health plan pays for a particular visit or service. For example, a policy-holder might pay a $45 co-payment for a doctor's visit, or to obtain a prescription. A co-payment must be paid each time a particular service is obtained.

Coinsurance:

In stead of paying a fixed amount up front (a co-payment) the policy-holder must pay a percentage of the total cost. For example, the member might have to pay 20% of the cost of a surgery, while the health plan pays the other 80%. Because there is no upper limit on coinsurance, the policy – holder can end up owing very little, or a significant amount, depending on the actual costs of the services, they obtain.

Exclusions

Not all services are covered. The policy holder is generally expected to pay the full cost of non-covered services out of their own pocket.

Coverage limits

Some health plans only pay for health care up to a certain dollar amount. The policy-holder may be expected to pay any charges in excess of the health plan's maximum payment for a specific service. In addition, some plans have annual or life time coverage maximums. In these cases, the health plan will stop payment when they reach the benefit maximum, and the policy-holder must pay all remaining costs.

Out-of-pocket Maximums

Similar to coverage limits, except that in this case, the member's payment obligation ends when they the out-of pocket maximum, and the health plan pays all further covered costs. Out-of-pocket maximums can be limited to a specific benefit category (Such as prescription drugs) or can apply to all coverage provided during a specific benefit year.

Capitation

An amount paid by an insurer to a health care provider, for which the provider agrees to treat all members of the insurer.

In- Network Provider

A health care provider on a list of providers reselected by the insurer. The insurer will offer discounted coinsurance or co-payments, or additional benefits, to a plan member to see in-network provider. Generally, providers in network are providers who have a contract with the insurer to accept rates further discounted from the "usual and customary" charges the insurer pays to out-of-network Providers. Prescription drug plans are a form of insurance offered through some employer benefit plans in the US, where the patient pays a co-payment and the prescription drug insurance part or all of the balance for drugs covered in the formulary of the plan.

Some, if not most, health care providers in the United States will agree to bill the insurance company if patients are willing to sign an agreement that they will be responsible for the amount that the insurance company doesn't pay. The insurance company pays out of network providers according to "reasonable and customary" charges, which may be less than the provider's usual fee. The provider may also have a separate contract with the insurer to accept what amounts to a discounted rate of capitation to the provider's standard charges. It generally costs the patient less to use an in-network provider.

Health Plan vs. Health Insurance

Historically, HMOs tended to use the term "health plan", while commercial insurance companies used the term "health insurance". A health plan can also refer to a subscription – based medical care arrangement offered through health maintenance organization, HMO, PPO, or POS plan. These plans are similar to pre-paid dental, pre-paid legal, and pre-paid vision plans. Pre-paid health plans typically pay for a fixed number of services (For instance, $300 in preventive care, a certain number of days of hospice care or care in a skilled nursing facility, a fixed number of home health visits, a fixed number of spinal manipulation charges, etc.) The services offered are usually at the discretion of a utilization review nurse who is often contracted through the managed care entity providing the subscription health plan. This determination may be made either prior to or after hospital admission (concurrent utilization review)

Comprehensive vs. Scheduled

Comprehensive health insurance pays a percentage (may be 100, 90, 80, 70, 60, 50, percent) of the cost of hospital and physician charges after a deductible (usually applies to hospital charges, but may apply to some hospital services) is met by the insured. These plans are generally expensive because of the high potential benefit payout $1,000,000 to 50,000,000 is common – and because of the vast array of covered benefits.

Scheduled health insurance plans are not meant to replace a traditional comprehensive health insurance plans and are more of a basic policy providing access to day-to-day health care such as going to the doctor or getting a prescription drug. In recent years, these plans have taken the name mini-med plans or association pans. These plans may provide benefits for hospitalization and surgical, but these benefits will be limited. Scheduled plans are not meant to be effective for catastrophic events. These plans cost much less then comprehensive health insurance. They generally pay limited benefits amounts directly to the service provider, and payments are based upon the plan's "Schedule of benefits". Annual benefits maximums for a typical scheduled health insurance plan may range from $1,000 to $ 25,000.

Inherent Problems with Insurance

Insurance systems must typically deal with two inherent challenges: adverse selection, which affects any voluntary systems, and ex-post moral hazard, which affects any insurance system in which a third party bears major responsibility for payment, whether that is an employer or the government. Some national systems with compulsory insurance utilize systems such as risk equalization and community rating to overcome these inherent problems.

Adverse Selection

Insurance companies use the term "adverse selection" to describe the tendency for only those who will benefit from insurance to buy it. Specifically when talking about health insurance, unhealthy people are more likely to purchase health insurance because they anticipate large medical bills. On the other side, people who consider themselves to be reasonably healthy may decide that medical insurance is an unnecessary expense; if they see the doctor once a year and it costs $250, that's much better than making monthly insurance payments of $40. (Examples figures).

The fundamental concept of insurance is that is balance costs across a large, random sample of individuals (see risk pool) For instance, an insurance company has a pool of 1000 randomly selected subscribers, each pay $ 100 per month. One person becomes very ill while the others stay healthy, allowing the insurance company to use the money paid by the healthy people to pay for the treatment costs of the sick person. However, when the pool is self-selecting rather than random, as in the case with individuals seeking to purchase health insurance directly, adverse selection is a greater concern. A disproportionate share of health care spending is attributable to individuals with high health care costs. In US, the 1% of the population with the highest spending accounted for 27% of aggregate health care spending in 1996. The highest-spending

5% of the population accounted for more than half of all spending. These patterns were stable through the 1970s and 1980s, and some data suggest that they may have been typical of the mid-to-early 20th century as will. A few individuals have extremely high medical expenses, in extreme cases totaling a half million dollars or more. Adverse selection could leave an insurance company with primarily sick subscribers and no way to balance out the cost of their medical expenses with a large number of healthy subscribers.

Because of adverse selection, insurance companies employ medical underwriting, using a patient's medical history to screen out those whose pre-existing medical conditions pose too great a risk for the risk pool. Before buying health insurance, a person typically fills out a comprehensive medical history form that asks whether the person smokes, how much the person weighs, whether the person has been treated for any of a long list of diseases and so on. In general, those who present large financial burdens are denied coverage or charged high premiums to compensate. One large US industry survey found that roughly 13 percent of applicants for comprehensive, individually purchased health insurance who through the medical underwriting in 2004 were denied coverage. Declination rates increased significantly with age, rising from 5 percent for individuals 18 and under to just under a third for individuals aged 60 and 64. among those who were offered coverage, the study found that 76% received offers at standard premium rates, and 22% were offered higher rates. On the other side, applicants can get discounts if they do not smoke and are healthy.

Moral Hazard

Moral hazard occurs when an insurer and a consumer enter into a contract under symmetric information, but one party takes action, not taken into account in the contract, which changes the value of the insurance. A common example of moral hazard is third-party payment – when the parties involved in making a decision are not responsible for bearing costs arising from the decision. An example is where doctors and insured patients agree to take extra tests which may or may not be necessary. Doctors benefit by avoiding possible malpractice suits, and patients benefit by gaining increased certainty of their medical condition. The cost of these extra tests is borne by the insurance company, which may have had little say in the decision. Co-payments, deductibles, and less generous insurance for services with more elastic demand attempt to combat moral hazard, as they hold the consumer responsible.

Other Factors Affecting Insurance Prices

A recent study by Price Water house Coopers examining the drivers of rising health care costs in the US pointed to increased utilization created by increased consumer demand, new treatments, and more intensive diagnostic testing, as the most significant driver. People in developed countries are living longer. The population of those countries is aging, and a larger group of senior citizens requires more intensive medical care than a young healthier population. Advances in medicine and medical technology can also increase the cost of medical treatment. Lifestyle-related factors can increase utilization and therefore insurance prices, such as: increases in obesity caused by insufficient exercise and unhealthy food choices; excessive alcohol use, smoking, and use of street drugs. Other factors noted by the PWC study included the movement to broader-access plans, higher-priced technologies, and cost-shifting from Medicaid and the uninsured to private payers.

Health Insurance in Australia

The public health system is called Medicare. It ensures free universal access to hospital treatment and subsidized out of hospital medical treatment. It is funded by a 1.5% tax levy. The private health system is funded by a number of private health insurance organisations. The largest of these is Medibank private, which is government- owned, but operates as a government business enterprise under the same regulatory regime as all other registered private health funds. The coalition Howard government had announced that Medibank would be privatized if it won the 2007 election, however they were defeated by the Australian Labour party under Kevin Rudd which had already pledged that it would remain in government ownership.

Some private health insurers are 'for profit' enterprises, and some are non-profit organizations such as HCF Health Insurance. Some have membership restricted to particular groups, but the majority has open membership. Most aspects of private health insurance in Australia are regulated by the Private Health Insurance Act 2007.

The private health system in Australia operates on a "Community rating" basis, whereby premiums do not vary solely because of a person's previous medical history, current state of health, or (Generally speaking) their age (but see Lifetime Health cover below) Balancing this are waiting periods, in particular for pre-existing conditions(usually referred to within the industry as PEA, which stands for "pre-existing ailment") Funds are entitled to impose a waiting period of up to 12 months on benefits for any medical condition the signs and symptoms of which existed during the six months ending on the day the person first took out insurance. They are also entitled to impose a 12-month waiting period for benefits for treatment relating to obstetric conditions, and a 2-month waiting period for all other benefits when a person first takes out private insurance. Funds have to discretion to reduce or remove such waiting periods in individual cases. They are also free not to impose them to begin with, but this would place such a fund at risk of "adverse selection, attracting a disproportionate number of members from other funds, or from the pool of intending members who might otherwise have joined other funds. It would also attract people with existing medical conditions, who might not otherwise have taken out insurance at all because of the denial of benefits for 12 months due to the PEA Rule. The benefits paid out for these conditions would create pressure on premiums for all the fund's members, causing some to drop their membership, which would lead to further rises, and a vicious cycle would ensue.

There are a number of other matters about which funds are not permitted to discriminate between members in terms of premiums, benefits or membership- these include racial origin, religion, sex, sexual orientation, nature of employment, and leisure activities. Premiums for a fund's product that is sold in more than one state can vary from state to state, but not within the same state. The Australian government has introduced a number of incentives to encourage adults to take out private hospital insurance These include:

Life Time Health Cover

If a person has not taken out private hospital cover by the 1st July after their 30th birthday, then when (and if) they do so after this time, their premiums must include a loading of 2% per annum. Thus, a person taking out private cover for the first time at age 40 will pay a 20 per cent loading. The loading continues for 10 years. The loading applies only to premiums for hospital cover, not to ancillary (Extras) cover.

Medical Levy Surcharge

People whose taxable income is greater than a specified amount (Currently $ 50,000 for singles and $ 100,000 for families) and who do not have an adequate level of private hospital cover must pay a 1% surcharged on top of the standard 1.5% Medicare Levy. The rationale is that if the people in this income group are forced to pay more money one way or another, most would choose to purchase hospital insurance with it, with the possibility of a benefits in the event that they need private hospital treatment – rather than pay it in the form of extra tax as well as having to meet their own private hospital costs.

Private Health Insurance Rebate

The Government subsidizes the premiums for all private health insurance cover, including hospital and ancillary (extras), by 30%, 35% or 40%.

Health Insurance in Canada

Most Health insurance in Canada is administered by each province, under the Canada Health Act, which requires all people to have free access to basic health services. Collectively, the public provincial health insurance systems in Canada are frequently referred to as Medicare. Private health insurance is allowed, but the provincial governments allow it only for services that the public health plans do not cover; for example, Semi-private or private rooms in hospitals and prescription drug plans. Canadians are free to use private insurance for elective medical services such as laser vision correction surgery, cosmetic surgery, and other non-basic medical procedures. Some 65% of Canadians have some form of supplementary private health insurance; many of them receive it through their employers. Private-sector services not paid for by the government account for nearly 30 percent of total health care spending.

In 2005, the supreme court of Quebec ruled, in Chaoulli.V.Quebec, that the province's prohibition on private insurance for health care already insured by the provincial plan could constitute an infringement of the right to life and security if there were long wait times for treatment as happened in this case. Certain other provinces have legislation which financially discourage but does not forbid private health insurance in areas covered by the public plans. The ruling has not changed the overall pattern of health insurance across Canada but has spurred on attempts to tackle the core issues of supply and demand and impact of wait health insurance across Canada but has spurred on attempts to tackle the core issues of supply and demand and the impact of wait times.

Health Insurance in the Netherlands

In the Netherlands in 2006, a new system of health insurance came into force. All insurance companies have to provide at least one policy which meets a government set minimum standard level of cover and all adult residents are obliged by law to purchase this cover from an insurance company of their choice. The new system avoids the two pitfalls of adverse selection and moral hazard associated with traditional forms of health insurance.

In the Dutch system, insurance companies are compensated for taking on the high risk individuals, because they receive extra funding for them. This funding comes from an insurance equalization pool run by a regulator which collects salary based contributions from employers (about 45% of all health care funding) and funding from the government for people whose means are such that they cannot afford health care (About 5% of all funding) Thus insurance companies find that insuring high risk individuals becomes an attractive proposition. All insurance companies receive from the pool, but those with more high risk individuals will receive more from the fund. The remaining 45% of health care funding comes from insurance premiums paid by the public. Insurance companies compete for this money on price alone. The insurance companies are not allowed to set down any co-payments or caps or deductibles. Neither, they are allowed to deny coverage to any person applying for a policy or charge any thing other than their nationally set and internet published standard policy premiums. Every person buying insurance from that company will pay the same price as every one else buying that policy. And every person will get the minimum level of coverage. Children under 18 are insured for free (the funding coming from the equalization pool).

In addition to this minimum level, companies are free to sell extra insurance for additional coverage over the national minimum, but extra risks for this are not covered from the insurance pool and must therefore be priced accordingly.

Health Insurance in the United Kingdom

The UK's National Health Service (NHS) is publicly funded health care system that provides coverage to everyone normally resident in the UK. It is not strictly insurance system because (a) there are no premiums collected, (b) costs are not charges at the patient level and (c) costs are not pre-paid from a pool. However, it does achieve the main aim of insurance which is to spread financial risk arising from ill-health. The costs of running the NHS are met directly from general taxation. Private health care has continued parallel to the NHS, paid for largely by private Insurance, but it is used by less than 8% of the population, and generally as a top-up to NHS services.

The NHS provides the majority of health care in the UK, including primary care, in –patient care, long-term health care ophthalmology and dentistry. Recently the private sector has been increasingly used to increase NHS capacity despite a large proportion of the British public opposing such involvement, According to the World Health Organization, government funding covered 86% of overall health care expenditures in the UK as of 2004, with private expenditures covering the remaining 14%.

Health Insurance in the United States

The US market – based health care system relies heavily on private and not-for-profit health insurance, which is the primary source of coverage for most Americans. According to the United States Census Bureau, approximately 84% of Americans have health insurance; some 60% obtain it through an employer, while about 9% purchase it directly. Various government agencies provide coverage to about 27% of Americans (there is some overlap in these figures)

Public programs provide the primary source of coverage for most seniors and for low - income children and families who meet certain eligibility requirements. The primary public programs are Medicare, a federal social insurance program for seniors and for low - income children and families who meet certain eligibility requirements. The primary public programs are Medicare, a federal social insurance program for seniors and certain disable individuals, Medicaid, funded jointly by the federal government and states but administered at the state level, which covers certain very low income children and their families, and SCHIP, also a federal – state partnership that serves certain children and families who do not qualify for Medicaid but who cannot afford private coverage. Other public programs include military health benefits provided through TRICARE and the Veterans Health Administration and benefits provided through the Indian Health Service. Some states have additional programs for low – income individuals.

In 2006, there were 47 million people in the United States (16% of the population) who were without health insurance for at least part of that year. About 37% of the uninsured live in households with an income over $ 50,000.

In 2004, US health insurers directly employed almost 470,000 people at an average salary of $61, 409. (As of the fourth quarter of 2007, the total US labour force stood at 153.6 million, of whom 146.3 million were employed. Employment related to all forms of insurance totaled 2.3 million, Mean annual earnings for full – time civilian workers as of June 2006 were $41,231; median earnings were $33,634.) The insurance industry also represents a significant lobbying group in the US. For the 2007 -2008 election cycle insurance was the 8th among industries in political contributions to members of Congress, giving $13,411,561, of which 56% was given to Democrats (lawyers and law firms were number 1, giving $ 59,205,616, of which 80% went to Democrats). The top recipient of insurance industry contributions was Senator Christopher Dodd (D-CT). The leading contributor from the industry – as measured by total political contributions - was AFLAC, inc., which contributed $907, 150 in 2007.

See also

- Injury cover
- Economic capital
- Government of ownership
- Health economics
- Health maintenance organization
- Healthcare reform
- Self - funded health care
- List of insurance topics
- Physicians for a National Health Program
- Public health
- Social health insurance
- Social security
- Social welfare
- Health care
- Health care politics
- Philosophy of Healthcare

Conclusion

The United Nations Declaration of Human Rights 1948 provides that "Everyone has a right to a standard of living adequate for the health and wellbeing of himself and his family, including food, clothing, housing and medical care and necessary social services and the right to security in the event of unemployment, Sickness, disability, widowhood or other lack of livelihood in circumstance beyond his control. In India, social security finds a place in our Constitution. Article 41 requires the State, within the limits of it's economic capacity and development, to make effective provision for securing the right to work, to education and to provide public assistance incase of unemployment, old age, sickness and disablement and in other cases of undeserved want. Part of the State's obligations to the poorer sections is met through the mechanism of life insurances. As per the law and the directions of the regulatory authorities, insurance companies in India are obliged to extend insurance benefits to economically weaker sections of the society in the unorganized sector.

19

Micro Insurance – An Overall View

Muthulakshmi, K

Micro-insurance refers to protection of assets and lives against insurable risks of target populations such as micro-entrepreneurs, small farmers and the landless, women and low-income people through formal, semiformal and informal institutions. Such products are often bundled with micro-savings and micro-credit, thereby allocating scarce resources to micro-investments with the highest marginal rates of return. Micro insurance is the most underdeveloped part of microfinance. Yet various schemes exist that are viable, been served two major purposes:

(i) they have contributed to loan security;

(ii) They have served as instruments of resource mobilization.

The greatest challenge for micro insurance lies in the combination of viability and sustainability with outreach. Although introduction of sound practices such as appropriate policy sizes and timely payment of installments of premium or positive incentives to renew on time in order to avoid policy getting lapsed can be feasible, the ultimate effectiveness of interventions focusing on institutional transformation and sound insurance practices will vary considerably, depending on the appropriateness of the regulatory environment. Development Goal to enable micro insurance to be an integral part of a country's wider insurance system, it is important for every insurer to adjust its costs of serving marginal clients in remote areas, collecting premiums and installments and offering doorstep services. It is also important to recognize a wide network of intermediaries in the rural and social sectors and notify regulations in order to guide and supervise the micro insurance service providers and their customers.

Today we have a variety of microfinance institutions with national and local outreach. Many of them have already become corporate agents or have entered into referral arrangements with insurers. However, semiformal institutions including savings and credit cooperatives, NGOs and self-help groups which have immense potential in carrying the message of insurance as also solicit insurance business are yet to be utilized in a manner where their true potential can be harnessed to increase the insurance penetration levels. This is due to restrictions in the existing agency regulations in terms of minimum eligibility norms in order to become an agent.

Depending on the existence and vigour of such institutions, the following alternatives have emerged for offering strategic entry points for micro insurance development:

(1) Adapting formal insurance arrangements to the needs of the micro-economy.

(2) Upgrading non-formal (comprising semiformal and informal) insurance arrangements with insurance companies.

(3) Linking formal and non formal insurance institutions with banks and self-help groups.

(4) Establishing new local institutions providing micro insurance services.

The first three strategies may be inter-connected:

(i) adapting insurance companies to the requirements of the micro-economy is a first step; then

(ii) linking them as wholesale institutions to self-help groups as retailers; and finally,

(iii) Upgrading self-help groups e.g. to the level of financial cooperatives or village banks.

If insurers are to serve customers who differ widely in terms of service costs and risks, the only viable inducement for them is an adequate margin, lest they exclude small farmers, -micro-entrepreneurs and people in remote areas. Only sound social insurance, which combines a social mandate with profit-making, has a chance of sustainability.

Institutional Adaptation .The experience so far has been that formal financial institutions serve but a fraction of the population, which typically lies within the upper quartile of the social hierarchy. Through adaptation to the microfinance market requirements, they may gradually expand into the second-highest quartile and into segments of the lower quartiles. Within the foreseeable future they will normally not be able to fully serve that market.

Non formal finance mostly rests on local institutions which are directly accessible to all segments of the population. Self-Help Groups (SHGs) are member-owned and member-controlled local institutions. They may either be financial groups, with financial intermediation as their primary purpose; or non financial groups, with financial intermediation as a secondary purpose, such as vendors' associations, family planning groups and numerous other types of voluntary associations.

Need for Developing Micro-Insurance in India

The functions that need to be focused must include: providing guidance to members, collecting premium installments from members, insurance services to members, communication and exchange of experience, providing linkages with banks,

NGOs or donors, supporting the proposals of individual members to insurance companies through recommendations.

Characteristics of Micro Insurance

Insurance is mechanism that user risk pooling to compensate individuals and groups adversely affected by a specified risk or event. As such, it is a way to transfer risk from an individual to a group so that each individual only pays the average of the loss for all members of the group.

- Micro insurance is a subset of insurance that provides protection to the poor in a way that reflects their cash constraints and coverage requirement. Its clientele is markedly different from the market served by the existing formal insurance companies.
- Micro Insurance clients are poorer and depend on the flow of income that can fluctuate considerably throughout the year. While the shocks experienced by the poor may be the same, they are more vulnerable to them because the have fewer reserves to draw upon. Once they reserve are gone, repeated shocks force them into a reactive mode, always responding after a crisis.
- Micro insurance, if designed appropriately, offers the poor an opportunity to be more proactive in managing risk by reducing the chance of a loss resulting from unanticipated risk events. To date, the experience with micro-insurance has been limited.

Basic Principles of Micro Insurance

Basic principles that should be observed by micro insurance provider are universal to insurance and risk management. They include:

1. Similar units are exposed to risk:

Insurers require that risk in a particular class or group of policies be similar. Insurers also require that the group, insured (or the "risk pool") includes a large number of this similar risk, relative to the total population.

2. There is limited policy holders control over the insured event:

Insurance protection cannot be offered if policyholders can control the occurrence of insured event.

3. Insurable interest exists:

Insurance cannot be provided to policyholders who have a vested interest in a loss occurring. A property insurance policy, for example, on a home cannot be sold to anyone other then the residents of the home.

4. Losses are determinable and measurable:

Insurance provider must have mechanism for verifying the occurrence of a loss and identifying its cause and value.

5. Losses should not be catastrophic:

The risk pooling mechanism of insurance breaks down against risks that cause large losses for a substantial portion of the risk pool at the same time.

6. Chance of loss can be calculated:

Setting insurance premiums requires estimating the size of the expected losses and the chance of loss.

7. Premiums are economically affordable:

In general, for an insurance policy to be attractive purchases, the cost of premiums must be substantially less than the benefit offered by the policy.

Linkage to Insurers

On a modest scale, various forms of life and health insurance have been successfully practiced by different institutions in different countries, particularly as part of loan protection schemes. Micro-insurance procedures and services should be set by insurers rather than the regulator. Appropriate procedures and services should be applied to attain;

(1) Sound financial management,
(2) Convenient and safe savings premium collection and deposit facilities
(3) Appropriate claim appraisal and processing procedures
(4) Adequate risk management,
(5) Timely collection of premium installments,
(6) Monitoring and
(7) Effective information gathering, all of which may include cooperation between different formal and non-formal intermediaries in fields where each is most effective.

Rural Health through Micro Health Insurance

Micro health insurance and community-based health insurance scheme are increasingly recognized as a preferred mechanism to finance healthcare provision. Access to health services is still inadequate among the majority of the rural populations and poses as one of the biggest challenges in Indian healthcare. In the private and urban centric healthcare scenario, approximately 70 per cent of the populations who are living in the rural area have little or inadequate access to healthcare. Currently, with an estimated 300 million BPL population or 60 million BPL families without any kind of social protection, affordable healthcare for the masses has emerged as an urgent need of the nation. To meet the healthcare crisis, micro health insurance and community-based health insurance scheme are increasingly recognized as a preferred mechanism to finance healthcare provision.

Types of Micro Insurance

There are two main types of micro insurance— one focused on extending social protection to the poor in the absence of appropriate Government schemes and the other offering a virtual financial service to low income households by developing an appropriate business model that enables the poor to be a profitable or sustainable market segment for commercial or co-operative insurers.

Need of Healthcare Financing

The total healthcare spending of India is around six per cent of the GDP, where the public health care expenditure is less then one per cent of GDP. So, the private expenditure on health in India is more then 80 per cent and most of it is out-of-pocket expenses. Rapid increase in healthcare cost and more of out of pocket expenses is increasingly pushing more households below poverty line. Studies have shown that there is a strong link between health and income (low-income levels). A health shock to the lower income group people has serious consequences as it not only leads to direct expenditures in terms of hospitalization, medicine, investigations, transport etc but indirectly lead to loss of wages.

Thus a health risks in lower economic people results in catastrophic financial loss and significant threat to the people. The problem can't be addressed by the regular claim because of its high cost. In order to overcome this paradox, the need of the hour is to find new and innovative solutions for ensuring quality and affordable healthcare and one way to address the same is to have a Micro Health Insurance Scheme, which has a very low premium.

Advantages

- Protection against the catastrophic financial burden resulting from unexpected illness or injury.
- Protecting the poor from indebtedness and impoverishment resulting from medical expenditure thus reduces poverty.
- Better access to cost effective quality healthcare by the BPL population.

- Protective social security for all the unorganized workers - BPL population.
- Non-commercial mutual 'micro health insurance schemes' are attractive because they enable the members to retain part of the profits. This is also an effective way to reduce free-riding, moral hazard and adverse selection, as well as insurance fraud.
- Women Empowerment -enhance contribution to household income, thus better control over household decisions.
- Reduces child mortality and leads to improved health especially among women.
- Dependence on non formal high cost intermediaries is reduced.
- Enables the poor to build assets and thereby reduce their vulnerability.
- Wholesome enhancement in quality of life.

Challenges

- One of the biggest challenges in micro-insurance is distribution and spread. The rural and informal sectors are not a homogenous category and geographically dispersed. So, distribution of micro insurance is very expensive. It has been estimated that, if the cost of the policy is Rs 300-400, the cost of distribution in rural areas would work out to Rs 600.
- The challenge of developing a policy that is affordable for its clients but also sustainable for the institution.
- Dealing with a small number of clients represents a challenge in terms of costs and sustainability.
- Inability of the people to pay a high premium upfront. Hence limited benefits, dissatisfaction and drop outs.
- Illiteracy and lack of awareness.
- No control on the numbers on enrollees, hence chances of 'adverse selection' and 'moral hazards'.

- Poorest quintiles are 2.6 times more likely than the richest to forgo medical treatment when ill.
- Presence and practice of multiple systems of medicine and medical practitioners (several of whom are not formally certified and recognized).
- Increasing per capita expenditure on health. Currently, the per capita income is Rs 997 (207 from public and 790 from private) and it is increasing as healthcare is becoming expensive.
- Absent of insurance branch network and relevant infrastructure to market the insurance and insurance related services (especially for health insurance).
- Requires specialized actuarial capacity, which is complicated by the lack of reliable data characteristic of low-income, informal markets
- Requires a robust distribution system that can handle small financial transactions efficiently in convenient locations, and engender trust
- Lack on trained intermediaries in rural areas.
- Healthcare is no longer a service— it is fully commercialized
- Potential insurance frauds by the provider and the consumer.
- Institutional weakness in the areas of management, marketing, administration and technical expertise, and data systems, which leads to weak communication and coordination between the partners, poor marketing of the products, lack of transparency and weak accountability.
- Reinsurance is usually not used because sums insured are too small.

Introduction of health insurance policies and any improvement must also be accompanied by the revival of healthcare facilities at all levels, increase in public health spending, reintegrating the public health system with the broad social security system meant for the poor which would also include safe drinking water, sanitation and family planning service. All these increase the cost of service.

Micro Insurance Models

Several models of micro insurance delivery are in use internationally. These models fall into the following groups.

Partner-Agent Model: An insurer is paired with a bank or Micro Finance Institution (MFI) to offer effective and efficient micro insurance products. Insurers utilize MFI's delivery mechanism to provide sales and basic services to clients. In this model, the insurer manages the insurance risk and the financial organization acts as the agent for the product(s)

Full Service Model: In some cases, regulated insurers develop products that effectively help them move down market without a marketing partner. They are responsible for all aspects of product design, sales, servicing, and claims assessment. The insurers are responsible for all insurance-related costs and losses and they retain all profits. In other cases, the MFI itself takes on the insurance risk.

Social Protection Model: In this model, the Government takes on the responsibility of insuring its citizen (or some portion of them) using 'contributions' usually from the employed populations. The key to spread of micro insurance is the presence of community initiatives and Self Help Groups (SHGs), which are aided by the Government and also by the banks and MFIs.

Community-based Model: The policyholders own and manage the insurance programme and negotiate with external healthcare providers. The multiple responsibilities, limited capacity of local people, and limited support make these programmes difficult to reach organizational sustainability

Provider Model: The service provider and the insurer are the same. Hospitals or doctors develop and offer their own insurance schemes with community groups. These have been difficult to manage because insurance skills are limited among hospital administrators.

Current scenario of micro-insurance in India

In India, there are leading Insurance Corporation / companies (e.g. the Life Insurance Corporation Ltd and the General Insurance Corporation) in the formal sector. A plethora of insurance schemes is available to the general public, though very limited products are available exclusively for women and the rural poor (Nalini et al., , 2007).

The Insurance products are designed for the purpose of attracting more clients, as a gift for getting them in to the bank's fold for security reasons (e.g. in event of loan defaults) and not for meeting the needs of the poor. The benefits are, if at all realized purely incidental and not intentional It is ironic that even the incidental distribution of insurance benefits are not even equally shared amongst the target clients. The overall picture on Micro Insurance indicates that insurance remains the 'Cinderella of Micro financial activities.'

Conclusion

Micro insurance is a young financial service with proven best practices; Demand is strong and indicative of an important potential market. Along with savings and emergency loans, micro – insurance has a role to play in poor 'people's risk management. There are challenges to provide micro insurance to the poor and there is a need for greater innovation and experimentation. Regulation with in the industry is also critical. Working together, micro insurance can be both a successful business venture and advantageous to the poor. However, the current move of IRDA towards effective regulations requires collective efforts otherwise the issue will not gain attention.

References

Deshpande, Ramesh and Verma Niraj. (2003) Review of Rural Finance Institutions in India,

Rural Health through Micro Health Insurance-Dr.Biswendu Bardhan microinsurance@irdaonline.org

Nalini Prava Tripathy, Prabir pal, Insurance Theory and Practice (2007) Prentice Hall of India pvt. Ltd. Publications

20

The Study on Consumer Acceptance Level Towards Private Insurance and LIC

N.Sumathi, J.Jayashree

Insurance sector has been opened up for competition from Indian private insurance companies with the enactment of Insurance Regulatory and Development Authority Act, 1999 (IRDA Act). As per the provisions of IRDA Act, 1999, Insurance Regulatory and Development Authority (IRDA) was established on 19th April 2000 to protect the interests of holder of insurance policy and to regulate, promote and ensure orderly growth of the insurance industry. IRDA Act 1999 paved the way for the entry of private players into the insurance market, which was either to the exclusive privilege of public sector insurance companies/ corporations. Under the new dispensation Indian insurance companies in private sector were permitted to operate in India on the fulfillment of certain prerequisites. A large number of public and private players are competing today in both life and general insurance segments. The FDI cap/ Equity in the insurance sector are 26 percent under the automatic route subject to licensing by the insurance regulatory and development authority. There exists huge scope of investment in the insurance sector in India. India has an enormous middle-class that can afford to buy life, health and disability and pension plan products. Further, insurance is one of the most important taxes saving instrument in the country.

Life Insurance in India was nationalized by incorporating Life Insurance Corporation (LIC) in 1956. All private life insurance companies at that time were taken over by LIC. In 1993 the Government of Republic of India appointed RN Malhotra Committee to lay down a road map for privatisation of the life insurance sector. While the committee submitted its report in 1994, it took another six years before the enabling legislation was passed in the year 2000, legislation amending the Insurance Act of 1938 and legislating the Insurance Regulatory and Development Authority Act of 2000. The same year that the newly appointed insurance regulator - Insurance Regulatory and Development Authority IRDA — started issuing licenses to private life insurers. In the year 2006, Apart from Life Insurance Corporation, the public sector life insurer, there are 17 other private sector life insurers, most of them joint ventures between Indian groups and global insurance giants.

Life Insurance

Life insurance in India made its debut well over 100 years ago.

'In our country, which is one of the most populated in the world, the prominence of insurance is not as widely understood, as it ought to be. What follows is an attempt to acquaint readers with some of the concepts of life insurance, with special reference to LIC. Life insurance is a contract that pledges payment of an amount to the person assured (or his nominee) on the happening of the event insured against.

The contract is valid for payment of the insured amount during:

1. The date of maturity, or
2. Specified dates at periodic intervals, or
3. Unfortunate death, if it occurs earlier.

Among other things, the contract also provides for the payment of premium periodically to the Corporation by the policyholder. Life insurance is universally acknowledged to be an institution, which eliminates 'risk', substituting certainty for uncertainty and comes to the timely aid of the family in the unfortunate event of death of the breadwinner. By and large, life insurance is civilization's partial solution to the problems caused by death. Life insurance, in short, is concerned with two hazards that stand across the life-path of every person:

That of dying prematurely leaves a dependent family to fond for itself.

That of living till old age without visible means of support.

ICICI Prudential Life Insurance

ICICI Prudential Life Insurance Company is a joint venture between ICICI Bank - one of India's foremost financial services companies-and prudential plc - a leading international financial services group headquartered in the United Kingdom. Total capital infusion stands at Rs. 33.62 billion, with ICICI Bank holding a stake of 74% and Prudential plc holding 26%.

We began our operations in December 2000 after receiving approval from Insurance Regulatory Development Authority (IRDA). Today, our nation-wide team comprises of over 1,000 offices, over 263,000 advisors; and 22 banc assurance partners.

ICICI Prudential was the first life insurer in India to receive a National Insurer Financial Strength rating of AAA (Ind) from Fitch ratings. For three years in a row, ICICI Prudential has been voted as India's Most Trusted Private Life Insurer, by The Economic Times - AC Nielsen ORG Marg survey of 'Most Trusted Brands'. As we grow our distribution, product range and customer base, we continue to tirelessly uphold our commitment to deliver world-class financial solutions to customers all over India.

Table 1

Market position of insurance companies

(Rs. in lakh)

Company Name	*Premium Up to Aug. 2004*	*Rank*	**Total Policies*	*Ranking on No of Policies*	*Avg Premium per policy (APPP)*	*Ranking on APPP*
Bajaj Allianz	14,395.73	4	70,237	4	20,495	5
ING Vysya	2,606.27	11	34,928	8	7,461	13
AMP Sanmar	1,823.25	12	12,321	12	14,797	8
SBI Life	12,768.21	5	34,128	9	37,412	2
Tata AIG Life	9,150.07	7	79,673	3	11,484	10
HDFC Standard Life	9,671.52	6	59,213	6	16,333	7

(Contd.)

(Contd. Table 1)

Company Name	*Premium Up to Aug. 2004*	*Rank*	**Total Policies*	*Ranking on No of Policies*	*Avg Premium per policy (APPP)*	*Ranking on APPP*
ICICI Prudential	39,977.55	2	81,635	2	22,009	4
Birla Sun Life	18,150.60	3	48,022	7	37,796	1
Aviva Life	5,623.20	9	29,521	10	19,048	6
Kotak Mahindra	3,626.48	10	16,225	11	22,351	3
Max New York	6,356.25	8	65,505	5	9,703	11
MetLife India	1,522.84	13	10,489	13	14,518	9
LIC	584471.09	1	7023186	1	8,322	12

Source: Reserve Bank of India.

Objectives of the Study

1. To test the acceptance level of private insurance in comparison with LIC among respondents at Coimbatore city.
2. To find out the reasons why people taking insurance policies.
3. To find out the reasons of why people prefer LIC or Private insurance companies for their investment.
4. To know the awareness of people regarding the products available with insurance companies.
5. To know the opinion of the people against some features of LIC and Private insurance companies
6. To find out awareness about the benefits of investing in Private insurance companies

Tools for Analysis

The data collected directly from the general public, taking into consideration various factors. The study can be made using various ways such as direct interviews, telephonic interviews, online interviews etc., but the population taken for the study was the questionnaires from 150 customers of Coimbatore city. Customers of different income levels, in the ratio of 50; 50 in which 50% constitute LIC and the rest is the private sellers. The private players include all the thirteen companies currently operating in the market. Kind of the products were not considered. For the purpose of this analysis the following tools are used, Simple percentage analysis, Tables and graphs were used to analyze for the data's collected.

As per the Table-2, out of 150 respondents the main reason based on which insurance decisions are made to take insurance policies in a company were ranked based on the responses taken and the results where that the tax benefit is the main reasons for people preferring insurance and the second reason for taking insurance for getting regular income and the third reason is

Table 2
Reasons for Taking an Insurance Policy

S.No	*Reasons for taking the policy*	*No of respondents*	*Ranking*
1	Product Features	20	4
2	Safety of scheme	25	3
3	Regular Income	34	2
4	Tax Benefit	38	1
5	Friends	11	5
6	Transparency	10	6
7	Meeting Emergency	7	7
8	Agents Recommendations	5	8
	TOTAL	**150**	

Source: Primary Data.

the safety of scheme provided. Meeting emergency purposes was given the least rank followed by agent's recommendations

Table 3
Initial Investment of the Respondents

S.No	*Initially invested in*	*No of respondents*	*Percentage*
1.	LIC	112	74.66
2.	PRIVATE INSURANCE	38	25.33
	TOTAL	150	100

Source: Primary Data.

The above Table-3 shows the initial investment of the respondents, which implied that s 75% respondents had invested in LIC and only 25% respondents did in private insurance.

Table 4

Mode of Awareness Regarding Insurance Services

S. No	*Awareness of insurance services*	*No of respondents LIC*	*%*	*No of respondents private insurance*	*%*
1.	Agents	30	40	41	54.66
2.	Advertisement	9	12	5	6.66
3.	Friends	29	38.66	21	28.33
4.	Others(auditor advice, bank managers)	7	9.33	8	10.66
	TOTAL	**75**	**100**	**75**	**100**

Source: Primary Data.

From the Table-4, In the case of private insurance the 55% of the respondents were aware of the insurance services mainly through the insurance agents and the 28% of the respondents were aware of the insurance services mainly through friends and relatives. In the case of LIC the 40% of the respondents were aware of the insurance services mainly

Table 5

Investment Details of the Respondents

S. No	*Kind of policy taken by the respondents*	*No of respondents LIC*	*%*	*No of respondents private insurance*	*%*
1.	ULIP	7	9.33	32	42.66
2.	WHOLE LIFE	5	6.66	5	6.66
3.	MONEY BACK	19	25.33	10	13.33
4.	PENSION PLAN	12	16	2	2.66
5.	ENDOWMENT	30	40	25	33.33
6.	MORTGAGE PLAN	2	2.66	1	1.33
	TOTAL	**75**	**100**	**75**	**100**

Source: Primary Data.

Figure 1
Investment Details of the Respondents

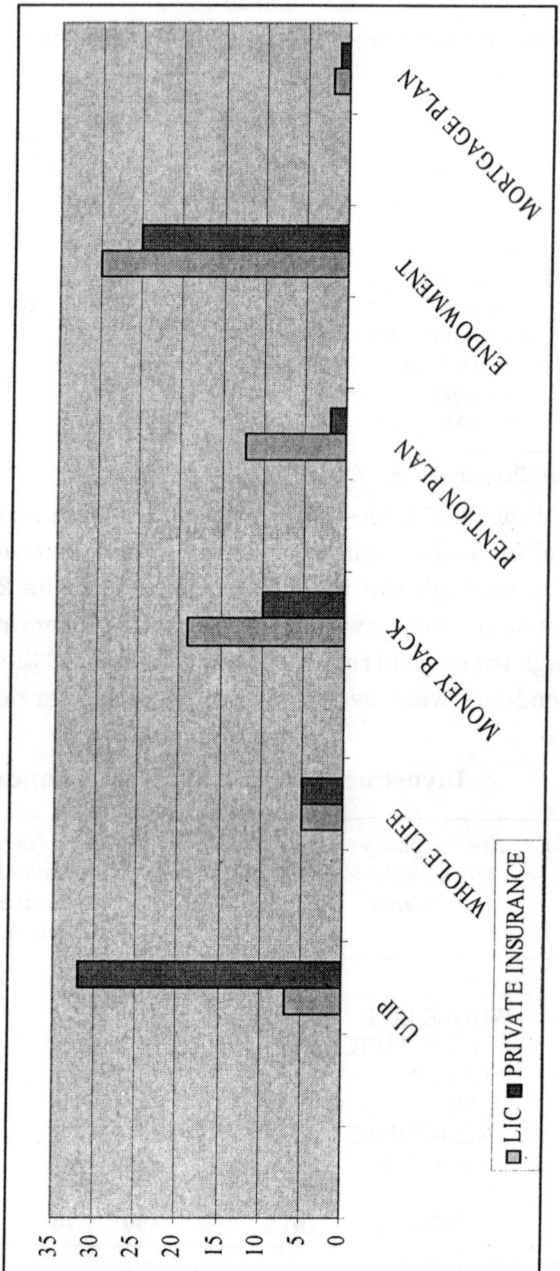

through agents and 39% of the respondents were aware of the insurance services mainly through friends.

The above Table-5 shows that the investment details of the respondents, which implied that the most preferred plan in the case of LIC was to be endowment policy with 40%, followed by money back policy 25% and followed by pent ion plan with 16%.In the case of private insurance that the most preferred plan is ULIP policy with 43%, followed by endowment policy with 33% and followed by money back policy 13%.

Table 6
Reason for Accepting Private Insurance

S.No	*Reasons*	*No of respondents*	*Percentage*
1.	High Returns	38	50.66
2.	Better service	18	24
3.	Transparency	9	12
4.	Flexible	10	13.33
	TOTAL	**75**	**100**

Source: Primary Data

Figure 2
Reason for Accepting Private Insurance

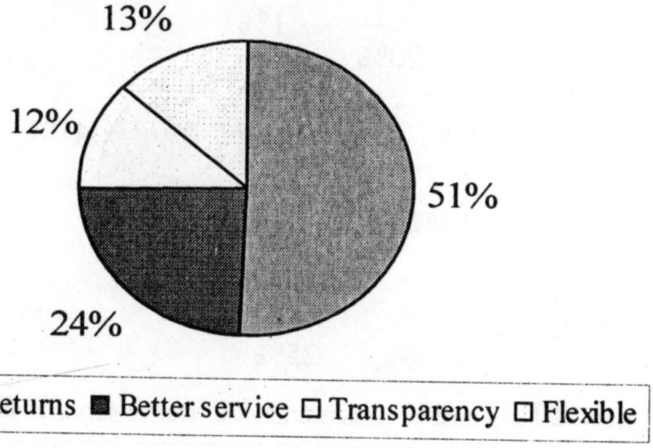

Source: Primary Data.

The above Table-6 shows that, the main reason for accepting private insurance was found to be higher returns with 51%,the next reason for accepting private insurance was better services with 24%,then next reason for accepting private insurance was flexible with 13%, then next reason for accepting private insurance was transparency with 12%.

Table 7
Reason for Accepting LIC

S.No	*Reasons*	*No of respondents*	*Percentage*
1.	Safety	30	40
2.	Less cost	19	25.33
3.	Less premium	10	13.33
4.	Better services	15	20
5.	More products	1	1.33
	TOTAL	**75**	**100**

Source: Primary Data.

The above Table-7 shows that, the main reason for accepting LIC was found to be safety with 40%, the next reason

Figure 3
Reason for Accepting LIC

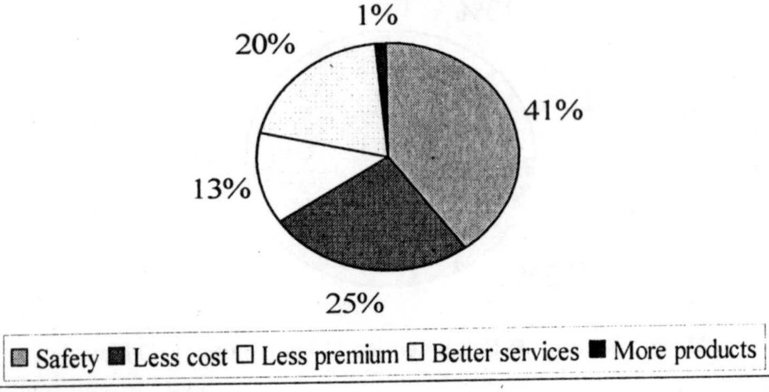

Source: Primary Data.

for accepting LIC was less cost with 25%, then next reason for accepting LIC was better service with 20%, then next reason for accepting LIC was found to be less premium with 13%, then next reason for accepting LIC was found to be more products with 1%.

Table 8
Opinion about the Procedure followed by the Insurance Companies

S.No	*Opinion about procedure followed*	*LIC*	*%*	*Private Insurance*	*%*
1.	Very simple	30	40	15	20
2.	Simple	23	30.66	33	44
3.	Difficult	17	22.66	25	33.33
4.	Very difficult	5	6.66	2	2.66
	TOTAL	**75**	**100**	**75**	**100**

Source: Primary Data.

The above Table-8 shows the opinion of the respondents about the procedure followed by the company. In the case of private insurance (40%) of the respondents feeling that it was very simple, then (31%) of the respondents feeling that it was simple, then (23%) of the respondents feeling that it was difficult, then (7%) of the respondents feeling that it was very difficult. In the case of LIC, (44%) of the respondents feeling that it was simple, then (33%) of the respondents feeling that it was difficult, then (20%) of the respondents feeling that it was very simple, then (3%) of the respondents feeling that it was very difficult.

Figure 4
Opinion About the Procedure Followed by the Insurance Companies

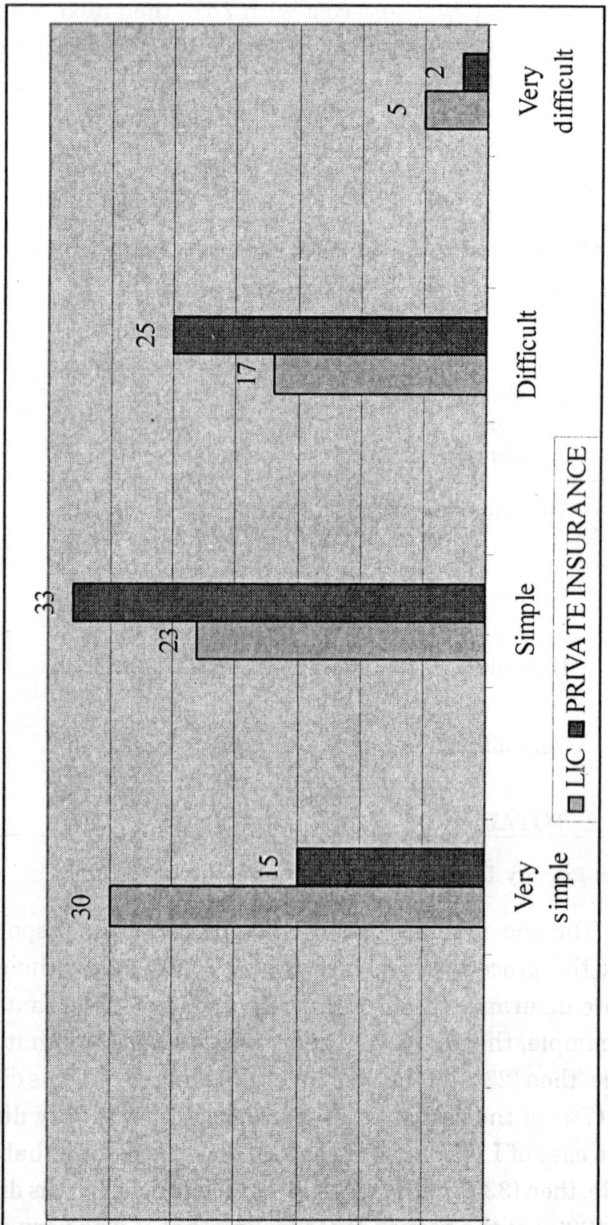

Source: Primary Data.

Table 9
Awareness of Private Insurance by the Respondents with Respect of Benefit

S.No	*Benefits*	*No of respondents*	*Ranking*
1.	Life coverage	37	**1**
2.	High returns	25	**3**
3.	Reliability	5	**8**
4.	Medical Claims	15	**5**
5.	Tax benefit	32	**2**
6.	Emergency	3	**7**
7.	Loan facility	13	**6**
8.	Flexibility of plans	18	**4**
9.	Services	2	**9**
	TOTAL	**150**	

Source: Primary Data.

The above Table-9 shows that the awareness of private insurance with respect of benefit of the various scheme in general. Though only 9% of them were not aware of private insurance .even though they were aware of benefits in general. The respondents ranked the life coverage as first then followed by tax benefit, high returns and flexibility of plans provided by the company.

Suggestions

To be successful in marketing of insurance products the company should have clear mission and values that should be clearly conveyed to all the stake holders of the firm. So that the company maintains sufficient transparency among the other entire competitor in the field.

To achieve greater penetration the insurance companies have to create vibrant and competitive industry, with greater efficiency, choice of the products and value for the customers. The suggestions regarding the insurance service are:

1. The services of the insurance companies can be improvised.
2. The penetration can be increased in the rural areas.
3. More awareness regarding the insurance and insurance product is needed.
4. Transparency of the companies can also be improved.
5. Companies can concentrate on more customized products.
6. Flexible premium payment modes can be made available to the customers.

Conclusion

Penetration of the life insurance is beginning to cut across the socio-economic classes and attract people who have never purchase insurance. with the heightening awareness and consumer education comes a willingness to view the life insurance an integral part of the financial portfolio. No longer is insurance a poorly understood product that is purchased over to people. Nor it is the product that is only bought hurried during the time of filing taxes. It's catching on as an important element in the financial basket. On that is purchased to fulfill specific emotional needs and has cleared benefits and trained advisors provide solutions to the customers to meet their financial needs. Life insurance is also regarded as versatile financial tool. It provides solution for three major needs have people namely accumulation needs, safety needs and retirement needs.

The privatization does not only benefit the customer alone it provides a huge employment opportunities to huge employees and have also hired more than 90,000 as financial advisors who council and recommend the products to the insurance buyers. The career as financial advisors provides huge flexibility in work and provides learning and earning opportunities. It is evident that only players with a long term vision and robust business strategies will survive. Whatever may be the developments, the future and the developments in the industry will exist.

References

1. Agarwala A N. "Life insurance in India: A Historical and analytical study". Allahabad. 1961
2. Insurance in India- a historical perspective
3. Rao B S R. "Functioning of the LIC an appraisal", Institute for financial Management and research, Madras, 1976
4. Ray R M, "Life insurance in Indian perspectives in social security", New Delhi ,1982.

WEBSITES

1. Life insurance http://www.indianinfoline .com
2. History http://www.irdaindia.org
3. LIC Act 1956 http://www.vakilno 1 .com
4. www.google .com

21

Information Technology in Insurance Sector

K. Abirami

The insurance industry today is passing through an exciting phase. The lure of the growth potential has already seen players drawing up aggressive plans for market and the mind share of prospective customers. The life insurance industry in India, which had been nationalised in the 1950's was liberalised in 1999 based on the recommendations of Malhotra Committee report (1993). After passing of the IRDA act 1999, the first private sector life insurance company started its business in 2001. Today they are 15 players in life insurance and 11 in non-life insurance in private sector. This huge expansion is possible mainly through technological improvement. In 1985, Information Technology (IT) capital investments represented 52% approximately of the total capital outlays made by insurance.

Information Technology

There has never been a time when the effective use of IT has been more crucial to the success of the insurance industry. The insurance markets are being revolutionized by technology at a high speed pace. It and software solutions, allowing cross-border trade to become electronic and paperless, are increasingly on offer to importers, exporters, shipping companies and financial institution. The computing technology, networking technology and advanced electronics together make today's IT The convergence of electronics and telecommunications created by devices like fax, telex which the business world-wide has been using extensively over last three decades. The convergence of computers and telecommunication has generated various computer networks making the business data transfer feasible. The computers with advanced electronics has provided the multimedia facilities i.e. apart from data in electronic format the voice (audio) and image (video) also can be a controlling input to and output from a computing device.

Hardware

Developments in Information Technology have been characterized by miniaturization and reducing cost with improved performance and better reliability combined with shortened product development cycles, due to advances in chip technology. The early use of huge computers during World War II was for military purpose. The computer technology went hand in hand with the advances in electronics. The computers for commercial use in 1960s, made use of transistors instead of vacuum tubes in the earlier computers. The integrated circuit (IC) technology of 1970s forms the backbone of latest computers. With the feasibility of circuits having large scale integration (LSI) and very large scale integrations (VLSI) powerful computers came to the table tops (Micro computers) and then to laptops and now to palmtops.

Software

Like the hardware, the computer languages (software) have also undergone change. The software transitions from very hard to use machine level language (MLL) through Symbolic / Assembly Level Language (ALL), High Level Language (HLL like COBOL, Basic etc.), fourth generation (4GLs like relational databases) have today reached to expert systems. This has brought the computer closer to business managers who may not be necessarily computer professionals. With complicated operating systems for mainframes and mini computers the personal computers came handy with operating systems like DOS, UNIX. This changed the concept of huge data processing centre into decentralized data processing units. The recent additions of user friendly interfaces like Windows brought menu driven, user friendly computing to the society. Word processing and spreadsheets made processes more efficient and one could edit documents or do calculations faster. But there was no sharing of information.

Computer Interface and Storage Devices

The dialogue with computer which is through input and output devices has changed its form and medium. The first interface with computer was the punched card (Holerith Card) Today the typewriter like keyboard or pointing and clicking device like mouse are in common use. Digitizers have introduced the flexibility of translating maps and figures to computer memory. Scanners have added image capture facility to computers. The touch screen add-ons and touch panels would accept finger touches as if they were mouse clicks.

The storage devices have changed from bulky and sequential access magnetic disks and tapes to handy and flexible floppy disks, hard disks. Optical disks offer mass storage capabilities. Today's compact disks with high storage capacity of 600 MB onwards are replacing concepts of publication information with relatively less cost.

Data Distribution and Networking

Advancements in IT have provided connectivity amongst computers of electronic data interchange. This enabled the organizations and individuals to spread messages within and outside the organizations at a very low price on electronic mail. Electronic data transmission enables information sharing within specific sites on Local Area Network (LAN) using coaxial or unshielded twisted pair (UTP) cables. Operating offices of a business house can be connected through leased telephone lines to form a Metro Area Network (MAN) allowing data transfer within different offices of a city. Electronic data transmission over long distances using satellite communication links or fiber optic cables forms WANs. The new client-server technology has provided an open systems environment with broad interoperability across diverse hardware platforms and connectivity between offices. The client-server computing also made distributed data possible, had workflow and office automation support as well as graphics user interface leading to customer-oriented information systems. Digital telephone lines (ISDN) provides for transmission of text, picture, film and sound to any remote place.

The Need for Information Technology

The rapid innovations in the field of information and communication technology have posed serious challenges for the insurance industry in India. The use and application of information technology in wide variety of insurance's operations has now become strategic in the sense that it has direct impact on the productivity of resources, and a sweetening impact on reducing the cost of various activities. The innovations in information technology can be effectively utilized in the following areas.

- Speedy and correct insurance of documents
- Expeditions disposal of claims
- Proper building of accounts and statistics

→

- Quality Assurance Efficiency

Technologies For Insurance

The insurance markets are being revolutionized by technology at a high speed pace. IT and software solutions allowing cross-border trade to become electronic and paperless, are increasingly on offer to exporters, importers, shipping companies and financial institutions. Following technological advancements can really enhance the performance of insurance companies.

- **Database Management Systems**

The principle of tracking and measuring responses can pay off for the commotional insurance industry. To find more clients, insurer needs to consider many factors, including lapsation, cash value, premium and competition. But the need to record and study the characteristics of persistency the length of time we retain policies, customers and agents is most important for insurance companies. clear advantages of new PC (Personal Computer) and RISC (Reduced Instruction Set Computer) technology gives companies power to keep tens of millions of policies on a device with thousands of bytes of data per Policy / Client / Agent.

- **Group Linking Software**

Group – Linking software enables sharing of information and particularly suits document heavy insurance business.

- **Mapping**

Insures to meet different needs, such as identifying loss prone areas or geographic claim analysis, can use mapping technology. It helps the insurer to analyse the extent of its network (i.e) the insurer can determine whether it has too many or too few agency force in a particular area.

- **Imaging and Workflow Technologies**

The proposal forms may be scanned into an imaging system, data may be extracted for updated to computer and for automated underwriting workflow may be implemented. It is estimated that imaging and workflow enabled underwriting could reduce the time taken to issue a policy as much as 60%. Under the imaging system, every document – be it correspondence, forms, photocopies of cheques, faxes etc. are all maintained in a sharable electronic folder-neatly indexed, updated and available simultaneously to all concerned.

- **Call Center Technology**

Good customer service is a crucial element in gaining, maintaining and retaining profitable customer. Call center concept based on Interactive Voice Response Services (IVRS) is gaining importance in this aspect.

- **Cat Models**

Catastrophic models use data from the recent spate of natural disasters that helps develop more predictions of insurers' property exposures in future disasters. Using this date curious "what if" scenarios of Probable Maximum Loss (PML) using the best estimate available at an insurer' exposures are tested. Finally an underwriting policy that limits the company's exposure to catastrophic losses is implemented.

- **Intranet, Extranet and Internet**

Intranet is the network connecting different offices of the same business to permit the internal data within the business. Extranet is a network allowing the business to communicate with business partners like suppliers, vendors, banners, regulations etc, on the electronic channel. Internet is a global network of many computer networks. Insurers can browse through many useful sites on the Internet.

Insurance And Electronic Commerce- E-Insurance

E-Insurance ispo-facto, not aloof, is one of the growth areas in India. Enormous opportunities are being created by the internet's new connectivity such as improving customer's service, reducing cycle time, becoming more cost effective, and selling goods, services, or information to an expanded global customer base. Globally, insurance on the net has lagged behind other financial service products such as banking and brokerage. Of the total online users only 5% used insurance service online.

Generally the largest insurers have been focused on static marketing presence online, encompassing product information, FAQ's and quotes. Only a few insurers have added the ability to submit applications online. This lack of participation in the e-business revolution is seen across lines. The Insurance companies attribute two factors for the slow take off. First and foremost, insurance is a product that is sold and not bought. The Internet is perceived to be a buyer's medium, with online customers able to search quickly and for the most competitive prices and variety of products. Insurance is one product that cannot be easily commoditized. The more personal the selling process the greater the difficulty in using the net as a medium for selling. Insurance is one product, which involves personalised selling. The process of insurance sales requires a series of face-to- face interactions.

International Trends

The convergence effect of IT is being felt by the insurance industry as well as in developed countries. The Global online insurance market is expected to achieve an exponential growth in the near future. In the life insurance segment alone, the total online business will grow to $ 21 billion by 2003. Premium income from then non-life policies will go up to $ 18 billion in the next three years. The Gartner Group in a study conducted by them says that in a year 25% of all customer contracts and enquiries for enterprises will come via the Internet, e-mail and online forms. Banc assurance customer service, which has been almost exclusively done via the telephone (96% of all transactions) will become increasingly e-mail based in the next four years; decreasing telephone related service by 28%. Similarly, by essentially outsourcing administrative and cost intensive processes such as policy administration to customers, the cost of administration and servicing the insurance policy also decreases sharply.

E-Insurance in India

The intriguing question before all associated with the insurance industry is that will it be possible for private companies or even public sector monoliths to sell insurance online in India in the near future ? Insurance companies will probably have to wait for internet penetration to increase and the still ambiguous e-commerce rules to take concrete form. However what is not debatable is that new private entrants will change the rules of the game for the Indian insurance business, both in the life insurance and the non-life insurance segment, unfolding opportunities for software engineers and professional agents.

To peep into the possibilities and opportunities emerging out of the integration of insurance and information technology, various organizations have organized seminars and conferences in the recent past to explore the possibilities of selling insurance on the Net and gauge the opportunities for the growing Indian software industry.

According to T.Ramanan of Assocham, life insurers were among the first to go online with informative content and features like actuarial calculators. However, according to him, they have been relatively slow to embrace online commerce, which currently makes up about 1% of the total tem life market. Only 12% of insurance companies globally sell policies online. The growth of global online insurance business augurs well for the Indian IT sector. The exponential froth in the online insurance business will unfold significant business opportunities for software companies / consultants.

The opportunities that rise out of this will be both global and local, because new entrants will have to either fine tune or prepare customized packages for the Indian Market. Online insurance will also help companies reduce costs and keep premiums low, a pre-requisite in a price sensitive market like India.

Benefits of Electronic Insurance

E-Insurance provides multiple benefits to the insurer and the existing and prospective insured:

- Information collected is better and cheaper.
- Speed of response – Insurance of policy and settlement of claims is faster.
- Provides new ways of doing business in competitive market.
- Flexible pricing and customized services.
- Global accessibility i.e. lapse of physical boundaries.
- Increased sales without additional sales force.
- Immediate premium collection and funds transfer.
- Reduced cost per transaction

Technological Challenges

One of the prominent challenges of e-commerce is security. It is very evident that many uses are reluctant to do business on the internet due to security reasons. Issues of transmission securities, host server security, confidentiality, authenticity and ways to counter these challenges are covered, in the following topics.

Security

- Database security : The business database security is utmost important this has to be monitored by security of the work server and web access.
- Web server Security : Security policies should be defined like who is allowed access, nature of the access and who authorizes such access ? who is responsible for security what kinds of materials are allowed on server pages ?
- Passwords sniffing : The most significant security risk on the internet today is the use of plain text, reusable

passwords that are sent over the internal and external networks. User names and passwords are the most common way of authenticating uses on the internet today. They are widely used by many internet protocols, including remote log in, file transfer, remote e-mail reading and web access. protection against password sniffing is to avoid using plain text, usernames and reusable passwords.

- Network sniffing programmes : Automated tools should be used to scan your network. These tools check for well known security-related bugs in network programmes such as sent mail and FTPD. Computers are certainly being scanned by crackers interested in breaking into the systems, therefore, network scanning programmes should be regularly run.
- Physical Security : One can ensure physical security by having an alarm system that calls the policy, having a key lock on the computer power supply. There should be adequate protection against fire, explosions, humidity and dust.
- Web access security : Organisations run web servers because they are an easy way to distribute information to people on the internet. But sometimes this information is not required to be distributed to everybody. Host based restrictions can be implemented using a firewall to block incoming HTTP connections to a particular web server.
- Transmission Security : Encryption is a key technology to ensure transaction security various types of encryption technologies are : single key cryptography/symmetric or Private key encryption : a private key is generated and is send to receiver to a secret channel every message is encrypted at the sending end and transmitted over the network. The receiver applies the private key to decrypt the message.

Public key cryptography : A key pair, public key and private key is generated sender sends the message using public key for encryption. The receiver who is the only person having private key can receive the message.

VPN-Virtual Private Networks : The current firewall technology includes VPNs, a way to enable secures communication across internet. VPNs are a less expensive alternative and an interoperable standard. A VPN link is very flexible and works with any applications that use TCP/IP, unlike SSL.

Privacy : Privacy is likely to be a growing concern as internet - based communications and commerce increase. Designers and operators of websites who disregard the privacy of users do so at their own peril. Users who feel that their privacy has been violated may leave the web. Thus it is important to protect personal privacy on the web. Every time a web browser views a page on the web, a record is kept in that web server's log files.

Legislations: can be passed to prevent the internet service providers from parting with personal information of the clients. Whether or not such legislation passes in the future web surfers should be aware that information about their activities may be collected by service providers, vendors, and site administrators and other on the electronic super highway.

Proxy server : one approach to privacy is to use an anonym zing web server. These are servers that are designed to act as proxies for users concerned with privacy . Using an anonymizer requires that you place faith in the person or organisation that is running the service, that's because the anonymizer knows who has connected to it and what pages they have seen.

Information Technology used in Insurance payments :

Front End operations	:	New payment related modules pertaining to both ordinary and SSS policies have been added to the Front End packages catering to loan,

		claims and development officers' Appraisal to reduce time lag and ensure accuracy
Metro area Network	:	More than 10,000 transactions area carried out over this Network on any given working day.
Wide area network	:	This enables the customers to view his policy data and pay premium from any branch of any MAN city.
Interactive voice response(IVRS)	:	It enables customers to the up LIC and receives information about their policies on the Telephone.
Information Kiosks	:	These Kiosks enable the users to provide policy details and accept premium payments.
Website	:	LIC has given its policy holders a unique facility to pay premiums through Internet, absolutely free and view their policy details on Internet premium payments.
Info centers	:	It has also set up call centers to provide information about our products, policy services, branch addresses and other organizational information.

IT Departments in an Insurance Sector

Generally the insurance organisation has three-tier set-up – Operating office (BO/DO), Controlling Offices (RD/DO) and Central Office (HO). The organisation and responsibilities of the IT department and its sub-departments is more or less in the hierarchical order of the various offices.

The IT department at HO is responsible to the chairman/ CEO of the organisation for implementation of IT plan. The department is responsible for procuring new technologies, conducting training and preparing the broad IT policy framework. The RO and BO are respectively responsible to the CO. The Head of the IT department may have the following functional managers with their respective tasks :

Technology Manager	• Evaluation and acquisition of new technologies in hardware, software, networking and packaged solutions. • Recruitment and supervision of system and network engineers • Conducting of various training programmes
System Manager	• Systems analysis and design • Functional specifications • Development of application and user manuals • Assignment of work to project leaders, system analysts and programmers • Evaluation of studies
Network Manager	• Network administration (Including WAN) • User administration, systems security, e-mail etc. • Controlling and supervision of network administration
Operations Manager	• Maintenance of hardware • Job scheduling, backups and file control • Assigning work to operators and DEOs • Training of users • Controlling of data flow

Conclusion

The supporting technology requirements will be a real time, rather than batch; longitudinal rather than episodic; will require connectivity rather than be self contained; will be interactive; will rely on large relational databases. Therefore the imperative for the all the insurers, especially LIC and GIC is to build up an efficient interface between the various departments and segments. This would reduce the paper work, improve efficiency of service delivery and provide competitive advantage to the insurance companies. Insurance is poised for substantial growth in the times to come. The current focus of insurance has been the acquisition of new business and market share. The real challenge is to retain and service these customers.

References

Dr. P.K.Gupta-*Insurance and Risk Management–Chapter 31, pp. 531–543, 2004.*

The Hindu survey of Indian Industry 2007.

S.D.Totade - *Editors : D.C.Srivastava, Shashank Srivastava-Indian Insurance Industry Transition and Prospects, 2002 – Chapter 19, pp. 312 – 327.*

Internet Sources

www.google.com

22

Human Resource Practices of Insurance Companies and Employee Work-life Balance Issues

Dr. A Kumudha, Ms. Shripria V, Dr.V Srividya

The global competition has changed the workplace dynamics. In the pursuit of improving performance, increasing productivity, reducing costs and enhancing profitability in the workplace, organisations are evolving new ways and means to build psychological relationships with employees. Work-life balance is a common challenge throughout the industrialised world. The changing demographics of work force are prompting many individuals to work harder at balancing work responsibilities, family needs and personal life demands. In today's fast paced society, people have started realizing that they need to strike a balance between their work life and personal life. In an effort to earn more money to reach the ultimate goal of having a quality life, the balance is lost somewhere along the way. Balancing the dual demands and responsibilities of work and family roles has become an increasingly widespread problem experienced by employees and employers. (Graham and Crossen, 1996). The concept of work life balance is based on the notion that paid work and personal life should be seen less as competing priorities than as complementary elements of a full life. Meaning and importance of quality of work life is assuming a new significance. The connotation of the term "work" has become different. It has more to do with the intellectual exercise than physical labour. Researchers have pointed out that a balance between work and life is maintained when there is no conflict between work and family demands. This is an idealistic situation however if there exists conflict between work and family then it affects the productivity of the employee and impacts his notion of balancing work-life. The interface between work and life is important to organizational researchers and to managers because of its potential to influence job satisfaction, job involvement and organizational commitment.

Insurance Sector in India

In India insurance business is broadly classified into two branches, life insurance and non-life insurance. Insurance companies are important players in financial markets as they collect and invest large amounts of premiums in various investment instruments. Lately, insurance companies have also ventured into pension schemes and mutual funds. Insurance market in India presents several striking features. Following the recommendations of the Malhotra Committee Report, in 1999, the Insurance Regulatory and Development authority (IRDA) was constituted as an autonomous body to regulate and develop the insurance industry. The IRDA opened the market in August 2000 with the invitation for application for registrations. Foreign companies were allowed ownership of up to 26% and later increased about 70%. A number of multinational and Indian companies have entered the market today, many of the multinational players have local partners and vice versa. At present there are 13 companies in the life insurance business and another 13 in the general insurance business. The penetration level of insurance business in India has increased up to 0.9 percentages which is 4.7 percent of global average. The growth in insurance is as 20 percent per annum that has made the insurance business a buyers market. This is due to the entry of the private companies. Today the beneficiaries are the customers with the insurance companies offering a wide range of products, customised services and professional advices, and these have become the mainstay of the industry. Only 22% of the insurable population in India possesses life insurance. Out of a population of more than one billion, only 1.8 percent of GDP constitutes the premium. Hence all the existing players and new entrants are competing with each other to tap the potential market. The work lives of employees have undergone a lot of changes. The work patterns of employees have undergone tremendous changes with target driven performance expectations and scope for quick growth in careers. The insurance industry is in a flux of stiff competition amongst players.

The insurance sector in India has come a full circle from being an open competitive market to nationalisation and back to the liberalised market again. Tracing the developments in the Indian insurance sector reveals 360 degree turn witnessed over a period of almost two centuries. Liberalised environment in India has seen a lot of private international players in the market offering insurance solutions. The environment is very competitive with all the players scaling up of operations. This has brought about a change in the work practices of the companies. Employees working at the service end are expected to exert themselves for the cause of customer servicing, this has become the central theme of any service sector today where insurance sector is no exception. On one end the employers are offering better environment and employee friendly work places in order to attract and maintain HR that is productive. Today's organisations are aware that (i) there is an increasing awareness of the employees to balance ones own work-life (ii) Organisational commitment of the employees comes from how the employees perceive the organisational offering to balance work-life. On the other end, employees look out for better work places in terms of career growth, compensation and that one that allows work-life balance.

Work-life balance policies are however more relevant today than ever before and Indian organisations are recognising this. Globalisation has created its own pressures on employees of travel and working across varied time zones and women are entering the workforce in a society where "most of the household chores and responsibility of bringing up the children are dumped on them". Career and competitive pressures are making more demands on the employee's time as a result of which attention to family and self is taking a back seat which is disturbing the mental equilibrium as well as deteriorating personal health." Moreover, employee aspirations are growing, both at work and at home. And above all, there are increasing demands on an employee's time from family and society. Most employers believe that work-life balance was relevant across all industries and across both genders, though a little more relevant to women and even more relevant if both the partners were working. However, it was felt that the combination of policies would vary by industry, job function and geographical locations. Most also seem to believe that it is middle managers who would be most receptive to these policies. There is recognition to the fact that work-life balance policies would create a healthier, more productive and motivated work force, help position the organisation as an employer of choice and give men more time to spend at home thus giving women a respite from the family work. Prior study also reveals that despite this recognition, almost most organisations had no stated formal work-life balance policies. They offered few policies for employees beyond employer owned options like canteen facilities, stress management workshops, more cheerful office interiors and programmes for children of employees.

Research Methodology

A study with an objective to understand the Human resource practices of insurance companies and employee work-life balance issues was undertaken in Coimbatore. The research design is descriptive in nature that includes surveys and fact finding enquiries of different kinds. The major purpose of descriptive research is description of the state of affairs as it exists at present. The population for the study included all the insurance companies in Coimbatore city. In the life Insurance sector 13 companies in total were covered among which one company is a public sector company and all other 12 companies were private sector companies. In the general insurance sector 3 public sector companies and 3 private sector companies were covered. For the purpose of the study secondary sources of data were used. Secondary data was used for collecting information of the insurance companies, their human resource practices.

Human Resource Policies and Practices

The Human resource policies and practices of organisations in general offer guidelines in management of human resources in the organisation. These may include the terms of employment, work timings, training and development provided by the organisation, performance review and appraisals, facilities at the work place like canteen, day care etc, leave from work allowed, social security measures like pension fund, gratuity, insurance schemes, grievance handling procedure etc. In the insurance sector most of the firms follow the statutory norms and the regulations of IRDA act. For the purpose of the study only those Human resource policies and practices that have a direct say in balancing work and life were analysed.

The following is the table that shows the Human resource Policies and Practices of insurance companies in Coimbatore that influence the work life balance of employees.

Discussions and Findings

Among the human resource policies and practices followed by Insurance companies, some of the policies and practices like

Human Resource Policies and Practices of Insurance Companies that Influence Work-life Balance

HR Policy	*Social Responsibility*	*Development Policy*	*Grievance Handling*	*Time Scheduling*
LIC	Quality of work-life, self respect	Performance appraisal and training	Redressal officers appointed	fixed 10 am-5 pm
UIA	Quality of work, self respect	Performance appraisal and training	Redressal officers appointed	fixed 10 am-5 pm
NIA	Quality of work, self respect	Performance appraisal and training	Redressal officers appointed	fixed 10 am-5 pm
OIC	Quality of work self respect	Performance appraisal and training	Redressal officers appointed	fixed 10 am-5 pm
BHARTI AXA	Quality of work, self respect	Performance appraisal	No separate system	Fixed-9.30 am-5-pm
RELIANCE	Quality of work, self respect	Performance appraisal	Redressal officers appointed	Fixed-9.30 am-6-pm

(Contd.)

(Contd. Table)

HR Policy	*Canteen Facility*	*Career Support*	*Insurance Policy*	*Leave Days*
LIC	private canteen	Incentives, awards/rewards, Product training	Covered	45 days per year
UIA	private canteen	Incentives, awards/rewards ,Product training	Covered	45 days per year
NIA	private canteen	Incentives, awards/rewards Product training	Covered	45 days per year
OIC	private canteen	Incentives, awards/rewards Product training	Covered	45 days per year
BHARTI AXA	Pantry	Incentives, awards/rewards, Need based training	Covered	10 days with pay
RELIANCE	Pantry	Incentives, awards/rewards, Need based training	Covered	24 days with pay, sat half day off

(Contd.)

(Contd. Table)

HR Policy	*Social Responsibility*	*Development Policy*	*Grievance Handling*	*Time Scheduling*
BAJAJ ALLIANCE	Quality of work, self respect	Performance appraisal and career planning and dev	Redressal officers appointed	fixed/flexible
TATA AIG	Quality of work, self respect	Performance appraisal	Redressal officers appointed	Fixed-9 am-6-pm
AVIVA	Quality of work, self respect	Performance appraisal and career planning and dev	Redressal officers appointed	Fixed-9.30 am-6-pm
BIRLA	Quality of work, self respect	Performance appraisal and career planning and dev	Redressal officers appointed	Fixed-9.30 am-6-pm
ICICI PRU	Quality of work, self respect	Performance appraisal and career planning and dev	No separate system	fixed 9.15 am-5.45 pm
ICICI LOM	Quality of work, self respect	Performance appraisal and career planning and dev	No separate system	Fixed-9.30 am-6-pm

(Contd.)

(Contd. Table)

HR Policy	*Canteen Facility*	*Career Support*	*Insurance Policy*	*Leave Days*
BAJAJ ALLIANCE	Pantry	Incentives, awards/rewards, product and Need based training	Covered	24 days with pay, sat half day off
TATA AIG	Pantry	Incentives, awards/rewards, product and Need based training	Covered	24 days with pay, sat half day off
AVIVA	Pantry	Incentives, awards/rewards, product and sales training	Covered	42 days with pay & sat, sun off
BIRLA	Pantry	Incentives, awards/rewards, training as per hierarchy	Covered	26 days with pay, sat& sun day off
ICICI PRU	Pantry	Incentives, awards/rewards, product and sales training	Covered	30 days with pay & Sunday
ICICI LOM	Pantry	Incentives, awards/rewards,	Covered	30 days with pay &

(Contd.)

(Contd. Table)

HR Policy	*Social Responsibility*	*Development Policy*	*Grievance Handling*	*Time Scheduling*
MET LIFE	Quality of work, self respect	Performance appraisal and career planning and dev	Redressal officers appointed	Fixed-9 am-6-pm
MAX NY	Quality of work, self respect	Performance appraisal and career planning and dev	Redressal officers appointed	Fixed-9 am-6-pm
HDFC	Quality of work, self respect	Performance appraisal	No separate system	Fixed-9 am-6-pm
KOTAK	Quality of work, self respect	Performance appraisal	Redressal officers appointed	Fixed-9 am-6-pm
ING VYSYA	Quality of work, self respect	Performance appraisal and career planning and dev	Redressal officers appointed	Fixed-9 am-6-pm
IFFCO TOKIO	Quality of work, self respect	Performance appraisal and career planning and dev	No separate system	Fixed-9 am-6-pm

(Contd.)

(Contd. Table)

HR Policy	*Canteen Facility*	*Career Support*	*Insurance Policy*	*Leave Days*
MET LIFE	Pantry	Incentives, awards/rewards, Product training	Covered	26 days with pay, sun day off
MAX NY	Pantry	Incentives, awards/rewards, training as per hierarchy	Covered	30 days with pay & Sunday
HDFC	Pantry	Incentives, awards/rewards, product and sales training	Covered	30 days with pay & Sunday
KOTAK	Pantry	Incentives, awards/rewards, product and Need based training	Covered	30 days with pay & Sunday
ING VYSYA	Pantry	Incentives, awards/rewards, training as per hierarchy	Covered	24 days with pay, sun day off
IFFCO TOKIO	Pantry	Incentives, awards/rewards, product and Need based training	Covered	24 days with pay, sun day off

Social responsibility, Development policy, Grievance handling, Time scheduling, Canteen facility, Career support, Insurance policy and Leave days are influencing the work-life balance efforts of the employees. These policies help reduce the work role conflict by being supportive to the work role of the employees.

Social Responsibility: Describes the responsibility of the company towards the society at large and the employees, for all the insurance companies it was found to be providing quality of work and self respect.

Development Policy: This describes the measures undertaken by the insurance companies to develop an individual in a role these include performance appraisal, training and career planning and development. Most of the companies follow performance appraisal to apprise employees of their performance and follow the system of career planning and development. This measure will enable the employees to know his performance and potential and enable them to be focused towards career advancement.

Grievance Handling: Grievance handling mechanism is very important as there needs to be a system in place to handle and redress the employee's grievances thereby promoting a supportive and conducive environment for the employees. Most of the insurance companies have systems in place to handle employee grievances.

Time Scheduling: Time is an important factor as mismanagement of time can cause stress. More time spend on work or no time flexibility can influence work-life conflict. Most of the insurance companies follow fixed time scheduling on an average 9.30 to 5.30 is the work timings.

Canteen: Availability of food and beverages in the work place also indicates a supportive environment of work and it is found that most of the insurance companies either have a pantry in operation or a canteen facility.

Career Support: Employees of insurance companies are provided with incentives, rewards and awards. Training is provided in product, sales and also need based training.

Insurance Policy: Social security measures like provision of insurance cover for employees enable them to ensure financial security in case of illness, disablement or death. Almost all the insurance companies provide insurance cover for the employees.

Leave Days: Leave from work is necessary for the employees to spend time away from work for family and interests. Insurance companies provide 45 days per year on the higher range and a minimum of 24 days per year with pay.

Conclusion

Human resource policies and practices play a vital role in enabling employees to balance their work and life. A balanced life is one where people spread their energy and effort, emotional, intellectual, imaginative, spiritual and physical – between key areas of importance. The neglect of one or more areas, or anchor points, may threaten the vitality of the whole. The human resource function has to cater to the well being of employees in order to ensure productivity and organisational growth. In India, especially in the insurance sector, the HR policies and practices that directly impact work-life balance of employees like flexible timing, child care, and use of IT like video conferencing to reduce travel, Leave time off etc are yet to be introduced. Moreover, work-life balance issues are seen only at a personal level and still it needs to be accepted to be an organisational problem.

References

Andrew Dutta, Manjeesh K Singh. Balancing the work and life of your employees, HRM Review, Februray, 2004

Anupama G.S, "Weekend Masti, Forget it! ,The week. March 11, 2007

Bhagat, Rasheeda, Next Step. Quaterly Journal on Management. Praxis, Vol.2:Issue 4. January 2, 2003.

DTI (Department of Trade and Industry). 2000 Work and parents: Competitiveness and choice. London DTI Green paper.

Graham E, Crossen C. 1996. Too many things to do, too little time to do them. Wall Street Journal, March 8: RI, R4.

Helen Lingard [a]; Valerie Francis [b] The decline of the 'traditional' family: work-life benefits as a means of promoting a diverse workforce in the construction industry of Australia, Construction Management and Economics, Volume 23, Issue 10 December 2005 , pages 1045 - 1057.

Indranil Banerjee. Harnessing work-life balance: A shared responsibility, HRM Review, December, 2007.

Lewis, S. (2001) Restructuring workplace cultures: the ultimate work-family challenge? Women in Management Review, Vol.16 No.1, pp.21-29.

Little, Andrew, National secretary of Engineering, Printing and Manufacturing Union, New Zealand. August 22, 2002.

Mallikarjun Krishnamurti. Work-life Balance: The art of Balancing, HRM Review, December, 2007.

Paramanad, Benedict. Are Indian companies striking a work -life balance. Management Next. Vol 1, Issue-3.July, 2003.

Raja Achanta, 2004. The work-life balance, HRM Review, March 2004

Sarah Wise. Work-life balance Literature and research review, Employment research institute, Napier University.

Saroj Parasuraman, Claire A simmers. 2001. Type of employment, work-family conflict and well-being: a comparative study. Journal of Organisational Behaviour, 22, 551-568(2001).

Srinivas, E.S. 2004, Rhythms of Life: Antecedents and outcomes of work: Family Balance in Employed Parents, Journal of Applied Psychology, pp.132-146.

Swamy. Work-life balance-Organisational Strategies for sustainable growth, HRM Review, October, 2007.

23

CRM in Life Insurance Corporation of India

G. Jothi

Every organization should have an integrated view encompassing production, marketing and service. The concept CRM is developed as a way to collect and manage customer service and sales information so the business would have more comprehensive view of their customer contact. CRM system provides unique opportunity with tremendous capabilities for sales management, sales forecasting, customer order processing and complaint handling supported by automated database and user-friendly solutions of information technology.

The insurance regulatory development authority bill passed in the Lok Sabha in December 1999 provides entry to the large number of player, addition of new distribution channels, modern technology and above all competition. The public sector LIC of India is an organization with largest customer base in the field. The brand image, the goodwill, the infrastructure, day-to-day technological up gradation and the dedicated work force make that an ideal organization for adopting the concepts of relationship marketing. The relationship with customers commence from the home of prospecting continues even after the settlement of claims. The need for CRM in LIC can be highlighted on the basis of following observations.

1. The market share of LIC for the year 2006-2007 was 96.21 percent with premium collection of Rs. 9,56,686.58 lakhs and 2,89,51,919 policies offered to its customers. Hence, there is a need to satisfy the customers and to have continuous relations with them. LIC is known for the policy holder trust and security.
2. By experience it was found that it costs 7 times to attract a new customer than to serve an old customer. Hence, the satisfaction of existing customer is required to reduce the promotional costs.
3. About 20 percent of the organization's loyal customers account for 80 percent of its revenue. In other words it implies that greater potential for cross functional selling and sell ups for the remaining 80 percent of customers.

These factors indicate that LIC needs CRM to meet growing competition in the market to gain the confidence of their customers.

CRM - Organization Set-up

The LIC of India has CRM machinery at Branch, Divisional and Zonal levels.

CRM at Zonal office

The Zonal Office has to play a very important role of actualizing the CRM concepts in the area of its jurisdiction. The effectiveness of the concepts depends on the support and encouragement provided by the Zonal office. It conducts programmes for the staff and field personnel of the zone with the help of CRM managers and trained zonal training center's faculty. It selects the manager and the staff of the CRM machinery at D.O. and B.O. levels. It assesses the customer satisfaction levels obtained at the various offices situated within the zonal area. It guides, monitors, recommends the various activities and appropriates measures for betterment. It keeps the central office informed of the various activities and progress achieved by the zone in the area of CRM.

CRM at Divisional Office

CRM machinery at Divisional Office level plays a great role to fulfill the objectives of the CRM. This level conducts awareness programmes for staff and field personnel for customer orientation. It has a grievance redressal machinery / complaints cell. This cell registers complaints from all sources including Web-based complaints. It forwards the complaint's to appropriate branch or service department at D.0 level for resolution and it closes the complaints. It has one more committee i.e., standing committee on customer relation.

CRM at Branch Office

At branch level, the Customer Relations Executives are (CRE) in-charge of CRM. He leads with linkages, customer satisfaction, customer meets, customer relation campaign, customer education, research survey etc. At branch level the main objectives of CRM are as follows:

(i) To champion the cause of the customer

(ii) To provide vital link between customer and organization

(iii) To obtain customer feedbacks for improving the systems and procedures.

The above objectives are achieved through the implementations of the following machinery at Branch Level.

(a) Customer Service Desk: Under this, they provide services through the single window system. At the counter of LIC, all the services are offered to the customers. They need not go round different sections for getting the information needed.

(b) Complaint Desk: Under this LIC register and follow up the complaints of the customer. They will be forwarded to manager CRM and to D.O., where decisions are to be taken at the standing committee. This desk make the customer feel that there is someone within the office to look after his complaint.

(c) **Correspondence Desk**: Under this desk, they record all letters received from customers and give reply by appropriate desks. They handle help line, telephone, E-mail, Fax, etc. They prepare reports on various types of requests received, time lag in resolving the requests, the pending requests etc.

(d) **Research and Survey**: LIC conducts market surveys, customer campaigns for exploring new business and retaining old customers. In this LIC studies revenue leakages, customer feed backs and measures customer satisfaction levels. They conduct awareness programmes to staff and field personnel for greater customer orientation.

(e) **Dealing with important customers**: At branch level, the officials concerned directly deal with high-end customers, take their complaints and solve them immediately. All these jobs are taken up in "Customer Relations Group (CRG)", under the guidance and supervision of the Customer Relations Executive (CRE). Depending on the workflow, one or more desks may be created.

The CRM machinery will be acting within the ambit of the financial powers granted to various authorities working in the branches as per the "Financial Powers Standing Orders". Thus, CRE at branch level personally handles the tasks like leakages, time lag study, customer satisfaction, customer meets, customer relationship campaign, customer 'education, research, survey, etc.

CRM - Organizational Procedures and Methods

The principle of "Uberrima fides" (utmost good faith) is the driving principle of LIC. It has capacity to act according to the needs and sentiments of the Indian people. The objective of social element is also an important element of LIC to prove itself.

Life Insurance business becomes successful when relationships take precedence over sales and when it places a higher priority on the policy holder. Like any relationship, good customer rapport requires 'care and feeding' and keeping in touch with the customer even after the sale is over. Following are the form of the initiatives to build relationships and retain them.

(i) Continuous mailer service regarding product knowledge and new CRM initiatives to policy holders and field force (Ex: Activities of capturing of mobile Nos. and e-mail IDs)

(ii) Segment-wise customer meets

(iii) Survey of the local market through selected Agents and Development Officers.

Operating Policies have been recognized as critical factors in CRM to meet the challenges in tune with the emerging trends in LIC

(a) Review and improvement of process-ECS (Electronic Clearing Service) method for payment into new business.

(b) Leveraging CRM to Marketing-Recycling of claim proceeds into new business.

(c) All survival benefits and maturity benefits are settled one month in advance.

(d) Non-early death claims are settled within 15 days from the date of receipt of intimation.

(e) Outstanding death claims ratio is brought to less than 0.5%. No claims-death or maturity to remain pending for more than 3 months.

(f) New policies are issued within 5 days. Whenever possible, policies are issued soon after completion of formalities.

(g) Revival of lapsed policies on a continuous basis, so as to retain customers and achieve growth in renewal premium income with effective usage of CRM module.

(h) Issue of policy status reports to all individual policy holders.

(i) Regular customer meets are held to get feed back in various servicing areas.

(j) Improvement of SSS servicing through special call 1ps in paying authority premises.

(k) Purification of policy masters is the important exercise, where LIC is trying for the data purity

(l) LIC is giving training to agents in technology to enable selling, data mining, providing competent services to customers.

(m) To increase the quality consciousness, empathy and responsiveness staffs are also being trained.

To be a customer oriented service organization LIC developed customer needed policies, products and procedures. To serve its customer best LIC initiated pre and post sale personalized service. They are viz.,

(1) CRM machinery is created at all levels for the implementation of CRM strategy

(2) Realizing the enrichment of attitude, LIC has initiated training programmes for the CRM personnel.

(3) Establishment of standing committee on customer relations in process of improvement and develop customer satisfaction index.

(4) Infrastructural support such as special counters,enquiry counters, etc, is provided to CRM machinery.

(5) Customer campaigns, customer relationship campaigns, revival campaigns, study of cash counters are initiated.

(6) Communicating the information to customer is the other important tool in CRM. LIC has established a unique training programme on customer communications.

(7) Other initiatives such as establishment of call centers at major cities, special training to managers, and working out a branch from office for a team based functioning.

(8) **Benchmarking:** Setting standard for various activities, reviewing and revising them is recognized as an essential

element in CRM. Standards 'have been fixed and communicated through manuals to all the branches for providing better services.

(9) **Total Service Quality**: Quality efficiency at every stage (End to End) of service activity leads to customer satisfactions. Any gap between the customer's expectation and services rendered leads to complaint. Hence, a constant surveillance on the processes (response time and consistency), customer grievances and system to plug the loopholes is of utmost importance. The service activity" of LIC is impressing upon quality/efficiency.

(10) **standing Committee**: LIC has taken up steps for instituting a separate committee comprising of HODs at Divisional Office and the Marketing Manager as the Chair Person. A decision which is not taken by a functional head (HOD) for various reasons can be taken by this Committee thereby avoiding a reference to Z.O.

(11) **Months of truth**: LIC has given at most importance to the policy holder grievances. They are what customers experience at contact points (Ex letters, telephones E-mail, in person). Organization "procedures are made sensitive enough to individual customer needs. Reliability and timely "response is being taken care of. LIC is giving importance to ambience of office is to be such that customer .is not only comfortable but he feels at home.

(12) **Customer's Satisfaction Index**: Unless a feedback system is devised it will not be possible to know the defects/ setback in working system. Therefore various methods by which the level of customer's satisfaction can be measured are adopted by LIC. fi1e feedbacks obtained are received positively.

(13) **Service Recovery**: Systems are adopted to satisfy an aggrieved customer and reduce the damage caused by an error or deficiency in products/ services rendered.

(14) **Single Window System:** Single window system adopted by LIC helps the customer to get all his demand met a

one point çounter). He is not made to run form pillar to post.

(15) **Handling complaints:** A complaint is the gap between services rendered and that expected by the customers. Expectations of a customer are created by his experience (with the same organization or some other organization), practices prevailing in the market, guidance provided by field personal or staff. LIC is giving preference to this aspect in finding alternatives to the problems.

e- CRM

Application of information technology and the computing resources if CRM is known as e-CRM. In fact, e-CRM provides manifold increased capabilities in customer relationship management and marketing. Speed, accuracy, single window, green channel, net working (internet connections) has become the order of the day without which it may not be possible to meet the customer's expectations. LIC has realized the need of the hour and implementing IT related changes in a big way.

LIC has set itself on the fast track of technology up gradation right from the year 1980. Communication to the staff and customers has become much faster and more frequent. Technologically, it is possible that a customer can deposit the premium at any of the networked franchise and the plans stand drawn to provide services to the policy holders from remote locations.

- **IT-Enhancing Efficiency**: FEAP (Front end application package) all the 2048 branches of LIC are equipped with in house developed programs covering all policy servicing aspects to" give prompt computerized services from introduction of proposal, completion, acceptance of renewal premium, revivals, loans etc. to final claim settlement.
- **IT-Developing Relationship** Bond: (Green Channel and Single Window) LIC is changing relentlessly and it

"changing face became evident to the customers with the introduction of the Green channel and single window modules. In fact these are not modules but are two concepts or geniuses. On single window person gets the cheque as an end result, therefore feels comfortable. On green channel a proposer gets the FPR and Policy Bond on the spot. Therefore, on his next visit to the office the customer looks for the some person or the single window, because he felt at ease during the last visit to office, Le., a memorable bond of relationship was developed. Hence the new initiatives taken by LIC should be adopted in true spirit.

- **IT - Connecting Employees/People**: A number of Mail Servers have been setup at Corporate and Zonal headquarters, to facilitate messaging solution. Net working of branches under a global master of policies is done to overcome physical barriers in servicing.

Zonal Training Centers are imparting training on new IT initiatives, being taken by Corporation with regard to new modules and new technologies being adopted, to update and enhance the technological knowledge of work force in LIC.

To be responsive to customer's needs / expectations, speed is the essence. The following customer contact services have been set up, by LIC enabling them to reach faster:

- LIC has commissioned Info Centers at Ahmedabad, Bangalore, Chennai, Delhi, Hyderabad, Kolkatta, Mumbai and Pune Divisional Offices. Customers desiring any information regarding their Life Insurance needs and about their policies can get the same by calling the Info center telephone number
- LIC has Interactive Voice Response system (IVRS) in 59 urban centers. This is menu driven service. Customers can get selected information regarding their policies by calling the prescribed telephone numbers.

- LIC has installed information Kiosks at 150 selected locations to give policy status reports and details about insurance plans, servicing aspects etc.
- LIC has tied up with some Banks and Service providers to offer an online premium collection facility to its customers in selected cities. It is intended to extend this facility to all the cities covered under network.

To maintain and optimize the relationships with customers and to develop customer retention through enhanced customer service, technology is said to be an effective tool in LIC. Apart from the Technological initiatives for the implementation of CRM strategy, e-service is a powerful tool in improving the quality of customer service. The benefits of e-service in LIC for the policy holders are:

LIC has geared its CRM strategy for education; it's customer for utilization of facilities provided by it such as:-

- facility to get the information about the policies through phone.
- Policy holder can pay his premium through internet
- Utilization of LIC Web site www.licindia.com to know the details about LIC and its mission.
- Premium payment can be made through ATMs of Corporation Bank and UTI Bank.
- Electronic clearing service can also be used for premium payment.
- Up gradation of technology should go hand in hand with training of staff in multifunction and all front end applications. For this purpose the training is imported to customer relations executives and customer relations groups.
- A customer folio number will be allotted to a policy holder having many policies. The aim is to improve the quality of the service and also do more need based selling of the policies.

- Popularizing the details of phone numbers of all centers, toll free telephone, and web site. address etc will help the policy holder to know more information regarding his policy.
- Taking advantage of mobile telephones implementation of "SMS Messaging Solutions" is also initiated.

Enhancing Data Base

Corporation is planning to go for data ware housing and data mining. With this tool, executives sitting in the chamber shall be able to drill down any information to minutest detail, with a click of mouse. Providing instant access and servicing to the policy holder under centralized data base management. This interactive system shall provide executives on easy access to decision models and data, which shall be helpful in decision making task, it combines data, models, software and user into an effective decision support and decision making system. What is required is careful implementation of modules / instructions after thorough discussions / deliberations. In technology the patience and faith in the systems, is of paramount importance.

Conclusions and Suggestions

LIC realized that enhancing customer value, delivering a higher level of service and enriching the brand all play a critical role in growing profitability and consistently pace the competition. The organization embraced customer relationship management concepts and technology during the part decade. LIC believes that keeping customer relationships strong and profitable in the future will require the right mix of innovative information technology, more effective business processors, better data management and new work-force initiations. LIC adopted the CRM philosophy at all levels and initiated necessary measures for providing better services to the policy holders. Computerization and networking of operating units is also taken up for better access. New methods like single windows. Green channel, customer service centers have received wide recognition and acceptance among users.

However, for LIC CRM could not meet the expected requirements due to skill gap_ lack of awareness among policy-holders, limited participation of the policy holder in marketing research and attitudinal problems at the front--end office. Introduction of on-line pass books or policy bonds with integrated data base can strengthen e-CRM. As the customers become more mobile, informed and demanding and competitors became more adept. LIC initiatives are not sufficient for the raising standard for CRM excellence. LIC has to deliver not only more sophisticated-sales and service capability, but also to deliver and manage these capabilities more quickly and cost effectively.

Policy holders' data enables the organization to build strong customer relationships and become, more customers-centric. The wealth of relevant customer data should be recognized and a central repository to manage the data with smart use of technology will lead to better customer relationships. Achieving the deep insights into customer needs, preferences, and behaviour is not doubt hard work. However, for a disciplined organization like. LIC at the collection, investigation and use of customer data from a strategic perspective stand has an excellent chance of generating superior customer loyalty and in the process, strong competitive advantage.

LIC has to implement its Knowledge Management Center program with adequate emphasis on communications, training, policies and procedures, knowledge proficiencies, incentives, a comprehensive measurement system and the creation of an organizational team to lead the knowledge management effort. This will provide employees with the tools and information needed to perform with increased efficiency. It also makes the employees more competitive and better suited to deliver value-based service to customers.

Today, customer relationship management requires different kinds of tools, many of them technology based. LIC has taken up all initiatives by the use of information technology for the better service and value to customers. When it comes to service to policy holders and relationship management, LIC is still ahead of the curve in terms of focus, culture and commitment. LIC, has been able to develop an approach that combines the latest technologies (i.e. internet, touch-screen kiosks, I√RS, single window, e-mail, green channel etc) with essential service to significantly enhance the corporation's ability to serve its, policy holders.

In order to enhance quality of services, LIC should encourage policy holders' participation in the CRM in a big way. CRM strategy sets the, agenda for what data is collected, how the data translated into information, customer intelligence and how that information is shared across the organization. The available customer information is to be strategically utilized and segmented to target the new customer prospects. Whenever new insurance needs have been discovered and new products have been developed LIC can expand its customer value both horizontally and vertically:

24

A Study on Banc Assurance Strategies

Dr. K. Subramanian

Insurance is the back borne of a countries risk management system. Insurance has assumed greater significance in recent times due to the increasing uncertainties. Insurance is a device by which losses suffered by a few are shared by many. Integration of the financial service industry in terms of banking, securities business and insurance is a growing worldwide phenomenon. The compound financial innovation in banking and insurance activities has evolved as a result of Banc Assurance.

Banc Assurance

One of the most significant advances in the financial services sector over the past couple of years has been the growth of Bancassurance – which, in simplest terms, means the distribution of insurance products through a bank's distribution channels. In other words, Banc assurance is a service which can fulfill both banking and insurance needs at the same time. Banc assurance as a concept first began in India with the opening up of the insurance industry to private sector participation in December 1999 which saw the entry of 20 new players - with 12 in the life insurance sector and 8 in the non-life sector. Banc assurance has also seen significant rise in other Asian markets. For example, banc assurance accounted for 24% of new life insurance sales by 'weighted' premium income in Singapore in 2002. This is a significant increase on the equivalent 2001 statistics of 15% and is as a result of growth in significant bank-centric banc assurance operations. The Universal Banking is evolving on these lines in India. Convergence has become the order of the day. It is the key stratagem for banks and insurance companies in India.

Even though the concept is simple to understand, it will come across lot of problems while implementation. Legislative differences, consumer behaviour, impact of history and culture, product complexity, employee work culture and many such other factors have contributed to significant differences in results across countries. For example, in France and Spain 60% to 80% of life insurance products are sold through bank branches compared to 10% in UK and USA.

Statement of The Problem

The insurance sector in India has come a full circle. Originally it was an open competitive market. Subsequently it was nationalized. It is back to liberalized market again. Entry of private insurance players in 2000- 2001has brought about alternate distribution channels to suit to the customer needs. Today, the interface between the customer and long drawn meetings with the insurance agent no longer identify the insurance company. Now the insurers are of the opinion that the day is not far when a customer will just to have a walk into a super market, a bank, a post office, an ATM, an internet or departmental store to pick up an insurance product virtually of the shelf. Tracing the development in the insurance sector reveals a 360 degree turn witnessed over a period almost 190 years. Banc assurance is one of the new concepts in India. Even though the system is good, however the problem in the implementation is inevitable.

Review of Literature

As it is a new concept being implemented in India, adequate studies have not been made. It is in the infancy stage. However an attempt was made by the researcher to collect information regarding banc assurance from the available sources.

Mukul K Gupta observes that "India has experienced a substantial growth in the life insurance business. The new business premium growth rate for the financial year 2004-05 over the previous financial year is 36%. This growth is primarily due to the aggressiveness witnessed in the private life insurance sector, which grew by 129% wherein banc assurance has simply outshined other alternate channels of distribution with a share of almost 25-30% of the premium income amongst the private players". With the dwindling down of rural branch networks in India, it is for sure that growth of banc assurance premium through rural insurance will not constitute much to the above growth statistics.

M. Shanmugam in his research paper presented in the International Seminar conducted by Cauvery College for Women. Trichy, on the topic entitled," **Recent trends in Insurance industry**" has pointed out that there should be better understanding between the banks and the insurance organisations in identifying the areas or potentials where the insurance and banking products are to be sold.

Dr. P. Palanivelu in his research paper presented in the International Seminar conducted by Cauvery College for Women. Trichy, on the topic entitled," **banc assurance, challenges and prospects in India** "has pointed out that banks and insurance companies has found banc assurance as an effective tool, attractive and synergistic option of offering a win to win situation.

Importance of the Study

With the opening up of the insurance sector and with so many players entering the Indian insurance industry, it is required by the insurance companies to come up with innovative products, create more consumer awareness about their products and offer them at a competitive price. New entrants in the insurance sector had no difficulty in matching their products with the customers' needs and offering them at a price acceptable to the customer. The study is important in the sense that it is a new concept in India. Our country is taking its race not only in the industrial field but also in the services sector. Hence an attempt was made by the researcher to analyse the scheme.

Objectives of the Study

(a) To assess the strength of Banc assurace in the competitive environment in terms of banking.

(b) To identify the untapped market opportunities of bank through righteous products with appropriate features to meet the needs of the various segments.

(c) To evaluate the role of Banc assurance in the context of threats of banking industry.

(d) To suggest certain ways and means for the betterment of Banc assurance model.

(e) To identify the righteous strategy for the effective promotion of Banc assurance model.

Hypothesis of the Study

1. Prevailing Competition in the area does not affect the implementation on the scheme.
2. No adequate steps were taken by the banks to offer attractive insurance products to the untapped areas.
3. The introduction of banc assurance scheme in no way affects the existing traditional banking operations.
4. The existing corporation agent customer model cannot make anymore developments.

5. Instead of following a common model, local needs of the clients should be considered.

Strength of Banc Assurace

According to a recent study, banc assurance is on the rise, particularly in emerging markets. Worldwide, insurers have been successfully leveraging banc assurance to gain a hold in markets with a limited variety of distribution channels.

Banc assurance, the provision of insurance services by banks, is an established and growing channel for insurance distribution. However it penetrates different markets in different ways. Europe has the highest banc assurance penetration rate. In Asia, however, banc assurance is gaining in popularity, particularly in China, where restrictions have been simplified. Success of the banc assurance is in a particular market is influenced by social and cultural factors, as well as regulatory considerations and product complexity, play a significant role in determining how.

The outlook for banc assurance remains positive. While development in individual markets will continue to depend heavily on each country's regulatory and business environment, banc assurers could profit from the tendency of governments to privatize health care and pension liabilities. New entrants have successfully employed banc assurance to compete with existing companies. Banc assurance will likely see further significant development in the coming years.

Vast Untapped Market

In a country of 1 billion people there is a huge potential market for life insurance products. In India the penetration of the insurance sector in the rural and semi-urban areas is low. There is a market of 900 million for life insurance and 200 million for householder's insurance policy. In addition to this the affluent section can be tapped for Overseas Med claim and Travel Insurance policies.

Huge Pool of Skilled Professionals

Whether it is banks or insurance companies there is no dearth of skilled professionals in India to carry out a successful banc assurance venture.

Weakness of Banc Assurance

However the followings are the shortcomings of the scheme.

Though it has aimed at mass market, banc assurance have begun to finely segment the market. As a result of this there was concentration on a fewer products and fewer areas.

The market has been becoming a tailor-made product for each segment. The aim to have a specific client segment has turned some banc assurers to shift away from using a standardized, single channel sales approach instead of adopting a multiple channel distribution strategy. If multi channels are used then results will be encouraging. Some banc assurers are also beginning to focus exclusively on distribution.

In some markets, face-to-face contact is preferred, which tends to favour banc assurance development. This naturally makes the road for favour to some segments.

Banks have started using direct marketing and Internet banking as tools to distribute insurance products. New and emerging channels are becoming increasingly competitive, due to the tangible cost benefits embedded in product pricing.

Lack of Networking Among Bank Branches

In spite of growing emphasis on total branch mechanization (TBM) and full computerization of bank branches, the rural and semi-urban banks have still to see information technology as an enabler. Complete integration of branch network involves huge investments for creating IT and communication infrastructure.

Low Savings Rate

Though we have a huge market for insurance policies, the middle class who constitutes the bulk of this market is today burdened under inflationary pressures. The secret lies in inculcating savings habit but considering the amount of surplus funds available with the middle class for investing in future security, the ability to save is very nominal.

Challenges

Recent developments are expected to challenge traditional banc assurers in the following ways:

The shift away from manufacturing to pure distribution requires banks to have better agreement with regard to the incentives of different suppliers.

Increasing sales of non-life products, will increase the risk involvement to the banker. The costs of servicing the policies have been increasing in the recent times.

Frequent non-life insurance claims will be a disturbance to the bankers for which they must be prepared with machine power as well man manpower.

Success in banc assurance venture requires a change in mindset. Though we have a large talent pool, the inability to sell complex insurance products on the part of bank professionals and their reluctance to learn has been a serious problem.

Non-response from the target groups can also pose a challenge as it happened in the USA in 1980s.

Advantages to Banks

- Productivity of the employees increases.
- By providing customers with both the services under one roof, they can improve overall customer satisfaction and there by customer retention level can be increased.
- Increase in return on assets by building fee income through the sale of insurance products.
- Can leverage on face-to-face contacts and awareness about the financial conditions of customers to sell insurance products.
- Banks can cross sell insurance products E.g.: Term insurance products with loans.

Advantages to Insurers

Insurers can exploit the banks' wide network of branches for distribution of products. The penetration of banks' branches into the rural areas can be utilized to sell products in those areas.

Customer database like customers' financial standing, spending habits, investment and purchase capability can be used to customize products and sell accordingly. Since banks have already established relationship with customers, conversion ratio of leads to sales is likely to be high. Further service aspect can also be tackled easily.

Advantages to Consumers

- Comprehensive financial advisory services under one roof. i.e., insurance services along with other financial services such as banking, mutual funds, personal loans etc.
- Enhanced convenience on the part of the insured.
- Easy access for claims, as banks is a regular go.
- Innovative and better product ranges.

Regulatory Framework of RBI

RBI guideline for banks entering into insurance sector provides three options for banks. They are: Joint ventures will be allowed for financially strong banks wishing to undertake insurance business with risk participation;

For banks which are not eligible for this joint-venture option, an investment option of up to 10% of the net worth of the bank or Rs.50 crores, whichever is lower, is available;

Finally, any commercial bank will be allowed to undertake insurance business as agent of insurance companies. This will be on a fee basis with no-risk participation.

The Insurance Regulatory and Development Authority (IRDA) guidelines for the banc assurance are:

- Each bank that sells insurance must have a chief insurance executive to handle all the insurance activities.

- All the people involved in selling should under-go mandatory training at an institute accredited by IRDA and pass the examination conducted by the authority.
- Commercial banks, including cooperative banks and regional rural banks, may become corporate agents for one insurance company.
- Banks cannot become insurance brokers.

Steps to be Taken to Make it a Success

The study provides a roadmap for designing winning convergence strategies through seven steps:

1. Complete a self-diagnosis and choose target regions.
2. Understand customer needs and dissatisfactions by segment.
3. Develop innovative products and services .
4. Improve product and distribution economics.
5. Determine an appropriate branding strategy.
6. Select the strategy to deliver the value proposition.
7. Quantify goals and incentives.

Models of Banc Assurance

Globally we have 4 kinds of banc assurance business models:

They are listed below

- Distribution alliance between the insurance company and the bank .
- Joint venture between the two.
- Merger between bank and insurer
- Bank builds or buys own insurance products

Most of the banc assurance operations in India fall into the first model, which in a way is quite a prudent decision. The Indian banc assurance scene as of now looks as promising area for expansion.

As banks are quite risk averse, they avoid going for any long term commitment. This is true in case of any radical changes in the minds of the public. The present regulatory framework prescribes that, one bank can tie-up with only one life and one non-life insurer, while insurers have the choice to tie-up with any number of banks. However there are many joint ventures between the bank and insurer such as SBI Life and ICICI Prudential.

Methodology

The data has been collected from both primary and secondary sources. More information was collected from secondary sources, web sites, research papers presented in the national seminar and international seminar on the topic of insurance.

Limitations of the Study

The study was conducted in a narrow sense due to the time constraints; the scheme is in the promotion stage only. Exhaustive list of clients are not available. Few banks have not at all opted this scheme. The private players are interested to implement the scheme. Information from few banks alone was collected and the inferences were drawn accordingly.

Analysis about the Scheme

Most of the public sector banks are not much concentrating on this new scheme. They concentrate on the regular business. Many private banks have been showing their interest to venture this scheme. Among the products on promotion health insurance has been very popular. This is due to the tie up arrangements with the hospitals in Tirunelveli. Some of the commercial banks show much interest in marketing their insurance schemes to their existing clients. One of the strategies adopted by the commercial bank is popularizing in the income tax benefits available to the clients with regard to health insurance. Most of the banks felt that, there is competition in marketing the insurance products among the clients. The exemption is motor vehicle insurance, which is being monitored by transport authorities.

Most of the clients are of the view that, an insurance product is available only with an insurance company. Of course this may be true with regard to life insurance. In order to avoid competition, suitable guide lines may be given in the inter-institutional meetings. Marketing of these products may be made popular by spending huge amount on product promotion during initial stages. Banks do not give importance for the amount of commission, but they give importance for client services. The present system of training is not adequate for the staff members of the commercial banks. Certain products are popular in certain segments and not all products promoted by the insurance companies. Convincing attitude of the insurance agents get business for them. During the introductory stages personal contact with customers will solve certain problems.

Results

(1) More than 80% of the respondents (8) have expressed that the prevailing competitions in the bank operations, implementation of ATM facilities offered by many banks affects the implementation of this scheme. Hence the null hypothesis is not proved. Therefore, the alternative hypothesis is accepted. That is, competition affects the operations of banc assurance.

(2) 70% of the respondent (7) bankers who have expressed that the authorities of commercial banks have taken steps to popularize the products even in small villages. Hence, null hypothesis is rejected. Therefore, it is concluded that, adequate steps were taken for canvassing new business in untapped areas.

(3) Around 90% of the bankers (9) have expressed that, due to shortage of man power, there has been lot of problems in the implementation of the scheme. Hence the null hypothesis framed, that is, the introduction of banc

assurance scheme in no way affects the existing traditional banking operations, is rejected. So, the alternate hypothesis is accepted.

(4) For the hypothesis, the existing corporation agent customer model cannot make anymore developments, around 70% of the respondent bankers (7) are of the opinion that, the agents are able to convince, explain and clarify regarding the features of an insurance product. So the null hypothesis is rejected. Therefore, it is concluded that, the present agent model is also working good.

(5) For the hypothesis, instead of following a common model, local needs of the clients should be considered, most of the respondent bankers have expressed that, instead of a common models framed by the top level authorities, by decentralization process, a suitable model which suits to the local requirements should be implemented. Hence the hypothesis framed is accepted.

Suggestions for the Effective Promotion

In spite of growing emphasis on total branch mechanization (TBM) and full computerization of bank branches, the rural and semi-urban banks have still to see information technology as an enabler. Complete integration of branch network involves huge investments for creating IT and communication infrastructure.

More and more joint ventures should be arranged between the insures and commercial banks. The human force in the banks should set their minds towards the new concept. Net working among bank branches should be increased. More training should be provided to the staff members of the commercial banks.

The existing groups in the village should be considered for group coverage of insurance, readily available groups will be existing customers of the bank, existing customers of the insurance company, existing employees of the institutions and other occupational groups.

Social Relevance of the Study

The study was conducted on a new concept, banc assurance. It gives multiple benefits to both the insurer and the bank. In the rural areas, where it is difficult to market an insurance product can be marketed by the bank manager who knows the local requirements of the rural people. As regular banking operations and insurance operations are performed under one roof, the cost of operations will come down drastically and as a result, more services can be provided. There is saving in advertisement cost also for both organisations. Multiple channel can be used for marketing the insurance products which will be really beneficial to the banks,, insurer and insured.

Conclusion

With huge untapped market and unexplored areas, insurance sector is likely to do lot of activity. Banc assurance, the emerging distribution channel for the insurers, will have a large impact on Indian financial services industry. Traditional methods of distributing financial services would be challenged and innovative. Banks will bring in customer database, leverage their name recognition and reputation at both local and regional levels, make use of the personal contact with their clients. This is not possible for the new entrant as they are new to the field. In customer point of view, a bundle of products would be available to him. More customized products would come into existence and that too all within hands reach with limited pain from the customer side. Finally Success of the banc assurance would mostly depend on how well insurers and banks understand each other's businesses and their capacity to gain the opportunities available.

References

(1) "Banc assurance: Challenges and prospects in India" Research paper of Dr. Palanivelu,.Karpagam Arts and Science college, Coimbatore.

(2) **"Recent trends in Insurance industry"** Research paper of M. Shanmugam, Salem.

(3) **"Micro Banc assurance Models for India"** by **Dr. S. Ganesan** Director & Dean, Park School of Business, Chennai **& Dr. S. Jayaprakash,** Consultant, i-flex solutions limited, Bangalore **Chennai.**

(4) Gupta K Mukul (2006), Banc assurance: Taking the lead, The Financial Express dated 1st Jan 2006.

25

Health Insurance - Wider Coverage Gains Urgency

Dr. G. Shanthi

Introduction

The greatest resource India has is its human re-source and with it come the health issues. Size is a corollary for 'potential'. Thus India obviously has a huge market for health care and health insurance is an integral part of it. The concept of medical insurance started catching up in India only during the mid 1980s. Initially, only the basic version of hospitalisation cover was offered. With the opening up of the industry and the resultant compe-tition, more innovative products have been introduced in the market. India spends about 6.5 to 7 per cent of its GDP on healthcare of which 1.3 percentage point is in the government sector (this accounts for 22 per cent of overall spending) and 4.7 percentage point in the private sector (78 per cent of overall spending). However, estimates show that government spending on healthcare has come down to 0.9 per cent in the last few years.

The low level of government spending on healthcare limits the extent and effectiveness of the coverage it can provide. The poor coverage has led to a large, private out-of-pocket spending on health-care. In fact, over 60 per cent of the Rs.86,000 crore spent on healthcare delivery in India is private out-of-pocket spendingsourced from either dissaving or borrowing. It is reported that healthcare expenses on major diseases is one of the causes of indebtedness in certain sections of India's urban and rural society.

Life and Non-life Covers

Insurance lines can be broadly classified into two -life and non-life. But health insurance occupies a peculiar position. Regulations apart, in a way, it fits into both life and non-life sectors as it is about humans. In the evolving scenario both life and non-life insurers are covering health risks. However the basic cover of hospi-talisation on indemnity basis is covered only by non-life insurers. The basic differences are that in case of non-life insurers it can be on indemnity basis that is, payment of actual expenses (subject to the limit of sum insured), whether cashless or reimbursement. In the case of life insurers these are agreed value policies, meaning that the pre-agreed sum will be paid to the insured person on the happening of the covered illness / conditions. Ex-penses need not be established.

The other difference is that non-life policies are short-term policies they are mostly for a year. However some non-life insurers issue two year policies also. But the products of life insurers are long term in nature. They may be for 10 years or 20 years. It is noteworthy that there is an emerging school of thought that health insurers have to be separately categorised as the third stream. Section 3 (2AA) of Insurance Act 1938 provides for special treatment for new insurance companies who opt to operate exclusively in health insurance. The trend setter in this line is Star Health and Allied Insurance Co. Ltd., which is the first stand alone health insurer in India. Now more companies such as Apollo DKV are coming forward to operate in this area.

Insurance is the business of collecting from many and paying a few should they need medical help. Thus insurance will be a win to win situation and benefit all stakeholders, namely insured, in-surer and even the regulator if the habit of buying insurance spreads.

Growing Awareness

With the emergence of new life styles and social order, awareness of health is growing at a faster pace, so also are the new types of health conditions, including occupation related ones. Developments in the health care sector have introduced sophistication though at a higher cost. Thus there are various reasons for health insurance to emerge as a fast growing segment of non -life insurance. These include :

- Increasing awareness among the public about medical insurance.
- Vast number of 'uncovered' population for health risk.
- Increasing cost of health care.
- Newer developments in the medical sphere.
- Corporatisation of health care providers.

Public expenditure on health care in India is now only 0.9 per cent of GDP. Though as a percentage this seems a fraction,

Table - 1

Central Outlay on Healthcare (Rupees in Crore)

Year	*Health*	*Family Welfare*	*Total*
2005-06	2908	6424	9332
2006-07	2305	9000	11305
2007-08	5416	12866	18282

Source : Annual Reports of Ministry of Health and Family Welfare, Government of India.

in actual terms a huge amount is allocated for health and family welfare in the annual budgets. Table 1 gives an idea of the amounts spent by the Central government towards healthcare in recent years.

In spite of the fact that the public spending is ever increasing, about 80 per cent of health costs is still paid by patients out of their pockets. For many, even minor illnesses can cause big financial setbacks, and hospitalisation is out of the question. The self-insured population in India is only about 3 per cent of the total. The basic reason is the claim of more basic needs such as food and shelter on people's incomes apart from the wrong confidence that they will not fall ill. With about 22 per cent of the population living below the poverty line, the priority for many lies with the basic needs. Thus, health insurance is a luxury for them.

Generally, health insurance plans take three forms.

State funded, employer funded and self funded. State funded insurance schemes are tailor made schemes (such as Rajiv Aarogyasri Scheme of Andhra Pradesh). The beneficiaries are mainly the poor. Other schemes such as the Employee State Insurance are implemented by the government with contributions from other stakeholders. The next form is from the employers. Nowadays, health insurance cover is an essential part of the package offered to employees.

Pattern of Health Spend

The pattern of spending towards health care, according to the World Bank's estimate, is shown in the Table-2.

It is clear that from Table 2, 75 per cent of the total healthcare expenditure is met from own funds. This offers a large scope for health insurance business. Moreover, the increase in average health care costs has outpaced the increase in average earnings. This results in either increased level of debt or erosion of savings or inadequate level of healthcare, resulting in death or reduced earning capacity. The prevalence

Table-2

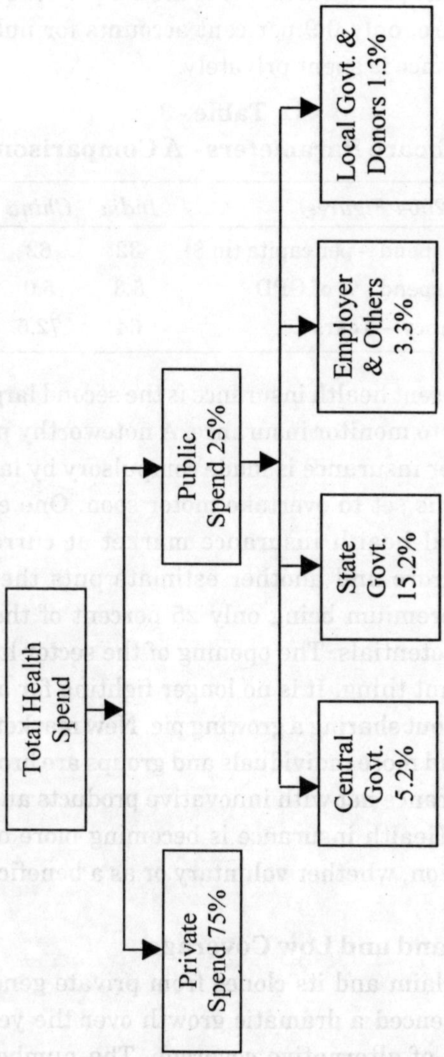
Total Health Spend
Private Spend 75%
Public Spend 25%
Central Govt. 5.2%
State Govt. 15.2%
Employer & Others 3.3%
Local Govt. & Donors 1.3%

of this trend has a larger impact on the social fabric. This all the more necessitates spread of the health insurance cover.

Table 3, also proves that health insurance business in India has vast potential as out of the 5.3 per cent of GDP spent on healthcare, only 0.9 per cent accounts for public spending and the balance is spent privately.

Table - 3

Healthcare Parameters – A Comparison (2004)

(2004 Figures)	*India*	*China*	*UK*	*USA*
Healthcare spend – per capita (in $)	32	62	3036	5365
Healthcare spend - % of GPD	5.3	5.0	8.4	13.2
Life expectancy – Years	64	72.5	78.3	77.4

At present health insurance is the second largest portfolio, second only to monitor insurance. A noteworthy point is that a part of motor insurance is made compulsory by law. In spite of this, health is set to overtake motor soon. One estimate puts the potential health insurance market at current levels at Rs.15,000 crore and another estimate puts the asset based insurance premium being only 25 percent of the real health insurance potentials. The opening of the sector has facilitated one important thing. It is no longer fighting for a share of the existing pie but sharing a growing pie. New markets are created and more and more individuals and groups are brought into the health insurance net with innovative products and by creating a feltneed. Health insurance is becoming more of a necessity than an option, whether voluntary or as a beneficiary.

Huge Demand and Low Coverage

Mediclaim and its clones from private general insurers have experienced a dramatic growth over the years, perhaps due to lack of alternative coverage. The number of persons covered under Mediclaim and other health insurance products has grown from 6.9 lakh in 1991-92 to 3.5 million in 1998-99 and

Table 4
Health Insurance Performance

Year	*Lives Covered (Million)*	*Gross Premium*	*Incurred Claims*	*Claims Ratio (%)*
		(Rs. Million)		
1995-1996	1.7	1,292	920	71.21
1996-1997	2.6	1,648	1,096	66.50
1997-1998	2.8	2,157	1,664	77.14
1998-1999	3.5	2,717	2,312	85.09
1999-2000	4.9	3,804	3,870	101.74
2000-2001	5.6	5,190	4,756	91.64
2001-2002	8.4	7,740	7,022	90.73
2002-2003	9.5	10,438	9,193	88.08
2003-2004	10.3	12,298	11,643	94.68
2004-2005	13.4	16,695	N.A.	N.A.
2005-2006	17.0	22,576	N.A.	N.A.

Source : IRDA and GIPSA (General Insurance Public Sector Association).

around 17 million in 2005-06. Translating this in terms of penetration, it was 0.084 per cent in 1990-91, 0.49 per cent in 1999-00 and 1.536 per cent in 2005-06. This indicates a low level of health insurance penetration besides a huge latent demand. The demand is being fuelled by increasing episodes of hospitalisation due to rise in lifestyle diseases and accidents, escalating cost of hospitalisation episodes, and the absence of any form of public health security net.

Health insurance has not been a profitable business segment for the general insurers. As a result, its dramatic growth has almost entirely been demand driven. The group health insurance segment, though a high loss grosser, has been used by insurers as a 'door opener' to the profitable corporate insurance business. Claims paid ratio is not an appropriate indicator of the profitability of Mediclaim. In fact, the ratio merely denotes the medical loss ratio without taking into account other allocable expenses on the policy such as acquisition costs and management expenses.

Although, from the point of view of medical loss ratios, the performance of Mediclaim appears satisfactory for the entire period under reference, the reality is somewhat different. Mediclaim has been profitable during the years when medical loss ratios were within 75 per cent, that is, up to 1996-97. Since then it has been loss making.

It is estimated that around 15 per cent of the population is covered under some form of pre-payment on healthcare, which includes employees and beneficiaries covered under ESIS, CGHS, Armed Forces, Central Police organisations, Railways, employer self-funded schemes, public sector undertakings and covered pensions under health insurance.

The Indian insurance industry, and the general insurance segment in particular, covers around 17 million persons under health insurance. Mediclaim, a medical expenses reimbursement policy of 1986 vintage, is the core product of general insurance. It is an indemnity based hospitalisation policy plagued with stringent pre-existence conditions exclusions and hence cannot be considered to provide comprehensive coverage. Health insurance coverage from life insurers in the form of health riders to life policies has had limited policyholder appeal.

Unprofitable Mediclaim

A main reason for Mediclaim becoming unprofitable after 1998-99 has been the major restructuring it underwent by removal of benefit sub-limits, making it instead a single benefit policy. This changeover encouraged over utilisation of policy benefits by healthcare providers and the policyholders. The claims ratio (medical loss ratio) peaked at 101.74 percent in 1999-2000. Since then it has moved in the range of 90 to 95 per cent.

Despite the IRDA's (Insurance Regulatory and Development Authority) non-statutory stipulations, private sector general insurance companies have been reluctant players in the health insurance market. Their performance in terms of developing and marketing of health insurance products has been dismal. Most of these players have cloned the Mediclaim policy and have restricted their health insurance spread primarily to meet IRDA provisions on health insurance. Though new products like hospital cash and critical illness policies have been introduced, these have had no significant impact in the market due of lack of aggressive marketing and 'skimming' by the private insurers.

During 2004-05 and 2005-06, health insurance premium grew by 35 per cent -26 per cent growth for public sector general insurers and 77 per cent growth for private sector general insurers. In terms of market share, the public sector share declined from 82 per cent to 76 per cent during 2004-05 and 2005-06, while that of the private sector increased from 18 per cent to 24 per cent. Companywise growth rates of health insurance premium were higher among private sector general insurers mainly due to a lower premium base. The highest growth rate during 2004-06 was achieved by ICICI Lombard at 131 per cent followed by IFFCO-Tokio at 84 per cent and Royal Sundaram Alliance at 68 per cent. Among public sector general insurers the highest growth in premium was attained by New India Assurance Company at 40 per cent followed by Oriental Insurance.

Individual and Group Health Insurance

The absence of reliable coverage and claims data has been a bane of health insurance. Hence, to facilitate a transparent picture of health insurance penetration, the IRDA should publish health insurance information for each type of policy to enable a meaningful analysis that will assist in an orderly development of the market. Health insurance currently is segmented into individual and group. The individual segment consists of individuals and households whereas the group segment consists mainly of employer groups. The share of individual Mediclaim in terms of premium is around 60 per cent. Individual health insurance is a large market segment which can be profitable provided insurers take measured steps to charge adequate premiums and manage anti-selection and moral hazard (both policyholder and healthcare provider).

The group health insurance is mainly used by most insurers as an entry route into corporate insurance portfolio. However, experience has shown that group health insurance business is mostly a losing proposition because corporate clients have squeezed out margins by seeking richer benefits (family floaters) and offering lower premiums (on account of discounts). This has led to spiraling claims outgo, which shows no signs of abating. The use of group health insurance as an accommodation cover is set to change on detariffing of the insurance market.

Role and function of Third Party Administrators (TPAs)

Introduction of Third Party Administrators (TPAs) to service health insurance policyholders was a significant step taken by the IRDA in 2001-02. The crucial reason for bringing in the TPAs was to provide cashless hospitalisation to Mediclaim policyholders.

A TPA is a service organisation under contract from an insurance company to administer its health insurance policies. It performs the role of a services integrator-a triage between the insurer, the insured / policyholder and the healthcare provider / hospital / nursing home and the like. Its range of services includes policyholder enrolment and benefits management, claims management, healthcare provider network management, medical management and customer relationship management. It is estimated that only around 70 per cent of the policyholders have been brought under TPA servicing.

The public sector general insurers, by virtue of their large health insurance market share, are the main users of TPA services. However, their experience with the TPAs has not been particularly encouraging. There have been innumerable complaints from policyholders about delay in enrolment and issuance of identity cards. Policyholders have also faced harassment from hospitals because of non-acceptance of pre-authorisations for hospitalisation issued by the TPAs. Healthcare providers on the other hand have complained against delays in claim settlements.

TPAs - an Evaluation

Based on policyholder and healthcare provider feedback, and borne out of its own experience, one of the public sector insurance companies recently undertook an evaluation of the functioning of its TPAs. It was found that claims outgo had not declined, instead it had spiraled. There was also a feeling that services to policyholders and claims settlement had not improved. Claims settlements had faced inordinate delays, despite insurers having provided 'claims float' to the TPAs. In an audit of the 'claims float account' by the insurer of some of the TPAs under it, discrepancies were found in the claims' settled and the amounts drawn from the claims float account. Further, TPAs had also been reluctant to submit claims data to the insurers, resulting in denial of post claims settlement verification by the insurers. Moreover, their failure to furnish claims data to insurers had resulted ill preventing them from loading premiums on accounts with high claims ratio.

Dissatisfied with their functioning and policyholder complaints, one of the private sector general insurers has internalized the functions of a TPA, while another has acquired an existing TPA to exclusively service its own policyholders. It is expected that some more private sector general insurers may follow suit. It is time the TPAs took corrective action to justify their role as healthcare facilitator failing which their survival may be at stake. They need to define service standards for every stage of interface with policyholders, be it enrolment, enquiry or hospitalisation. Customer satisfaction surveys need to be carried out at regular intervals to allow feedback on service deficiencies.

A weak link in the TPA chain has been the healthcare provider. The Indian healthcare sector is unregulated and lacks any widespread form of accreditation, clinical protocols and guidelines, quality benchmarks, predictability and uniformity of hospital charges. Besides, healthcare providers have adopted an adversarial posture towards TPAs, whom they perceive as harbingers of accountability a fear not misplaced, since healthcare providers have long been accustomed to operating in an unfettered environment.

There are also instances of cartelization by health providers to resist price negotiation. This form of collective bargaining, in the absence of health sector regulations, spells disaster for the efforts of TPAs and insurers to control claim costs and provider fraud. The insurance industry through TPAs has experienced pricepadding or differential pricing against insured patients, thus artificially raising health insurance claims ratio and proving detrimental to sustainable growth of the market. TPAs need to work hard to gain the confidence of healthcare providers and to bring them into the fold of health insurance, ideally as risk sharers, so that claims outgo for insurers is reduced. This is critical since insurers cannot be expected to sustain a perennially loss making health insurance portfolio.

Accreditation of Hospitals

Accreditation of health providers is a critical requirement for enabling quality benchmarking of services and healthcare facilities, a necessary step towards uniformity of provider charges. The services and facilities provided at the diagnostic centres, nursing homes, and hospitals need to be standardized. The introduction of a rating mechanism that is mandatory for participation in insurance schemes can fulfill this need. The system of grading is necessary to differentiate healthcare organisations based on their ability to deliver quality patient care. The organisations graded higher are expected to have better facilities, superior quality levels and consistency in service delivery. All efforts in the last few years to promote a voluntary health provider accreditation agency have not borne fruit. The health sector is divided over the issue. A system of rating of health providers has been introduced by credit rating agencies, ICRA and CRISIL.

These agencies have not met with much success since only a few tertiary level hospitals have got themselves rated, mainly to source domestic and foreign funding. The drawback with the rating process is that it is voluntary, expensive and apparently does not add value to health providers in the absence of a general apathy towards quality. The accreditation process needs to percolate down to at least the secondary level of care for it to make any significant impact on the quality of health delivery. In a positive development, the Quality Council of India (QCI) has recently laid down guidelines for accreditation of hos-pitals and healthcare providers. It has also constituted a

National Accreditation Board for Hospitals and Healthcare Providers (NABH). Unfortunately, the requirement for accreditation has not been mandatory, which in effect dilutes its purpose. Despite opening up of the insurance sector, no global health insurance company has shown interest in entering the Indian market.

Entry of global players

The presence of niche global players is necessary to deepen the market by bringing in contemporary practices relating to underwriting, product development, claims management and healthcare provider contracting. The IRDA appointed a committee in late 2004 to examine regulatory issues that have discouraged registration of stand alone health insurance companies. The committee recommended specific measures to encourage entry of stand-alone companies, which include

(i) Reduction of minimum capital requirement to Rs. 50 crore.

(ii) In-crease in FOI cap for stand-alone health insurers to at least 50 per cent.

(iii) Separate licensing for stand-alone health insurers.

(iv) Introduction of risk based capital norm and the like.

The recommendations, if accepted and legislated by the government, are expected to pave the way for the entry of niche global health insurers in the Indian insurance space. In the interregnum, one stand-alone health insurance company commenced operations in April-May 2006, while Apollo Hospitals Group has announced its tie-up with DKV, a Germany based health insurer for a possible venture in the next couple of months.

Innovative Products

With increased competition, the mantra will be 'innovate or evaporate' and 'perform or perish'. Already newer concepts are being introduced in the market, a great journey from the times of the basic hospitalisation cover. Critical illness cover, hospital cash, family floater, special policies for diabetics, HIV patients and even cashless settlements made directly to the treating hospitals are only a small beginning. The Indian market will take cue from its western counterparts and will soon introduce more innovative products such as health saving accounts, health annuities, managed health care including health maintenance organisations (HMO), preferred provider organisations (PPO) and point-of-service (POS) plans. In future, the focus of insurers will be on 'holistic health' rather than 'financing for health'.

They will strive for and the market will expect reasonable and adequate cover at optimum premium through innovative products. With increased activities and innovative plans, the roles of the regulator and the Government will only go up. It is the primary role of the regulator to ensure that policyholders get what they were promised at a fair price. After all, insurance remains only a promise unless the unfortunate event occurs. The Government will have to play a more facilitating role with the required legislations and administrative mechanisms. For example, the concept of health savings accounts will be successful only if there is a suitable legislation for tax and other benefits.

Post liberalisation, both general and life insurers have introduced critical illness (CI) covers. CI insurance is a health benefit intended to provide policyholders with a lump sum payment upon diagnosis of anyone of the 'covered' critical or life threatening illnesses. Commonly covered critical illnesses are heart attack, stroke, cancer and kidney failure. The number of critical illnesses covered varies from insurer to insurer, ranging from a basic four to over a dozen.

CI covers by life insurers are in the form of CI riders to life policies, while those by general insurers are in the form of stand-alone critical illness or dreaded disease policies. These covers have met with cautious response from consumers. There is also a wide difference in definitions of critical illnesses from insurer to insurer. From policyholders' protection point of view, it is essential that the IRDA undertakes standardisation of medical definitions across all critical illness products from different companies.

Hospital cash plan is another new product that has been introduced in the insurance market. Hospital Cash is a cover that provides a daily allowance to the policyholder during the days he spends as an in-patient in a hospital. The daily allowance is payable as a benefit amount, for which no proof of expenses needs be shown to the insurer. The amount is normally meant to be utilised by the policyholder in meeting out-of-pocket expenses incurred during the days of hospitalisation, which are not payable under most hospitalisation policies.

The future will also see the regulator regulating not only the health insurers but also health service providers such as hospitals, doctors and diagnostic laboratories. However, the relationship between quality and cost has no rational basis and there is a tendency to overcharge, particularly if insurance cover is available.

Scope for New Products

Transforming and evolving societies demand different security instruments and insurers have risen successfully to the challenge by offering evernew products. Development of managed care in the U.S. is an example of evolution of products when increasing claims made it difficult for employers to keep up with employee healthcare benefits. India's healthcare system has changed substantially over the last decade and continues to evolve. Medical cost inflation and changing medical technology require the development of strategies that make healthcare accessible and affordable to larger sections of the society. There is a crying need for products that address the requirements of old age healthcare, long term care, disability income, mental care and hospital plans.

Old Age Healthcare

Old age healthcare is a critical need of the society, more so in the absence of a comprehensive social security regime.

Insurers restrict entry of new policyholders at an older age to avoid anti-selection against them. Techniques need to be developed to counter anti-selection while providing this cover. Bundling pension products with health insurance riders can provide old age financial and healthcare security. This needs to be tested through a pilot. Defined contribution health plan dovetailed with a defined contribution pension plan may well be an option.

Long-term care insurance plans cover physical or mental incapacity that prohibits the insured's activities of daily living. Though age lessens an individual's ability to fully take care of oneself, most elderly persons require no assistance with their activities of daily living, whereas there are instances of younger persons requiring assistance. LTC insurance not only has relevance to the rapidly ageing population but it also has a bearing on middle age and younger persons experiencing similar exposures due to accidents or medical conditions such as critical illnesses and debilitating diseases.

Disability Income Products

Disability income insurance seeks to provide income benefit to the insured where physical or mental incapacity prevents him/her from being able to work. A growing number of individuals, at least in urban India, are concerned about the possibility of incurring high medical expenses and, therefore, are seeking to maintain medical expense insurance coverage's. In fact, financial consequences of a disability can be more debilitating for the family of the patient than his death itself. Similarly, large proportions of the wage earning population are purchasing group and life insurance to relieve or mitigate their dependents of financial hardships following upon their (wage-earner's) possible death.

However, as there is no disability income product in the market, the wage-earners population is not able to cover the possibility of losing their income due to disability caused by accident or disease. The need for disability income insurance and LTC is increasing per se, more so due to declining family support as a result of disintegration of the 'extended family' and economic development. The institution of joint family, which provided social security for centuries to Indian families, is fast withering away. Tragically, it is not being replaced rapidly enough with a 'social security net' sufficiently wide to take in its fold all those who are the worst affected.

Changes in policy design

The health insurance market in India has witnessed significant qualitative changes since insurance liberalisation. Apart from introduction of new products, policy designing and rationalisation has made rapid strides to catch up with contemporary international practices. With the rise in tertiary level medical costs due to medical inflation and newer technologies, the maximum benefit limit of Rs. 3 lakh provided by Mediclaim was insufficient. A few private insurers took the lead to increase the benefit limit up to Rs. 10 lakh. Now, it is possible to get health insurance beyond the Rs. 10 lakh benefit limit.

The pre-existing conditions provision was stringent in addition to being a life-time exclusion. These provisions have now been relaxed to a three or four year exclusion period. Some policies now reimburse expenses related to daycare procedures taken at hospitals which due to advancements in medical technology, do not require hospitalisation. The procedures relate to laparoscopic surgeries, cataract operations and the like.

Health insurance underwriting now includes pre-enrolment health checks for persons above 45 years of age to trace pre-existing conditions. This step also aims to restrict adverse selection by a percentage of policyholders who purchase health insurance with a pre-determined purpose to make a claim. It should be understood that insurance covers contingent liability and not a known certainty. A large segment of pre-determined claim seekers, if not weeded out though underwriting controls, pose the possibility of uncontrolled high claims resulting in increased premiums for other policyholders.

Health insurance has been a loss making proposition for Indian insurance companies. Stung by continued losses since 1999-2000, the four public sector general insurance companies have recently initiated steps to rationalize their health insurance policies. Some of these changes include putting limits on hospital room rent, clearer definitions of exclusions and pre-existing diseases, increasing the minimum benefit limit to Rs.50,000, loading premiums for higher age-groups and stricter under-writing for persons above 55 years. All these will help longterm sustain ability of health insurance. These will also pave the way for product innovation and newer coverages that have just not happened.

Conclusion

Health issues are acquiring urgency due to factors like medical inflation, increasing life expectancy, increasing load of lifestyle diseases and uncertainties in individual employability and earnings. Paradoxically, living long and dying young are both creating new tensions in the society. With virtual absence of a public health security system and a high proportion of national health spending being met by households, the need for a widespread health insurance system is urgent and pressing. Each set of players in the game needs to play his part honestly. Vigorous and robust development of the health insurance sector requires resolute actions taken by all players in healthcare financing - the regulators, the insurers and the healthcare providers. Some such actions are :

- Encourage entry of stand-alone health insurers to deepen the market and increase underwriting knowledge and capacity.
- Encourage hospital promoted health plans which combine healthcare financing and delivery.

- Develop specific regulations for such 'managed care entities' relating to minimum capital requirements and policyholder/member protection, among others.
- Disseminate greater information relating to premiums, penetration, claims, disease profile and regional variations in healthcare costs.
- Support bolder initiatives by insurers in developing newer products to cater to the changing needs of the society. These may include policies covering disability income, major organ transplant, mental disease and old age health. Similarly, expenses incurred on infertility treatment, on organ donor in case of organ transplants also need to be covered. Medical expenses arising out of AIDS is an exclusion at present in all health insurance policies, unlike in western societies.

Incessant high claims outgo has been a worrying issue with the insurers. Unfortunately, no concerted steps have been taken by them to introduce claims management techniques. Despite healthcare provider resistance, insurers need to stress adoption of DRG based contracting with providers to contain spiraling claims costs. Insurers also need to impress upon the TPAs to effectively implement claims costs management techniques such as pre-admission testing, pre-authorisation prior to admission and utilisation and continued stay reviews. In addition to the supply side changes being envisaged, it is of equal importance to spread awareness about the need to plan for healthcare financing exigencies. Let not health insurance be promoted as a tax-planning instrument. Further, let not the paradigm any more hold true that a majority of persons become aware of the need and availability of health insurance only after someone in the family or friends underwent financial hardship due to an episode of expensive hospitalisation.

26

CRM Perspective in Insurance Sector

I. Narsis

Insurance is a written contract or certificate of insurance that provides protection against future loss. Following a promise of reimbursement in the case of loss sum assured is paid to people or companies (insured) so concerned about hazards that they have made prepayments (premiums) to an insurance company (insurer). Insurance in India started without any regulation in the Nineteenth Century. It was a typical story of a colonial era: a few British insurance companies were dominating the market and serving mostly large urban centers. After independence, it took a dramatic turn (Annexure-I). Insurance was nationalized.

Life Insurers i.e. Life Insurance Corporation of India (LIC) and General Insurers i.e. General Insurance Corporation of India (GIC) GIC had four subsidiary companies. With effect from Dec'2000, these subsidiaries have been delinked from parent company and made independent insurance companies. They are Oriental Insurance Company Limited, New India Assurance Company Limited, National Insurance Company Limited and United India Insurance Company Limited.

First, the life insurance companies were nationalized in 1956, and then the general insurance business was nationalized in 1972, only in 1999 private insurance companies were allowed back into the business of insurance with a maximum of 26% of foreign holding. The first batch of licenses was issued by the Insurance Regulatory and Development Authority (IRDA) in 2001. IRDA issued Certificates of Registration to five new companies in May-June 2008, to undertake insurance business in India. Total number of life insurers registered with the Authority has gone up to 21. While, the total number of general insurers registered with IRDA has gone up to 20 (Annexure-II).

After telecom and banking, it's the turn of insurance companies to deploy customer relationship management (CRM) solutions. As competition intensifies, insurers are trying every tick in the book to retain existing customers, with a wide range of services driving the market for CRM applications in the process.

What is CRM?

The CRM is not a product or service. Rather, it is a strategy used to learn more about customers' needs and behaviour in order to develop stronger relationships with them. From the IT perspective, it provides an integrated view of a company's customer to everyone in the organization so that the customer can be served effectively. In simple terms, CRM is the use of a wide range of marketing, sales and promotional techniques and processes to identify create and manage customers. 'To manage' here implies retaining customers by providing appropriate services for them in time. Of late, it has been widely felt that companies can beat its industry leader in terms of product, quality, pricing, promotion and placement of its product. Hence, to build a customer base, it is not just sufficient to be good at the four Ps, but it is more essential to build a relationship with the customer. This increased focus on managing relationship with the customer in the long-run has led to a new approach known as CRM.

Hence, CRM is defined as a comprehensive strategy and process of acquiring, returning and partnering with selected customers to create superior value for the company and the customer. The CRM basically centers on the combination of technology and human resource with an aim to gain insights into the behaviour of customers and to cater to their perceived values.

Characteristics of CRM

The important characteristics of CRM are as follows:

- Facilitates personal, one-to-one relationship.
- Each customer is viewed as a market and is served differently, according to his/her specific requirements.
- Focuses on building long-term and lifetime relationships.
- Makes optimum use of information technology to build the profile of each customer in detail and updates the same promptly.
- Success of marketing is measured from the long-term point of view, i.e., lifetime market share and lifetime profitability, rather than based on short-term objectives.
- Customer plays an important role of an ambassador for the company and its products, rather than being just a buyer and consumer.

Need for CRM

The concept of CRM is not new. The customer has been the prime concern for companies since the time of the industrial revolution over the years, the management approach, that viewed customer relationship as its key asset, has gained increased prominence in the priorities and practices of many profit and non-profit organizations. Companies have been doing it since the beginning of trade. However, the focus was more on selling rather than on customer orientation. Competition, driven by globalization, has changed the entire perspective. Customers now have varied choices, are more knowledgeable and demanding too. Now they need to be handled with utmost care by the companies because the question is not only to acquire them but to satisfy and to retain them for long. Both from the academicians and the industry experts' perspective, the importance attached to customer relationship building is increasing by leaps and bounds from day to day.

Inclination of CRM in Indian Insurance Sector

While the insurance sector is seeking to maintain a balance between acquiring customers and developing existing ones, customer acquisition is vital, as no retention strategy will entirely stem from customer defection. That said insurance companies are experiencing unacceptable levels of customer churn, thanks to which they are focusing on keeping the customers they already have in a bid to ensure a net growth in their customer base. Today, the focus is on selling more products to existing customers to improve profitability. Customer-focused strategies require CRM (customer relationship management) to help acquire customers through various touch points and to translate operational data into actionable insights for proactively serving customers. CRM is playing a significant role in acquiring new customers. CRM helps to obtain granular details about customers, to design better products, to improve service levels and to reduce operational costs.

Customer Focus

Customer focus is a customer centric organization. It is about getting each and every one of your employees to look at their job through the eyes of your customers and understanding what they must do to add value. It is about continually listening to the voice of your customers, getting their input and feedback and using this information to make changes which they value – changes to your products and services and your business. It is about adding value at all levels of your organization – from IT to sales and the shop floor to customer service and every department in between. It is much more than good or great customer service...and it's true that Customer Focus will give you a competitive advantage.

Current Market Scenario

Insurance firms are tactically rolling out an application here and there rather than strategically implementing a complete CRM suite. In this, they are on the right track. They (insurance firms) are taking baby steps, starting with operational CRM to increase sales force automation. Once they have a sufficiently large customer database, they use BI (Business Intelligence) tools to mine data from various sources (such as contact centers and from banks with which they align) pushing the need for analytical CRM solutions. CRM technologies such as sales force automation, contact centre segmentation and campaign management tools are maturing and finding wider adoption with large insurance companies. The banking, financial services and insurance sector and telecom will continue to drive the CRM market, but the uptake of CRM in the insurance vertical will climb steeply in 2004 and growth will be rapid and higher. The need to integrate customer data from multiple channels and to increase sales force productivity (including that of agents) and running productive marketing campaigns will continue to drive demand for CRM software.

Enhanced Spending on CRM

Insurance firms spend close to 12 percent of their IT budgets on CRM software and services. Insurance firms are looking for CRM initiatives with budgets ranging from Rs. 50 lakhs going right up to Rs. 3 crores. The sector is busy compiling data on individuals, including their purchasing patterns and buying preferences of policies, pension plans and the like. In many cases, proceeding from policy renewal marketing to existing customers remains an unsophisticated exercise, often amounting to little more than a request to renew, with no attempt at putting a value proposition before the customer. With a little help from CRM software, insurance firms can sell multiple insurance policies and pension plans to the same customer.

Business drivers for CRM

A couple of years ago, LIC dominated the insurance market with the help of its sales force and channels and margins were reasonably high. Today, there are close to 20 companies offering both life and general insurance products. All of them have equally strong international and local partners (Annexure-III); all are focusing upon similar geographies and target audiences. Insurance companies are joining hands with banks by becoming channel partners for insurance. Tata AIG has a marketing alliance with HSBC, Birla Sun Life has one with Citibank and IDBI and LIC ally with Corporation Bank, while Kotak Life Insurance has an arrangement with Kotak Bank. This strategy helps insurance firms increase their footprint to cover a larger part of the customer base in the 20-30 years demography. CRM helps to connect a bank's high net worth customers with insurance firms.

Broad CRM Perspective – CRM module and Areas where it can be applied in Insurance Sector.

1. Collaborative CRM

Collaborative CRM is an approach to customer relationship management (CRM) in which the various departments of a company, such as sales, technical support and marketing share any information they collect from interactions with customers. It facilitates interactions with customers through all channels (personal letter, conferencing, chat, fax, phone, web, e-mail) and supports co-ordination of employee teams and channels. The purpose of collaboration is to improve the quality of customer service, and, as a result, increase customer satisfaction and loyalty. It is a solution that brings people, processes and data together so that companies can better serve and retain their customers.

Collaborative CRM provides the following benefits:

- Enables efficient productive customer interactions across all communications channels.
- Enables web collaboration to reduce customer service costs.
- Integrates call centre enabling multi-channel personal customer interaction.
- Integrates view of the customer while interacting at the transaction level.

2. Operational CRM

Operational CRM means supporting the "front office" business processes, which include all customer contact (sales, marketing and service). Tasks resulting from these processes are forwarded to employees responsible for them, as well as the information necessary for carrying them out. Interfaces to back-end applications are provided and activities with customers are documented for further reference.

Operational CRM provides the following benefits:

- Delivers personalised and efficient marketing, sales, and service through multi-channel collaboration.
- Enables a 360-degree view of your customer while you are interacting with them.
- Sales people and service engineers can access complete history of all customer interaction with your company, regardless of the touch point.

3. Analytical CRM

Analysing data created on the operational side of the CRM equation for the purpose of business performance management. Analytical CRM is tied to data warehouse architecture; it is most often evident in analytical applications that leverage data marts. The Analytical Data mart is customer centric and contains the following data: Demography (age, sex, cultural level, marital status, etc.). Ownership of Insurance product/services. Product/ services usage (balance, transactions, etc.). Global variables: profit, cost, risk, assets, liabilities. Relationship with the Insurance companies: segment, portfolio, etc. Customer analysis typically leads to targeted campaigns that increase the share of the customer's spend. Examples of Campaigns directed towards customers are the following:

- Acquisition: Cross-selling, up-selling
- Retention: Retaining customers who leave due to maturity or attrition.
- Information: Providing timely and regular information to customers.
- Modification: Altering details of the transactional nature of the customers' relationship.

Conclusion

According to a report from Indian Infoline (January 2004). India has the highest number of life insurance policies in force in the world. The industry is pegged at Rs 400 billion in India. Gross premium collections stand at 2 percent of the GDP and this has been growing by 15 to 20 percent per year from the Life Insurance Corporation of India (LIC) and other government-owned insurers. At present, 312 million middle class consumers in India have enough financial resources to purchase insurance products like pension, health care, accident benefit, life, property and auto insurance. Only 2.5 per cent of these insurable populations, however, have insurance coverage in any form. The potential premium income is estimated at around US $80 billion. This will place India as the sixth largest market in the world (after the US, Japan, Germany, UK and France). Privatization has led to new players entering this market and it is expected to grow at a rapid pace. Competition in pricing is yet to emerge. Once that happens, as with all dynamic customer-oriented service industries such as banking and telecom, the race to gain and retain customer mind share will be on.

Annexure 1
Milestone of Insurance Regulations in the 20th Century

Year	*Significant Regulatory Event*
1912	The Indian Life Insurance Company Act
1938	The Insurance Act: Comprehensive Act to regulate insurance business in India
1956	Nationalization of Life Insurance business in India
1972	Nationalization of General Insurance business in India
1993	Setting up of Malhotra Committee
1994	Recommendations of Malhotra Committee
1995	Setting up of Mukherjee Committee
1996	Setting up of (interim) Insurance Regulatory Authority (IRA) Recommendations of the IRA
1997	Mukherjee Committee Report submitted but not made public
1997	The Government gives greater autonomy to LIC, GIC and its subsidiaries with regard to the restructuring of boards and flexibility in investment norms aimed at channeling funds to the infrastructure sector
1998	The Cabinet decides to allow 40% foreign equity in private insurance companies-26% to foreign companies and 14% to NRI's, OCB's and FII's.
1999	The Standing Committee headed by Murali Deora decides that foreign equity in private insurance should be limited to 26%. The IRA bill is renamed the Insurance Regulatory and Development Authority (IRDA) Bill
1999	Cabinet clears IRDA Bill
2000	President gives Assent to the IRDA Bill

Annexure II
Updated list of all Insurance Companies in India

Non-Life Insurers	*Life Insurers*
Bajaj Allianz General Insurance Co. Ltd.	Bajaj Allianz Life Insurance Company Limited
ICICI Lombard General Insurance Co. Ltd.	Birla Sun Life Insurance Co. Ltd
IFFCO Tokio General Insurance Co. Ltd.	HDFC Standard Life Insurance Co. Ltd
National Insurance Co.Ltd.	ICICI Prudential Life Insurance Co. Ltd
The New India Assurance Co. Ltd.	ING Vysya Life Insurance Company Ltd.
The Oriental Insurance Co. Ltd.	Life Insurance Corporation of India
Reliance General Insurance Co. Ltd.	Max New York Life Insurance Co. Ltd
Royal Sundaram Alliance Insurance Co. Ltd	Met Life India Insurance Company Ltd.
Tata AIG General Insurance Co. Ltd.	Kotak Mahindra Old Mutual Life Insurance Limited
United India Insurance Co. Ltd.	SBI Life Insurance Co. Ltd
Cholamandalam MS General Insurance Co. Ltd.	Tata AIG Life Insurance Company Limited
HDFC ERGO General Insurance Co. Ltd.	Reliance Life Insurance Company Limited.
Export Credit Guarantee Corporation of India Ltd.	Aviva Life Insurance Company India Limited
Agriculture Insurance Co. of India Ltd.	Sahara India Life Insurance Co, Ltd.
Star Health and Allied Insurance Company Limited	Shriram Life Insurance Co, Ltd.
Apollo DKV Insurance Company Limited	Bharti AXA Life Insurance Company Ltd.
Future Generali India Insurance Company Limited	Future Generali India Life Insurance Company Limited
Universal Sompo General Insurance Co. Ltd.	IDBI Fortis Life Insurance Company Ltd.

(Contd.)

(Contd. Annex-II)

Non-Life Insurers	*Life Insurers*
Shriram General Insurance Company Limited	Canara HSBC Oriental Bank of Commerce Life Insurance Company Ltd.
Bharti Axa General Insurance Company Limited	Aegon Religare Life Insurance Company Limited
	DLF Pramerica Life Insurance Company Limited
REINSURERS	
GENERAL INSURANCE CORPORATION OF INDIA.	

References

Kumari, Vaswati, "India Insurers Seek Perfect Partners." National Underwriters, March 5, 2001, 38-39.

Signa. "World Insurance in 1999." No. 9/2000. Published By SwissRe. Available at www.swissre.com.

Roy, Samit. "Insurance Sector: India." Industry Sector Analysis, National Trade and Development Board, US Department of State, Washington, DC, December 1999.

Berry, M.J.A. & Linoff G.S., 2000, Mastering Data Mining: The Art and Science of Customer Relationship Management, John Wiley & Sons, Inc.

Peppard, J., 2000, Customer Relationship Management (CRM) in Financial Services, European Management Journal, Vol. 18, No. 3, pp. 312–327,

Ryals, L., & Knox, S., 2001, Cross-Functional Issues in the Implementation of Relationship Marketing Through Customer Relationship Management, European Management Journal, Vol. 19, No. 5, pp. 534–542.

Winer, R. S., 2001, A framework for Customer relationship Management, California Management Review, 43(4): 89-105.

Johnson, E.M., 1981, Personal Selling in Financial Institutions, in J.H. Donnelly and W.R. George (eds), Marketing of Services, Chicago: American Marketing Association, pp. 21-24,

Berry, Leonard L., 1983, Relationship Marketing, in Emerging Perspectives on Services Marketing, L.L. Berry, G.L. Shostack, and G.D. Upah, eds. Chicago: American Marketing Association, pp. 25-28.

27

Attitude of Policy Holders Towards SBI Life Insurance Schemes

Dr. R. Eswaran, Dr. M. Balasubramaniam

Life is full of surprises, some pleasant and some not so pleasant. Each and every family has to live with these uncertainties. Preparing for the uncertainties of life is what insurance is all about. Why the human beings will waste precious moments contemplating tomorrow, when we have to live today? Insurance is a tool, a solution for delegating the worries concerning tomorrow onto a trustworthy institution so that we can start living today. With State Bank of India (SBI) life we could smoothen the rough edges of life make it a bit easier, so we needn't worry about our children's educations, or our family's future. Whether we are looking for a safe investment vehicle with good returns or life cover with regular returns in the future, all it needs is one small action on our part.

Origin of SBI Life Insurance

SBI Life Insurance Company Limited. Is a joint venture between India's largest bank, State Bank of India and S.A. Cardiff a leading Life Insurance Company in France. State Bank of India (SBI) is a household name, and it stands as the last word for financial strength and security in the country. SBI'S illustrious background dates back to the year 1806 when it started business, as a presidency bank, known as Bank of Bengal. Over the long journey, it has learnt to combine the best of banking practices handed down from the imperial management with the more dynamic ways of doing banking in the modern India. It has grown as a responsible giant in the banking field over the years.

Today, it has a branch network of over 9000 branches, an aggregate deposit base of nearly Rs.196821 crore and a total balance sheet size of Rs. 261504 crore. Together with its 7 associate banks, SBI commands about 30 per cent of the market share in banking. SBI is the strongest and most profitable bank in the country. It has a tangible networth of Rs.12146 crore as at March 2000, and it earned a pre-tax profit of Rs.2051 crore for ending that date.

Cardiff is a wholly owned subsidiary of BNP Paribas, which is one of the top 10 banks in the world, and the third largest in Europe. BNP is one of the oldest foreign banks with a presence in India dating back to 1860. It has 9 branches in major metros across the country. Cardiff came into being in the year 1973. Since then it has grown into a vibrant company specializing in personal lines such as long-term savings, protection products and creditor insurance. Cardiff had a premium income of over US$ 4 billion in 1999, and more that US$ 23 billion of funds under its management. Cardiff has been specializing in the art of selling insurance products through commercial banks in France and 23 other countries.

France is the mother of bank assurance in the world. Over 65 per cent of life insurance business is done through banks and financial institutions countries in France, and the trend is rapidly catching up in other countries. It operations joint ventures in developed as well as developing countries, such as Brazil, Chile and the Czech republic.

SBI Life Insurance Company Ltd is registered as a life insurance company with the insurance regulatory and development Authority of India (IRDA) and has been issued License number 111 on 29th March 2001. The company's authorized capital is Rs.250 crore, and the paid-up capital at present is Rs.125 crore. SBI owns 74 per cent of the total equity, and Cardiff the balance 26 per cent.

Statement of the Problem

A person buys insurance for one or more reasons. Realizing that the policyholder may die before their dependents can become self-supporting, they may want to purchase a policy that will provide their family due to their death of with an amount of money that will cover funeral and other last expenses, or pay off debts, or provide an income for the family, or pay off the house mortgage. They may, in addition, wish to use insurance as a way to accumulate a sum of money for the college education of his children or for the retirement income.

Despite the many uses to which insurance is put, it remains, like other forms of insurance, a means of protecting against financial loss. The loss in the case of Life insurance is the amount of income that the deceased would have produced, beyond that used for their personal needs, had they who suffer this loss. It is to protect them that life insurance is written. Life insurance also may provide living benefits for the policyholder himself to provide retirement income. For example, in such instance, the insurance becomes, in addition to protection a form of investment.

SBI life products are developed recently they are introduced in the year 2002. At present, these products have an excellent demand and response from the customers. There are several factors, which influences the customers to invest in this policy. After the privatization of insurance there is keen competition in the field of insurance business in India. Hence, in the present study an attempt has been made to ascertain the level of attitude of the policyholders towards SBI life insurance and its various schemes.

Objectives of the Study

The following are the main objectives of the present study:

1. To trace the origin, growth of SBI Life.
2. To study the various schemes of SBI life insurance
3. To study the level of attitude of policyholders towards SBI life insurance schemes.
4. To offer suggestions based on the observation of the study.

Hypothesis

"A Socio-economic factor of the policyholders' does not influence their attitude towards life insurance schemes".

Methodology

The present study is based on the survey method. Primary data were collected directly from policyholders who have taken SBI life insurance policies of SBI branch in Madurai. A structured interview schedule has been used for collecting primary data. Convenience sampling method was employed. In sampling only 150 representatives were examined and conclusion were drawn thereon.

In this study the researcher has identified to measure the level of attitude. As there is no readymade scale to measure the level of attitude, a scale namely "The attitude scale" has been developed by awarding scores to the components, with the help of this scale. The level of attitude of policyholders towards the life insurance has been measured the various components and their scores.

Various Policies in SBI Life Insurance

Life Long Pension Plan: Life expectancy is improving rapidly. People live longer. We cannot work throughout our life. We will have to retire from work. In the post retirement period we have lot of time for ourselves. We would like to do things we have not done while we were working.

Sudarshan: Sudarshan is an Endowment Policy designed to provide savings and has protection to our family. We can save regularly for the future. Thus at the end of the plan, we will receive a substantial amount of saving along with the accumulated bonuses declared. At the same time, our family will be protected for death risk for the full Sum Assured.

Money Back Plan: As an individual our life is fueled by dreams. We experience different special moments in life like wedding, birth of child, child's education or purchasing a new home. We have to be financially prepared for these special moments. What we need is easy liquidity at regular intervals with Life Insurance Protection to take care of these special moments.

Swardan: Happiness and security for our family is what we want. However life has its uncertainties and risks. All that were interested in is how best to afford a secure future for our loved one. Have we ever wished for a low premium insurance policy that is not only provides security to our loved ones but also returns back the premium paid.

Setubandhan: Setubandhan - investment - cum – life insurance opportunity, a unique life bond that helps, we the NRI living abroad, build a bridge between we and our dear ones in India.

This paper deals with the level of attitude of policyholders and factors influencing the attitude of policyholders towards SBI life insurance policies. The world attitude means "Settled Behavior" the analysis is based on the primary data collected from the policyholders. The level of attitude various from one policyholders to another and from time to time. A comprehensive study has been made to highlight the level of attitude, the variation of attitude and their relative importance of each component identified for measuring the level of attitude. The level of attitude of policyholders towards SBI life insurance policy had been obtained from the respondents by way of replies to fifteen statements by using five points scale. The statements are;

1. Premium rate
2. Remittance rate
3. Bonus rate
4. Policy document
5. Customer service
6. After sales service
7. Branch office (SBI)
8. Responses to inquiries
9. Documents for tax purposes
10. Loan procedure
11 Surrender value
12. SBI LIC policies and Social security
13. Advertisement
14. Risk and Nature of death
15. Interest paid by SBI

The attitude of policyholders has been measured with the help of the scale constructed with 15 components identified. The impact of these 15 components on the attitude varies since some components are more significant and some others are less significant. The level of attitude of the sample respondents was analysed through the scores obtained by using Likert's scaling technique. The scores for the statements were allotted as strongly agree-5, agree-4, undecided-3, disagree-2 and strongly disagree-1.

After giving scores for each component, total scores of each sample respondents is computed. Attitude scores of 150 sample policyholders were computed as per the scores stated above. Arithmetic mean ($\bar{X}$) and standard deviation(s) of the total attitude scores of 150 respondents have been computed. Score above ($\bar{X}$ +s) is considered to be high level of attitude.

Score below ($\overline{X}$ -s) is considered to be low level of attitude. Scores in between ($\overline{X}$ +s) and ($\overline{X}$ -s) are considered to be medium level attitude. Arithmetic mean score is 44.57 or 45 and standard deviation score is 5.80 or 6. Respondents whose attitude scores above 50 (44.57 + 5.80 = 50.37) are considered as having high-level attitude and those whose level of attitude scores below 39 (44.7 – 5.80 = 38.77) are considered as having low level of attitude. The respondents whose levels of attitude scores are in between 40 and 49 are classified as having medium level of attitude.

Factors Influencing the Level of Attitude

There are some factors which influence the attitude of policyholders. There are two factors which were identified as factors influencing the attitude of policyholders towards SBI Life insurance policy. The relationship between dependent variable and independent variable has been studied by means of chi- square test.

One of the important conditions of applying chi-square test is that the cell frequency should not come less than five. Since only 150 policyholders alone were interviewed, there is a possibility that the cell frequency may be less than five, in case of three way classification. So for the purpose of chi-square analysis, the women respondents were classified into three categories namely, high, medium and low. The following seven factors which were influencing the level of attitude were tested.

1. Age of the policyholders
2. Gender of the policyholders
3. Educational qualification of the policyholders
4. Income of the policyholders
5. Size of the family of the policyholders

Relationship between Level of Attitude and Socio-Economic Background of Policyholders

The age factors are to be considered as an important factor as the people realizes the necessity of security to their dependents. We cannot expect the same level of realization from the aged people. Thus the age group of policyholders has a direct relationship with their attitude. Age is also a factor, which influence policyholders to select the type and amount of policy.

The SBI life insurance schemes are applicable to both male and female members. Male members, as the head of family, have more responsibilities than the female members. They earn money from various sources to maintain their families. Investment decisions are generally taken by man. Generally female members look into the domestic affairs of the family and hence they find lesser time to know about the benefits of the various SBI life insurance schemes. Therefore, sex of the policyholders has been identified as one of the important factor which influences the attitude level.

SBI life insurance protection is a necessary service required both for educated and uneducated persons. The educated persons understand the important of the insurance when compared to he uneducated. Educated man lead well planned life whereas the uneducated is ignorant of it. So they are not aware of benefits and important of insurance schemes. Education widens the knowledge of understanding. Therefore, educational qualification is identified is one the factors influencing the attitude of the policyholders towards the SBI life insurance schemes. Generally income is the main factor, which decides many matters. There may be various sources of income for person. But insurance service is needed for all irrespective of their income and the income plays the key role in motivating the attitude level.

Policyholders having big family will have more desired to take up life insurance policies, as feeling of security is a must for them. Policyholders having smaller family will have only limited desired to take up policy when compared to policyholders having big family. So the size of the family of the policyholders has been identified as one of the factors influencing the attitude

TABLE 1: Level of attitude and Socio-economic Factors

Sl. No.	*Socio-economic factors*	*Level of Attitude*			*Total Members*
		Low	*Medium*	*High*	
1.	Age				
	20 – 30 years	6	13	19	38
	31 – 40 years	10	15	30	55
	Above 40 years	5	42	10	57
2.	Gender				
	Male	12	54	50	116
	Female	9	16	9	34
3.	Educational level				
	Up to school level	7	33	27	67
	Graduates	9	22	25	56
	Others	5	15	7	27
4.	Income				
	Up to Rs.15,000	5	25	11	41
	Above Rs.15,000	16	45	48	109
5.	Size of the family				
	Up to 3 members	11	30	30	71
	4 to 6 members	5	23	9	37
	Above 6 members	5	17	20	42
	Total Members	21	70	59	150

Source: Primary data.

of policyholders. The Table 1 shows the socio-economic factors of the policyholders.

The age and level of attitude of the respondents are depicted in Table 1 of the total 150 respondents nearly 55 respondents belong to the group of 31 to 40 years. The numbers of respondents above 40 years were 57. From the table 1, it is understood that out of 150 respondents 116 male and 34 are female. In this modern world women are given equal important in all aspects, but in this study it has been founded that only meager amount of policyholders are from women.

Table 1 shows that 67 respondents are unto school level, 56 from graduates and 27 are others. It could be observed from Table 1 that 41 respondents are unto Rs.15,000 income group and out of which 25 members are having medium level of attitude. The 109 respondents are above Rs.15,000 income group and out of which 48 members are having high level of attitude. Table 1 reveals that 71 of the policyholders belong to the category below 3 members, 37 of the policy holders belongs to the category of 4 to 6 members and the remaining 42 of the policy holders belongs to the category of above 6 members.

To find out the association between the socio-economic factors of the respondent and the level of attitude towards SBI life insurance policy the Chi-square test was applied and the results were analysed.

Null Hypothesis Stated: (H_0)

H_0: Level of attitude is independent of socio-economic background of Policyholders in SBI Insurance policy.

The attitude level and the contribution of each components and factors influencing the attitude level have been discussed. Fifteen components and five factors have been identified to measure the attitude of policyholders towards SBI life insurance schemes. The calculated value is less than table value, the null hypothesis (H_0) is accepted and it is concluded that there is no significant relationship between the educational qualification, income and size of the family and the attitude of policyholders.

TABLE 2: Results of Chi-square test on Level of Attitude

Factors	*Calculated χ^2 value*	*Table value of χ^2*	*d.f*	*Inference*
Age	27.714	9.49	4	Ho: rejected
Gender	6.735	5.99	2	Ho: rejected
Educational qualification	4.027	9.49	4	Ho: accepted
Income	4.850	5.99	2	Ho: accepted
Size of the family	5.802	9.49	4	Ho: accepted

Source: Calculated on the basis of Primary Data.

The calculated value is more than table value, the null hypothesis (H_0) is rejected and it is concluded that there is a significant relationship between the age, gender and the attitude of policyholders.

Suggestions

- All the policyholders should be well informed about the premium rate
- It is found that the customers are not having awareness of the bonus issued by the SBI life insurance. Since it has been introduced in the year 2002. So the insurance company should inform about the bonus while taking policy.
- In this study it is found that more branch offices should be opened especially for the SBI life insurance. Because it has been now engaged by the State Bank of India.
- If a separate branch has been opened it will be more convenient for the policyholders for remitting for their premium.
- SBI life insurance agent provides prompt inquiries in order to increase their policyholders.
- All the policyholders who come under the tax bracket are provided with necessary documents for claiming tax concession.

- Loans for the policyholders are sanctioned only after the completion of third year. So the policyholders are not known about the loan procedure.
- Since the SBI life insurance has been introduced recently most of the policyholders are not known about the surrender value.
- By taking policies from SBI life insurance, "Social Security" for the policyholder has improved.
- Even though the policyholders say that the advertisement is more appealing it has not reached every nook and corner of the country. So all types medium for advertisement should be adopted.
- SBI life insurance covers risks for all kind of death.
- The SBI life insurance policyholders are not satisfied with the interest rate provided by the SBI life. So interest rate for the policyholders should be increased.
- At present the SBI life insurance policyholders are from educated group. Others are not well known about the SBI life policy. So it should be reached all kinds of people.

Conclusion

One of the major objectives of SBI life insurance is to carry the message of life insurance to the common man. Adoption of new insurance schemes, modification to suit to the needs of the people are possible by measuring the present level of attitude of various insurance schemes available.

28

Utilizing the Services of General Insurance Sector

Dr. C. Arjunan, Dr. L. Manivannan, M. Murali

Insurance is defined as the simple mechanism of some people who are exposed to the same level of risks of suffering destruction of damage to their properties, that are likely to be caused by perils like accident, fire, floods earthquakes, etc., coming together and agreeing to share the loss sustained any one of the members'; that is, the loss of one or more members is spread among all. Risk is uncertainty of a financial loss. It should not be confused with the chance of loss which is the probable number of losses out of a given number of exposures. It should not be confused with peril which is defined as the cause of loss or with hazard which is a condition that may increase the chance of loss. Finally, risk must not be confused with loss itself which is the unintentional decline in or disappearance of value arising from a contingency. Wherever there is uncertainty with respect to a probable loss there is risk.

Emerging Trends

With the onslaught of the September 11th 2001 attack on the U.S. and the terrorist attack in India at Amaranth there has been a dual impact on the insurance industry. On the one hand, it had to suffer losses by paying the huge claims of the aggrieved parties including the third party as well and on the other hand, the realization amongst the people as to the importance of insurance coverage is in the present scenario of uncertainty. And with the aggressive advertising by the various insurance companies the mindset of an individual is being magnificently changed from “I don’t need insurance” to “I need insurance”.

Importance of the Study

In our country the General Insurance companies, part of financial sector, are expected to show profits, though they are service-oriented organisations. The days are gone, when the General Insurance companies were set up with an exclusive motto of “service” instead of profit. The recent economic reforms urge the General Insurance Companies to introduce various insurance schemes in order to make profits by directing the schemes at target group of customers. The need for development of health insurance is thus once again recognized and it will now be possible to introduce a variety of insurance schemes similar to those in the overseas markets and as per demand of the clients in our own market. This study will help the public sector and private sector Insurance Companies to analyse its performance and to take corrective measures in the sphere of their insurance products.

Need for the Study

In our country, the General Insurance companies, part of financial sector, are expected to show profits, though they are service-oriented organisations. The days are gone, when the

General Insurance companies were set up with an exclusive motto of "service" instead of profit. The recent economic reforms urge the General Insurance Companies to introduce various insurance products in order to make profits by directing the schemes at target group of customers. The need for development of various insurance schemes is thus once again recognized and it will now be possible to introduce a variety of need based various insurance products in our own market, similar to those in the overseas markets. This study will help the Public and Private Insurance Companies to analyse its performance and to take corrective measures in the sphere of various Insurance products.

Objectives of the Study

The following are the main objectives of the study :

1. To study the performance and operations of various Insurance schemes in public and private sector Insurance Companies.
2. To study the customers' awareness and behaviour on various services offered by the Public and Private General Insurance.
3. To analyse the factors influencing the utilization of the services of Public and Private General Insurance companies.
4. To identify the major problems faced by the customers of Public and Private General Insurance in the study area.

Methodology

This study has used both primary data and secondary data. For collecting primary data field survey technique was undertaken in the study. The researcher has collected two hundred and fifty samples by means of interview using questionnaires.

Research Design

In this study descriptive research design is made use of which describes the demographic characteristics of policy holders in Public and Private Insurance Companies and the frequency of two variables.

Tools for Analysis

Simple statistical tools like Percentage, and Chi-square test were employed appropriately. Henry Garrett Ranking Techniques also employed for finding the reasons and problems.

Period of the Data Collection

The sample collected for the period of past three months.

Limitations of the Study

- The study was restricted to the Erode town.
- The sample collected has been restricted to 250 samples.
- The bias in samples could not be controlled because policy holders' attitudes differ.

Data Analysis

1. Simple percentage analysis :

Age Level of the Insurer

S. No.	*Age*	*No. of Respondents*	*Percentage*
1.	Below 25 years	72	28.8
2.	26 – 35 years	76	30.4
3.	Above 35 years	102	40.8
	Total	250	100.0

The sample consists of 72 respondents (28.8 percent) in the first group, 76 respondents (30.4% percent) in the second and 102 (40.8 percent) in the third group.

Educational Qualification of the Insurer

S. No.	*Educational Qualification*	*No. of Respondents*	*Percentage*
1.	School level	29	11.6
2.	UG	129	51.6
3.	PG	57	22.8
4.	Professional	35	14.0
	Total	250	100.0

The sample consists of 29 (11.6%) school level, 129 (51.6%) UG level, 57 (22.8%) PG level and 35 (14.0%) professional level of respondents.

Occupational Status of the Insurer

S. No.	*Occupation*	*No. of Respondents*	*Percentage*
1.	Business	37	14.8
2.	Govt. Employee	39	15.6
3.	Private employee	147	58.8
4.	Professional	27	10.8
	Total	250	100.0

The sample consists of 37 (14.8%) business, 39 (15.6%) Govt. Employees, 147 (58.8%) Private Employee and 27 (10.8%) professional respondents.

Marital Status

S. No.	*Marital status*	*No. of Respondents*	*Percentage*
1.	Married	188	75.2
2.	Unmarried	62	24.8
	Total	250	100.0

The sample consist of 188 (75.2%) respondents who were married and 62 (24.8%) respondents who were unmarried.

Awareness Level About the Insurance

S. No.	*Awareness*	*No. of Respondents*	*Percentage*
1.	Low	61	24.4
2.	Medium	126	50.4
3.	High	63	25.2
	Total	250	100.0

The sample consists of 61 (24.4%) respondents having low level of awareness, 126 (50.4%) respondents with medium level of awareness and 63 (25.2%) respondents having high level of awareness.

Preference of Insurance Sector

S. No.	*Sector*	*No. of Respondents*	*Percentage*
1.	Public	52	20.8
2.	Private	198	79.2
	Total	250	100.0

The sample consists of 52 (20.8%) respondents utilizing the services of public sector insurance and 198 (79.2%) respondents utilizing the services of private sector insurance.

Period of Utilizing the Insurance Services

S.No.	*Period*	*Level of satisfaction*			*Total*
		Low	*Medium*	*High*	
1.	Below 1 year	2 (10.0)	11 (55.0)	7 (35.0)	20
2.	1 – 3 years	53 (30.6)	47 (27.2)	73 (42.2)	173
3.	3 – 5 years	3 (7.5)	21 (52.5)	16 (40.0)	40
4.	Above 5 years	2 (11.8)	7 (41.2)	8 (47.1)	17
	Total	60	86	104	250

The sample consists of 20 (8.0%) respondents are below one year, 173 (69.2%) respondents are 1-3 years, 40 (16.0%) respondents are 3-5 years and 17 (6.8%) respondents are above 5 years.

Number of Policies Taken

S. No.	*Number of policies*	*No. of Respondents*	*Percentage*
1.	1 policy	155	62.0
2.	2 policies	84	33.6
3.	Above 2 policies	11	4.4
	Total	250	100.0

The sample consists of 155 (62.0%) respondents are having one policy, 84 (33.6%) respondents are having two policies and 11 (4.4%) of the respondents are having above two policies.

Problems Faced by the Respondents

S.No.	*Opinion*	*No. of Respondents*	*Percentage*
1.	Yes	209	83.6
2.	No	41	16.4
	Total	250	100.0

It is highlighted from the above analysis that 83.6% of the respondents are faced some problems in utilizing the services of General Insurance companies and only 16.4% of the respondents are not facing any problems in utilizing the services of General Insurance companies.

2. Two-way Classification Analysis

Age And Level of Satisfaction On Utilizing Services of General Insurance

S.No.	*Age*	*Level of satisfaction*			*Total*
		Low	*Medium*	*High*	
1.	Young (Below 25 years)	26 (36.1)	20 (27.8)	26 (36.1)	72
2.	Middle (26 – 35 years)	9 (11.8)	31 (40.8)	36 (47.4)	76
3.	Old (Above 35 years)	25 (24.5)	35 (34.3)	42 (41.2)	102
	Total	60	86	104	250

It is found from the table that the percentage of the respondent's high level of satisfaction in utilizing the services rendered by General Insurance was the highest (47.4%) in middle

Educational Qualification and Level of Satisfaction on Utilizing Services of General Insurance

S.No.	*Educational Qualification*	*Level of satisfaction*			*Total*
		Low	*Medium*	*High*	
1.	School level	5 (17.2)	8 (27.6)	16 (55.2)	29
2.	UG	26 (20.2)	46 (35.7)	57 (44.2)	129
3.	PG	19 (33.3)	13 (22.8)	25 (43.9)	57
4.	Professional	10 (28.6)	19 (54.3)	6 (17.1)	35
	Total	60	86	104	250

aged respondents and the same was the lowest (36.1%) among the old aged respondents. The percentage of medium level of satisfaction in using the services was the highest (40.8%) among the middle aged respondents and the lowest (27.8%) among the young aged respondents. On the other hand, the percentage of the low level of satisfaction in utilizing the services of General Insurance was the highest (36.1%) among the young aged respondents and the lowest (11.8%) among the middle aged respondents.

It could be observed from the above table that the percentage of the respondents' high level of satisfaction on utilizing the services rendered by General Insurance was the highest (55.2%) in school level respondents and the same was the lowest (17.1%) among the professional level respondents. The percentage of medium level of satisfaction on utilizing the services was the highest (54.3%) among the professional level respondents and the lowest (22.8%) among the PG level respondents. On the other hand, the percentage of the low level of satisfaction on utilizing the services of General Insurance was the highest (33.3%) among the PG level respondents and the lowest (17.2%) among the school level respondents.

Occupation and Level of Satisfaction on Utilizing Services of General Insurance

S.No.	*Occupation*	*Level of satisfaction*			*Total*
		Low	*Medium*	*High*	
1.	Business	6 (16.2)	9 (24.3)	22 (59.5)	37
2.	Govt. Employee	6 (15.4)	19 (48.7)	14 (35.9)	39
3.	Private employee	43 (29.3)	51 (34.7)	53 (36.1)	147
4.	Professional	5 (18.5)	7 (25.9)	15 (55.6)	27
	Total	60	86	104	250

It is noted from the above table that the percentage of the respondents' high level of satisfaction on utilizing the services rendered by General Insurance was the highest (59.5%) among business respondents and the same was the lowest (35.9%) among the Government employee. The percentage of medium level of satisfaction on utilizing the services was the highest (48.7%) among the Government employee and the lowest (24.3%) among the Business respondents. On the other hand, the percentage of the low level of satisfaction on utilizing the services of General Insurance was the highest (29.3%) among the private employee and the lowest (15.4%) among the Government employee.

Marital Status and Level of Satisfaction on Utilizing Services of General Insurance

S.No.	*Marital status*	*Level of satisfaction*			*Total*
		Low	*Medium*	*High*	
1.	Married	49 (26.1)	66 (35.1)	73 (38.8)	188
2.	Unmarried	11 (17.7)	20 (32.3)	31 (50.0)	62
	Total	60	86	104	250

It is divulged from the above table that the percentage of the respondents' high level of satisfaction on utilizing the services rendered by General Insurance was the highest (50.0%) among the unmarried respondents and the same was the lowest (38.8%) among the married respondents. The percentage of medium level of satisfaction on utilizing the services was the highest (35.1%) among the married respondents and the lowest (32.3%) among the unmarried respondents. On the other hand, the percentage of the low level of satisfaction on utilizing the services of General Insurance was the highest (26.1%) among the married respondents and the lowest (17.7%) among the unmarried respondents.

The following table reveals that the percentage of high level of satisfaction perceived in utilizing the services of General

Insurance was the highest (57.1%) among the respondents having high level of awareness on insurance services and the same was the lowest (35.7%) among the respondents having medium level of awareness on insurance services. The percentage of medium level of satisfaction perceived by the respondents utilizing the services of General Insurance was the highest (38.1%) among the respondents having medium level of awareness on General Insurance and the same was the lowest (28.6%) among the respondents having high level of awareness. On the other hand, the percentage of low level of satisfaction perceived by the respondents utilizing the services of General Insurance was the highest (29.5%) among the respondents having low level of awareness on General Insurance and the same was the lowest (14.3%) among the respondents having high level of awareness.

Awareness and Level of Satisfaction on Utilizing Services of General Insurance (Two-way Table)

S.No.	*Awareness*	*Level of satisfaction*			*Total*
		Low	*Medium*	*High*	
1.	Low	18 (29.5)	20 (32.8)	23 (37.7)	61
2.	Medium	33 (26.2)	48 (38.1)	45 (35.7)	126
3.	High	9 (14.3)	18 (28.6)	36 (57.1)	63
	Total	60	86	104	250

The above table shows that the percentage of high level of satisfaction perceived in utilizing the services of General Insurance was the highest (59.6%) among the respondents who prefer public sector and the same was the lowest (36.9%) among the respondents who prefer private sector. The percentage of medium level of satisfaction perceived by the respondents utilizing the services of General Insurance was the highest

(36.9%) among the respondents who prefer private sector and the same was the lowest (25.0%) among the respondents who prefer private sector.

Preference of Insurance Sector and Level of Satisfaction in Utilizing Services of General Insurance

S.No.	*Sector*	*Level of satisfaction*			*Total*
		Low	*Medium*	*High*	
1.	Public	8 (15.4)	13 (25.0)	31 (59.6)	52
2.	Private	52 (26.3)	73 (36.9)	73 (36.9)	198
	Total	60	86	104	250

On the other hand, the percentage of low level of satisfaction perceived by the respondents was the highest (26.3%) among the respondents who prefer private sector and the same was the lowest (15.4%) among the respondents who prefer public. From the above analysis it is found that majority of the respondents prefer public sector General Insurance.

Period of Utilizing the Services and Level of Satisfaction on Utilizing Services of General Insurance

S.No.	*Period*	*Level of satisfaction*			*Total*
		Low	*Medium*	*High*	
1.	Below 1 year	2 (10.0)	11 (55.0)	7 (35.0)	20
2.	1 – 3 years	53 (30.6)	47 (27.2)	73 (42.2)	173
3.	3 – 5 years	3 (7.5)	21 (52.5)	16 (40.0)	40
4.	Above 5 years	2 (11.8)	7 (41.2)	8 (47.1)	17
	Total	60	86	104	250

The above table indicates that the percentage of high level of satisfaction perceived in utilizing the services of General Insurance was the highest (47.1%) among the respondents who utilize for above 5 years and the same was the lowest (35.0%) among the respondents who utilize for below one year. The percentage of medium level of satisfaction perceived by the respondents utilizing the services of General Insurance was the highest (55.0%) among the respondents who utilize for below one year and the same was the lowest (27.2%) among the respondents who utilize for 1-3 years. On the other hand, the percentage of low level of satisfaction perceived by the respondents was the highest (30.6%) among the respondents who utilize for 1-3 years and the same was the lowest (7.5%) among the respondents who utilize 3-5 years.

Number of Policies Purchased and Level of Satisfaction on Utilizing Services of General Insurance

S.No.	*Number of policies*	*Level of satisfaction*			*Total*
		Low	*Medium*	*High*	
1.	1 policy	40 (25.8)	51 (32.9)	64 (41.3)	155
2.	2 policies	18 (21.4)	32 (38.1)	34 (40.5)	84
3.	Above 2 policies	2 (18.2)	3 (27.3)	6 (54.5)	11
	Total	60	86	104	250

The above table infers that the percentage of high level of satisfaction perceived in utilizing the services of General Insurance was the highest (54.5%) among the respondents who purchase above 2 policies and the same was the lowest (40.5%) among the respondents who purchase two policies. The percentage of medium level of satisfaction perceived by the respondents utilizing the services of General Insurance was the highest (38.1%) among the respondents who purchase two policies and the same was the lowest (27.3%) among the respondents who purchase above two policies. On the other hand, the percentage of low level of satisfaction perceived by the respondents was the highest (25.8%) among the respondents who purchase one policy and the same was the lowest (18.2%) among the respondents who purchase above two policies.

3. Chi-Square Test

Level Of Satisfaction On Utilizing The Services Rendered By The Insurance Companies And Demographic Factors Of The Insurer

S.No.	*Factor*	*Chi-square Result*
1.	Age	Significant at 5% level
2.	Educational Qualification	Significant at 5% level
3.	Occupational Status	Significant at 5% level
4.	Marital Status	Not Significant
5.	Awareness	Significant at 5% level
6.	Preference on insurance Sector	Significant at 5% level
7.	Period of utilizing the services	Significant at 5% level
8.	Number of policies taken	Not Significant

The above table shows the result of chi-square test for level of satisfaction on utilizing the services of General Insurance Company with selected independent factors. It is identified from the above analysis that the six independent variables are closely associated with the dependent variable and remaining two is not closely associated with.

4. Henry Garrett Ranking Technique

The resons for selecting a particular insurance company has been shown in the following table and it is noted that most

Reasons for Selecting the Particular Company

S. No.	*Reason*	*Total score*	*Mean score*	*Rank*
1.	Proximity (Nearest place)	11066	44.3	III
2.	Good service	16053	64.2	I
3.	Courteous behaviour of staff	14011	56.0	II
4.	Need satisfactory product	10699	42.8	V
5.	Dealer / Financier tie up	10986	43.9	IV

of the respondents preferred 'good service' was ranked first with a Garrett score of 16053 points. It is followed by the 'Courteous behaviour of staff' which ranked second with a Garrett score of 14011 points. The third rank was placed for the factor 'Proximity' with Garrett scores of 11066 points. The factor such as 'dealer / financier tie up' was ranked in the fourth position with a Garrett score of 10986 points. The last rank is placed for the 'need satisfactory product' obtained by General insurance with a Garrett score of 10699 points. From the above analysis that majority of the respondents are selecting the General Insurance company for the reason of its 'Good Service'.

Problems Faced by the Respondents - Ranking

S. No.	*Problem*	*Total score*	*Mean score*	*Rank*
1.	No proper response of officers / agents	11282	54.0	II
2.	After Sales Service	11034	52.8	III
3.	Not proper intimation of next renewal period	11995	57.4	I
4.	Delay in claim settlement	9466	45.3	V
5.	Not proper explanation of unknown policies	8702	41.6	VI
6.	Lack of knowledge of the agent / officer	10230	48.9	IV

It is noted from the above table that the problem 'Not proper intimation of next renewal period' was ranked first with a Garrett score of 11995 points. It is followed by the problem of 'No proper response of officers / agents' with a Garrett score of 11282 points. The third rank goes to the problem of 'After Sales Service' with a Garrett score of 11034 points. The problem 'Lack of knowledge of the agent / officer' occupies fourth rank with a Garrett score of 10230 points. 'Delay in claim settlement' is the fifth problem with a Garrett score of 9466 points and 'Not proper explanation of unknown policies' is the sixth problem with a Garrett score of 8702 points. From the above analysis it is found that majority of the respondents faced the problem 'Not proper intimation of next renewal period'.

Findings

1. It was found from the analysis that, above 35 age respondents were having maximum level of satisfaction for utilizing the services of General Insurance then the young and middle category of respondents. The results of chi-square test also proved that there is a close relationship between the age of the respondents and their level of satisfaction on utilizing the services of General Insurance.
2. While analyzing the Educational Qualification of the respondents and their opinion on the services offered by the General Insurance, it is found that the maximum level of satisfaction perceived on the services was among the respondents who have acquired education at school level and the results of chi-square test also proved that there is a close relationship between the Educational Qualification of the respondents and the level of satisfaction on utilizing the services of General Insurance.
3. Occupational level of the respondents was studied under four categories such as business, Govt. employee, Private employee and Professional. These varying nature of

respondents opined that the maximum level of satisfaction perceived by the customers in utilizing the Services of General insurance was by the business people and professionals and which is proved by chi-square test at 5% significant level of association.

4. It was found from the analysis that the respondents are having unmarried have perceived maximum level of satisfaction on utilizing the services of General Insurance.
5. The analysis of awareness factor shows that the maximum level of satisfaction perceived on Services of General Insurance was among the respondents having high level of awareness regarding the various services offered by the General Insurance. The calculated Chi-square value is found to be higher than the table value and the result is significant at 5% level. This reveals that there is a close relationship between the respondents' level of awareness and the level of satisfaction perceived in utilizing the services of General insurance.
6. It is highlighted from the analysis that maximum level of satisfaction perceived on services of General Insurance was among the respondents who prefer public sector General insurance and it is proved by the analysis of Chi-square at 5% significance level.
7. The Chi-square result also showed 5 per cent level of significance, for utilizing the services offered by the General Insurance among the respondents who utilize the services for above 5 years.
8. Among the number of policies purchased by the respondents was analysed that above two policies purchased respondents have perceived maximum level of satisfaction on utilizing the services of General Insurance.
9. While analyzing the major reasons for selecting the insurance companies, it is found that majority of the respondents preferred General Insurance companies by the reason of its 'Good Service'.

10. The major problems faced by the respondents based on the level of difficulty in utilizing the Services of General Insurance are analysed through Henry Garrett Ranking Technique, which gives the result of the problem 'Not proper intimation of next renewal period' attend by the sample respondents.

Suggestions

(1) The General Insurance Companies in the study area should concentrate towards young and middle aged customers and establish a good relationship by providing an attractive service. Since the young respondents' relationship with the insurance can be longer due to their age factor, simultaneously the middle aged respondents create a good relationship properly whenever they approach to avail their services in the selected General Insurance Companies.

(2) The respondents have received the detailed information of the General Insurance through their advertisement and company agents / officers. Hence, it is suggested that the General Insurance companies may give a wide service in the customers and maintain the attractive advertisement through television (local channel), wall painting and radio (F.M). By doing so, more number of people may be aware of the services and utilize the service of General Insurance.

(3) The General Insurance companies, should gives the proper intimation of the renewal of policies and giving proper response of company officials and agents for avoid making false promises and misleading information to the customers in terms of premium amounts, due date and bonus facility.

(4) There is an opinion that the private sector General insurance companies should provide better service compare to public sector insurance companies by avoiding

improper communications, misleading and contains ample hidden conditions which are not properly communicated to the clients. Hence, it is suggested that a crystal clear communication with complete information should be provided by the companies to their present and prospective customers.

Conclusion

The competitive climate in the Indian insurance market has changed dramatically over the last few years. At the same time, changes have been taking place in the government regulations and technology. The expectations of customers are also changing. The existing General Insurance companies have to introduce many new products in the market which have competitive advantage over the products of Private Insurance. The Private Insurance companies have introduced some new innovative services to attract the customers by offering more bonus facilities and attractive services. The General Insurance sector is expanding and big international players are entering into the arena. The New Private Insurance Companies are consolidating themselves and innovating new methods of customer delight.

Index

D

M

T

U